PURO MEXICANO

PURO MEXICANO

edited by

J. FRANK DOBIE

DALLAS
SOUTHERN METHODIST UNIVERSITY PRESS

**TEXAS FOLKLORE SOCIETY
PUBLICATION NUMBER XII**

D EDICATED to my dear friend, Don Alberto Guajardo, sage learner from parchments out of the antiquity of his own land, from books of four languages, and from the medicine men of the Lipans and Kickapoos; general of Mexican wars; naturalist of deserts and sierras; acute observer and tenacious rememberer of all things of the *campo* and all ways and tales of the *campesinos*; generous-hearted gentleman; a tree of both nourishing fruit and pleasant shade that belongs, root and all, to the soil of Northern Mexico.

To this dedication are added thanks to H. Stanley Marcus, of The Book Club of Texas, for designing the format of the book and advising the artisans who set the type for it and printed it; and other thanks to Bertha McKee Dobie for skilled and prolonged assistance in editing the copy, proof-reading and indexing.

Prefatory Wisdom

By THE EDITOR

OCCASIONALLY it is wise to have a preface to a book; more often, probably, not to have one; but certainly it is never wise to have an unwise preface. And now with respect to wisdom and prefaces, the two wisest courses of action I can contemplate are, first, to be foolish, and, secondly, to become a patron of the Texas Folk-Lore Society.

As regards foolishness, there are divers professors of History—branded with more letters than Nig Add's old cow—who delight in nonsense but not one of whom will stand for a gleam of it in history. Folk-lore in the hands of scholars bent solely on comparative studies and analogues is fully as bad off as history. It is as if those two great kings of the Hebrews had lived only the latter half of their lives. Yet, as everybody knows, in their palmy days—

> King Solomon and King David
>> Led merry, merry lives
> With their many, many sweethearts
>> And their many, many wives.
>
> But when at last they both grew old,
>> With many, many qualms,
> King Solomon wrote the Proverbs
> And David wrote the Psalms.

I did not write "Los Animalitos." I don't have enough "qualms" yet. Indeed, of the many, many *versos* chanted and rattled off by Mexican children under the title of "The Little Animals," some are doubtless as old as Mother Goose rhymes. However, upon considering in this book Dan Storm's wonderful *chirrionera* and Riley Aiken's dog that ran clear to the moon and Sarah McKellar's naïve coyote and Hugh McGehee Taylor's very odd white dog and the doves containing such fatal eggs in the tales told by Elizabeth DeHuff—upon considering these and other wonderful creatures in the pages that follow, it seemed to me proper that at least some of "Los Animalitos" should precede them, even if the rhymes are my own.

> *Señores*, I wish to tell you
>   What the animals did.
> Some were building *jacales*,
>   And not a one was hid.
>
> I saw two billing doves
>   A-fighting with their teeth
> That shone as white as marble
>   And clicked *peeth, peeth.*
>
> A dying louse was digging
>   His grave in a mound,
> And a mole sowed potatoes
>   In the wind above the ground.
>
> I saw a frog with his guitar
>   Tuning up for to please;
> The guitar was made of milk
>   And the strings were made of cheese.
>
> A chicken-eating owl
>   Was buying a pair of specs
> So as to catch the fleas
>   On a family of polecat necks.

PREFATORY WISDOM

I saw also a cricket
  In a tavern drinking wine,
While a cockroach cooked some yams,
  On which both did dine.

I saw a nanny goat
  A-sitting in a chair
And as solemn as an owl
  A-combing out her hair.

I saw two furious rabbits
  Snarling at two coyotes,
And a rattlesnake reclining
  Twirled his long *bigotes* (mustaches).

I saw two stubborn burros
  Writing at a table,
While a parrot cooked *tortillas*,
  For she was very able.

A grasshopper I saw ploughing
  With a yoke of javalines,
And a bullfrog mounting a horse—
  High boots hid his jeans.

Just as the sun was coming up
  Night before last at midday,
A blind man sat writing
  What a deaf-mute had to say.

All this is made up;
  Yet it's composed of facts,
Because, although the truth,
  True things are what it lacks.

So go across that bridge
  Made of the ribs of a louse,
And stepping on the beak of a rooster,
  Arrive at your own house.

PURO MEXICANO

As editor and as a writer who has just finished a book of his own that is a pattern of Mexican folk, folk ways and folk-lore, I am exceedingly proud of this volume of purely Mexican lore; it is the best book the Texas Folk-Lore Society has issued since *Legends of Texas,* which came out in 1924 and is now virtually unprocurable. To no small degree · the patrons of the Texas Folk-Lore Society have made possible the issuance of such a large collection as *Puro Mexicano* in such a decent format. It takes fifty dollars to become a patron. The names of the patrons of the Texas Folk-Lore Society follow:

R. L. Blaffer, Houston
Mrs. R. F. Byler, Mathis
Sam P. Cochran, Dallas
Mrs. R. J. Dobie, Beeville
James R. Dougherty, Beeville
J. E. Farrell, Fort Worth
D. A. Frank, Dallas
John E. Green, Houston
George A. Hill, Jr., Houston
Miss Ima Hogg, Houston
Mrs. Richard M. Kleberg, Corpus Christi
Mrs. A. B. Looscan, Houston
H. Stanley Marcus, Dallas
Roy Miller, Corpus Christi
Mrs. Thomas O'Connor, Victoria
Mrs. J. R. Parten, Houston
J. R. Parten, Houston
Mrs. E. L. Perry, Houston
W. A. Philpott, Jr., Dallas
Carl Sandburg, Harbert, Michigan
Floyd Smith, Brady
Leslie Waggener, Dallas
C. C. Walsh, Dallas
Clarence R. Wharton, Houston
Frost Woodhull, San Antonio

Austin, Texas
The Fifth of May, 1935

CONTENTS

ix

PURO MEXICANO

A Pack Load of
MEXICAN TALES

By Riley Aiken

CONSCIOUSLY I began collecting the tales here offered in 1929. Yet some of them date in my memory as far back as 1907. I now have one hundred and four in my collection; I am planning to quit hunting when the number reaches one thousand and one.

The *cuentos* are from the Mexican states of Tamaulipas, Nuevo León, Coahuila and Chihuahua, all of the frontier, and from the Texas border counties of Cameron, Maverick, and Presidio. Getting the tales has depended upon a deep interest in folk-lore, patience, and coincidence. Some of them fell from a clear sky; some came by way of illustrating a point in conversation; others I got by pumping and lying in wait. Six of them I heard by camp-fires, three from washerwomen at work over their tubs, three in a railroad camp, two on a train, four from a man cook at the hacienda of Las Rucias in Coahuila, and a considerable number in saloons. The little group of Kickapoo tales I heard one rainy evening at the *ranchería* of Kickapoo Indians called Nacimiento, Coahuila.

The best stories I have were told me by one Santiago Garza, a teamster from the Sierra del Carmen region of Coahuila. He told me the stories of " 'Mana Zorra y 'Mano Coyote," "El Diente de Oro," and "The Dog That Ran to the Moon." The story of "La Cucaracha" came from a veritable Munchausen or Don Cacahuate named Doroteo living at a ranch thirty miles above Brownsville, Texas; he told me the parrot tale also.

In recording the tales I have employed the method used by Giuseppi Pitre, the Sicilian folk-lorist, writing down word for

1

word what the tale-teller told, including much repetition of *dijo* (said) and quaint corruptions like *ai 'ta, pos, a-a-a viene.*

While I have made extensive notes in comparative folk-lore, I have not here included them. For instance, I might have noted that the story of "La Madrina Muerte" is found in Germany and has been recorded in various forms in more than one Spanish-American country; indeed I have a very different version of it myself. I might have traced "Repaying Good for Evil" back to the Ganges, quoted a version of it written by Marie de France about the twelfth century, and pointed out the use of it in La Fontaine's fables, although, of course, the use of *sotol* and the coyote is purely Mexican. I have so many references to "Blanca Flor" that if written out they would be nearly as long as the story itself. Again I might have traced Pedro de Urdemalas back to Cervantes, noted the many collections of Mexican folk tales in which he appears, his name varying, and located him in Chile, Cuba and elsewhere. Books have been written on the picaresque theme in Spanish literature, and one might be written on the same theme in Spanish-American folk tales. Popular tales of "The Two Compadres" comprise a genre in themselves. Perhaps in the end I shall record these studies.

Now the *cuentos* stand by themselves, for themselves, and I hope they will give others as much pleasure as they have given me.

A Time for Everything

"*Mamacita,* tell us a story," said Juanito.

"This is no time for stories, *hijito,*" responded the mother. "For instance, it is about time that you fill this tub with water so I can finish the washing and get the clothes on the bushes to dry."

"First a story, *mamacita,* then the water," teased the boy.

"This is no time for stories, Juanito: You must learn to be patient." Then, with a laugh, she continued: "If once upon a time people had been patient, none of us would have to die and stay dead, but, just as a worm changes into a butterfly, we would come from death slightly changed but would still continue to live."

"*Más, madrecita;* tell the rest of it," said Juanito.

"Well, Solomon, the wisest of all men, discovered just how it could be done. He told his most faithful servant that on a certain day he would die. 'You must wrap me in a certain way, and after I have been three weeks in the grave you must dig me up and unwrap me. After having spent that time in the sleep of death, I shall come alive again,' said Solomon.

"*Bueno, pues,* the people missed Solomon. They asked questions and wanted to know why he was no longer on his throne.

" 'He is visiting another kingdom,' said the faithful servant. 'Within three weeks he will return.'

"At first the people were satisfied with the answer to their questions, but soon a rumor swept the kingdom like a plague. It was told that the servant had murdered their ruler, and before he could escape from the kingdom to wait for the three weeks to pass, he was captured by a mob. The people demanded to see their king without delay.

"Now, if you had been the servant, Juanito, what would you have done?"

"I would have told them all about it," said the boy.

"I forgot to tell that Solomon had asked that no one be told. In that case, Juanito, just what would you have done?"

"I don't know," said the boy.

"Very well, while you are thinking about it you may fill this tub with water," said the mother.

Juanito, very thoughtful, sat for a moment. Then he sprang to his feet and quickly filled the tub. "Now tell, *madrecita;* what did the faithful servant do?" he asked.

"He told the people it wasn't time for Solomon's return. They asked to know where the king had gone and the servant, refusing to tell, was threatened with death.

" 'Tell us,' they said, 'or we shall kill you.'

"The servant realized that if he told them, Solomon would never come alive again. He knew too, that if he didn't tell, both he and his king would be dead forever. So he took them

3

to the grave, showed them their ruler, and told them the story. The people were heartbroken and wept and prayed for forgiveness, but it was little good that this did. They had not been patient with time, and just for that the secret for coming alive from death was lost forever and ever.

"Now, if you had waited until some other time, this story would have been better," said the mother.

Repaying Good with Evil

"This was a wise man who, while walking along the trail, found a serpent in a trap.

"Let me out," begged the serpent. "It's wrong to keep me here."

"You are right," said the wise man. "It is wrong to keep one trapped." Thereupon he released the snake.

Immediately the serpent coiled about his benefactor and prepared to eat him.

"This is not right," said the wise man. "It is wrong to repay good with evil."

"Perhaps," replied the serpent, "but I am hungry."

"That I regret," said the wise man. "It is wrong to repay good with evil. Before you devour me, let's ask the opinion of someone else."

"That would only prolong your worry, for he would agree with me," said the serpent. "However, to please you, we will call a judge."

They spied a horse passing near. "Come here," called the wise man. "Come here, Señor Caballo. We want your opinion in a serious dispute."

The horse approached and heard impartially the pleas of each. "It is indeed not right for one to repay good with evil," said he. Then, fearing the wrath of the serpent, he added, "But on the other hand, *es la costumbre* (it is the custom) that good be repaid with evil. Behold myself, for example. Once I was young, had the best of food, and was happy, and it was with my energy that my master became a rich man. Now that I am old, he has turned me out to starve. Yes, *es la costumbre* to repay good with evil."

Then they called the ox. "Brother Ox," said the serpent, "we have called you to hear our cause and give an opinion. My friend here contends that it is wrong to repay good with evil. What is your judgment?"

The ox looked the facts calmly in the face and meditated and chewed his cud. Then with a tired sigh he said, "Whether it is right or wrong is not the case. *Es la costumbre* to repay good with evil."

"Fine," said the serpent to the wise man. "Now I shall devour you."

"We are but little wiser than we were," pleaded the wise man. "Grant that we hear the opinion of one more judge."

Thereupon they called the coyote. " 'Mano[1] Coyote," said the wise man, "my friend the serpent contends that it is right to repay good with evil. *Qué dices?*"

"I had rather not say without due thought. I am just *gente corriente* (common folks), a wild animal from the chaparral. My judgment at best may be of little use. What is the trouble?"

The story was told how the snake was released by the wise man and then how the former was wanting to devour the latter when the wise man said that it was not right to repay good with evil.

"That is not enough," said 'Mano Coyote. "I desire to study the case more in detail. Now just how was the serpent trapped? Show me where and show me the trap and show me just how he was fastened, for it might be that he was never trapped at all."

The serpent feared the suggestion that the trap was only a trick. He placed himself as the wise man had found him.

"Now is that really the way you were fastened in, Mr. Snake?" asked the coyote.

"It is," said the snake.

"Is that really the way he was caught?" he asked the wise man.

---

[1] *'Mano*, abbreviation of *hermano* (brother).

"It is," said the wise man.

"Then it is my judgment that the situation as it stands is better than it was when I found it. That is all."

"But it isn't right to leave him to die," said the wise man.

"If it isn't," said the coyote, "it's his own affair."

The wise man and the coyote walked away.

When out of hearing, the coyote said to the wise man, "Brother Wise Man, you will not deny that I have saved your life."

"No," said the wise man. "Though your decision was not definite, at least you saved my life. Look! I own a ranch near here. Come there at eight every morning from now on after I have tied up the dog and I shall give you a hen."

"Good!" said the coyote. "That is better; that is repaying good with good."

The coyote found life so easy he became lazy and took to strong drink, insisting that his appetite was bad and that he needed a *traguito* each morning before eating a hen. Then within a few days he complained that the *traguito* of *sotol* increased his appetite so much that one hen would not do. The wise man was compelled to add a bottle of *sotol* and another hen to the daily menu.

"It seems," meditated the wise man, "that, after all, good is repaid with evil. It was right to give the coyote something but now my friend is resorting to blackmail."

"And that isn't all," growled the dog. "Ere long he will call for another hen. I know him; he lives by his wits."

"That would be my ruin," said the wise man. "What should one do?"

"Put him off one day," said the dog; "then put me in the sack with the hens and when he calls for another chicken, let me out. I will attend to him."

Before long the coyote began to hint that one bottle of *sotol* and two hens were poor pay for the saving of a life. "It seems you have forgotten that good must be repaid with good," said he to the wise man.

"It seems, 'Mano Coyote," answered the latter, "that you have forgotten that at one time you said one hen a day was enough."

"But time changes all. The first contract is now unsatisfactory," answered the coyote. "It is my desire now that I be paid three bottles of *sotol* and three hens daily."

"Very well," said the wise man, "tomorrow I shall begin the new arrangements."

The following morning at the appointed time the wise man came to the meeting place with three bottles of *sotol* and three sacks.

"*Ay, carray!* Toss me out a hen."

This the wise man did. The coyote devoured her, feathers and all, and then drank another bottle of *sotol*.

"*Ay qué carray,*" he shouted. "Toss me out another hen."

The wise man released another hen. The coyote pounced upon her and ate her quicker than the first.

"*Caramba!*" he said, "with age and experience my appetite grows. Now give me the other bottle of *sotol*."

After finishing the third bottle, he shouted, "Let her out."

The wise man released the dog from the sack. The poor coyote was too drunk and stuffed to run. He was caught, but before the fangs of the dog had found their mark he called to the wise man, "It isn't right to repay good with evil. Call off your dog."

"Perhaps it isn't right," answered the wise man, "but *es la costumbre*."

The Three Counsels

This was a boy who ran away from home. Though at heart not bad, he had three habits that were by no means good, for he would stick to no purpose, was always asking about people's affairs, and would not control his temper.

Sí, señor, he ran away from home, but, do you know, he was hardly beyond the horizon when he left the highway for a trail, called to an old man to know his business, and flew into a rage when the latter did not answer.

Presently, however, the *viejito* spoke. "I am a peddler of advice," said he.

"What kind of advice?" asked the boy.

"It will cost you one peso to find out," was the answer.

The boy had only three dollars, but curiosity induced him to give one to the *viejito.*

"First," said the old man, "don't leave a highway for a trail."

"Is that what you call advice?" asked the boy. "You are a fraud."

"Don't you like that one?" asked the *viejito.* "Then give me another peso and lend an ear."

The boy reluctantly handed over the second of his three pesos and waited. "Second," said the *viejito,* "don't ask about things that don't pertain to you."

"Mal ladrón," shouted the boy, "for one peso I would kill you."

"Calm yourself, *hijito,*" said the old man. "I have among my wares one more bit of advice you need. Will you buy it or not?"

The boy's curiosity was too much for him. He gave his last peso to the stranger and listened attentively for the third time.

"Don't lose your temper," laughed the old man, and before the boy could gather his wits, he had vanished into the chaparral.

Sad and empty of pocket, the youth continued on his way.

He took to the road again just as a stranger mounted on a large black horse galloped up.

"Where to, *joven?*" called he.

"To the city," said the boy.

"Then you need advice," responded the man. "Look, I will help you. One league up the road you will find a short cut. You will recognize it by my horse's tracks. It will save you many miles."

The boy thanked him and continued on his journey with the purpose of leaving the highway for the path. However, never being able to keep to a purpose, he disregarded the path.

At noon he came to a ranch house. A bandit sat beneath an arbor in front of it.

"Pase, joven," he called. "You are just in time for dinner."

The boy entered the house and took a chair at the table.

8

He had waited no time when a servant placed before him a dish containing the head of a man. He was at the point of asking a question when he remembered suddenly one of his three costly bits of advice. "I had better ask no questions," thought he.

"Young man," said the bandit, "what do you think of this head?"

"It is a good head," replied the boy.

"Have you no questions?" queried the bandit.

"No, *señor*, none."

"Would you like to see some of my keepsakes?" asked the bandit.

"If it is your pleasure to show them," said the boy, "then it will be my pleasure to see them."

A closet was opened and the boy was shown many skeletons hanging by the neck.

"How do you like my men?" asked the host.

"They are good men," answered the boy.

"*Joven*," said the bandit, "I kill all my guests. These men, like you, each in his turn stepped across my threshold to have dinner with me. Each was shown a head, but, different from you, they wanted to know all about it. Their curiosity brought them to their present condition. You, however, have asked nothing about things that do not concern you, and for that reason my servants will conduct you safely from the ranch. In my corral there are three mules and a horse. The mules will be loaded with gold, and the horse will be saddled. These are yours."

Six bags of gold were tied *mancornado* (in pairs) and placed on the mules. The boy mounted the horse and with the help of the servants was soon on the highway again. "Indeed," he said to himself, "it pays to keep to the main road and it pays to ask no questions about things that do not concern one. Now I am rich."

"Halt!" called a voice from the roadside.

There stood a bandit with his arms crossed.

"What have you in those sacks?" he asked.

The boy was at the point of cursing with rage when he recalled the third bit of advice.

"It is a secret I prefer not to tell," he answered calmly.

"Speak or I shall kill you," threatened the bandit.

"If you feel that is best," said the boy, "then follow your conscience."

"Ha!" said the man, "you are a wise boy. *Adiós;* may you have a pleasant journey."

This *joven* entered the city. Before many weeks had passed he had built and stocked the best store in town and was making barrels of money. Furthermore, he met and married a wealthy girl. However, the best of all was that she, too, did not leave the main road for a path, asked no questions about things that did not pertain to her, and always kept her temper.

La Cucaracha

Juan de Toluca had been a good man. Therefore it was to the gates of Paradise that he directed his steps upon leaving this life.

"Buenos días, San Pedro," said he. *"Con su permiso* I wish to enter here."

But before St. Peter gave his permission, he began asking questions. He wanted to know how much money Juan had, his name and age, and his religion. At last he asked, "What is your race?"

"Mexicano," answered Juan.

"That is too bad," said St. Peter. "We don't keep Mexicans here."

"Why?" asked Juan. "Isn't it enough that one has kept the commandments and attended church?"

"Generally speaking, that is true," said St. Peter, "but the Lord has asked me to keep to the letter of the law. It is nowhere written in our constitution that heaven was made for Mexicans; therefore, I must ask that you step out of line and go to the regions below."

Juan was insistent, however. It had never been his plan to live in the infernal regions. Besides, he had gone to considerable expense upon leaving the vale of tears and had paid sixty pesos for a new hat. This useless expense San Pedro regretted sincerely, but he maintained that he could do nothing about the matter.

"Well, if I must take the other trail, I shall go," said Juan. "However, San Pedro, please do me one and only one favor."

"And what favor is that, Juan?"

"Permit me, please, to take one little peep at the City of Paradise."

San Pedro refused, saying that the memory of the sight of heaven would make hell hotter for him.

"You had better run along," he continued. "You are blocking the line."

Juan fell upon his knees and pleaded so earnestly that St. Peter said, "Well, if that's all you want, have your way."

Thereupon he allowed the Mexican to stick his head through a small opening in the gate of pearls.

Juan saw all that he had ever imagined he would see and even more. He realized the bitter truth of St. Peter's remarks to the effect that he would regret, and determined quickly to resort to cunning. He removed his hat, and at a moment when St. Peter's back was turned sent it rolling down the main street of heaven.

"My hat fell off!" he cried. *"Ay, ay, ay, sombrero de mis entrañas!* I will never leave this place without the sombrero so dear to my affections."

Peter was greatly perplexed. Some contend he had taken a liking to the Mexican. However this may be, the fact is he opened the gate and bade Juan get his hat and hurry back.

Once in Paradise, however, Juan found it convenient to lose himself in the great crowds of angels, and since St. Peter was having trouble at the gate, the illegal entrance to heaven was overlooked.

Everything had gone smoothly in God's kingdom until one day an angel asked to speak privately to the Lord.

"What do you want?" asked Nuestro Señor.

"No, nothing, *Señor,*" replied the angel reverently, "except, *Señor,* I have lost a ring and I suspect someone of having . . ."

11

"Sh—," said the Lord. "Not so loud. Never mention the ring again."

The angel bowed, apologized, and left immediately.

Three days later another angel would speak privately with the Lord.

"What do you want?" asked the Lord.

"No, nothing," said the angel, "only, *Señor*, I have lost a diamond brooch, and I suspect someone of having . . ."

"Sh—," said the Lord, "not so loud; it will ruin the reputation of my place. Go now and never mention the brooch again."

Three days passed and still another angel requested to speak to the Lord in private.

"What do you want?" asked Nuestro Señor.

"No, nothing," said the angel, "only, *Señor*, just this morning I lost my earbobs and . . ."

"I know," said the Lord; "I know."

Nuestro Señor looked sad and perplexed. At last, he said in a whisper, "Do you know, I believe there is a Mexican in heaven."

He went immediately to St. Peter. "Don't waste your breath, St. Peter," said He. "It isn't a question of denial. A Mexican is among us, and we must find some way to rid the place of him without a scandal. Look, the Texan is his neighbor. He knows the Mexican; go quickly to the devil and borrow him for a few moments."

Presently the Lord and St. Peter were asking all manner of questions.

"What are his weak points?" asked Nuestro Señor.

"Well, well," said the Texan.

"Ah, ah," said Nuestro Señor, "no spitting here."

"Well," continued the Texan, "first, I would say women."

"We won't bother about that," said the Lord. "Go on, go on."

"Second, I would say *tequila*."

"Go on," insisted the Lord.

"Third, I would say *La Cucaracha* and his native land."

"Good," said the Lord, "you may go now. St. Peter, get François, the French fiddler."

"*Bueno, Señor,*" said St. Peter.

"François," said the Lord, "can you play *La Cucaracha?*"

"*Mais, oui, Monseigneur,*" said the Frenchman.

Immediately he tuned his instrument.

"Come out here on the balcony where the angels can hear you," said Nuestro Señor. "I'm anxious to know if they like the piece."

"*Très bien, Monseigneur,*" bowed François.

He put his instrument beneath his chin and, after tightening his bow and getting a long breath, he began:

> "*La cucaracha, la cucaracha,*
> *Ya no puede navegar.*
> *Porque le faltan, porque le faltan*
> *Sus patitas de detrás.*"

Suddenly away out in the crowd a hat went sailing into the air, and someone yelled, "*Viva México!*"

"There he is, St. Peter," said Nuestro Señor. "Get him."

And that is the true story, *amigo,* of the only Mexican who ever went to heaven, and you see why they kicked him out.

Sister Fox and Brother Coyote[2]

For weeks 'Mana Zorra had been stealing a chicken each night from a ranch not far from her abode when one night she found a small man standing near the opening she had made in the wire of the chicken house. The man was only a figure of wax put there by the *caporal* to frighten the thief. 'Mana Zorra, unaware of this, was afraid, but, being very hungry, she decided to speak to the little man and ask permission to borrow a chicken.

"*Buenas noches,*" said 'Mana Zorra.

There was no answer.

"He is either too proud to speak or doesn't hear," said the

[2]Compare this story with "Br'er Coyote," by Sarah S. McKellar, and with the fable of the coyote and the coon in "Ranchero Sayings of the Border," by Howard D. Wesley, both in this volume.—*Editor.*

fox to herself. "If he isn't *mal criado* (ill-bred), then he didn't hear. I will speak to him again."

Going nearer the wax man, she said, *"Buenas noches, señor."*

The little man made no response whatsoever, and the fox, after sizing him up from feet to head, decided that she had been insulted.

"Ay, the things I'm going to tell this *hombrecito,*" said she. "He shall speak to me this time or I will slap his face."

She walked up to the figure and shouted at the top of her voice, "Step aside, please, and let me pass."

The wax man stubbornly stood his ground and refused to speak.

"'*Ora verás como yo te hago a un la'o*" (now you shall see how I make you move to one side), said 'Mana Zorra.

She struck the little man in the face and much to her surprise her foot was caught and held fast.

"Let me go!" shouted 'Mana Zorra, "or I shall hit you again."

The wax man refused to let go and 'Mana Zorra hit him full in the face with a hard right swing. The result was that this foot too, like the other, was caught and held.

"*Ay, como eres abuzón,*"[3] grumbled 'Mana Zorra. "Listen, *amigo,* either you let me go or I shall give you a kicking you will never forget."

The wax man was not impressed by the threat and refused to let go. 'Mana Zorra made good her word as to the kicking, but the little man didn't seem to mind at all and added insult to injury by holding her hind feet too.

"I'll bite," she threatened; "I'll bite." And quickly she bit the neck of the wax figure only to find herself caught not only by four feet but by her mouth as well.

"You think you have me," she scolded. "All right, how do you like this for a belly buster?" She pushed him so hard with her stomach that both of them fell rolling to the ground.

Just then who should appear on the scene but 'Mano Coyote?

"What are you doing there, 'Mana Zorra?" he asked.

"No, nothing," she answered. "This Christian and I have

---

[3]A provincialism meaning *an abusive person.*

come to blows over a chicken. I have a contract with the *ranchero* which provides me a hen a night, but this little fellow can't read and has made up his mind to interfere. Hold him for me, 'Mano Coyote, and I will get a hen for both of us."

The coyote, a gullible fellow, caught the wax man in a clinch and held him while the fox pulled loose, and continued to hold tight until she stole a hen and escaped into the chaparral. Then, much to his chagrin, he found that he had been tricked, and as a result would likely lose his life.

Dawn found 'Mano Coyote struggling with the wax man, and he was there and still fighting when the *caporal* arrived.

"*A' amiguito*," said the *caporal*. "This is what I have been wanting to find out for a long time. So it is you, Señor Coyote? And I had always thought you my friend. If you wanted a hen to eat, why didn't you come to me like a gentleman and ask for her? However, though greatly disappointed in you, I will give you another chance."

The *caporal* freed the coyote from the wax man and placed him in a little room with one broken window.

"Don't jump through this window till I call you," said the ranch foreman to the coyote. "My dogs will catch and kill you. Wait until I tie them up and get us a snack to eat. Then when I call, jump through the window and come to the kitchen."

The *caporal* heated water and poured it into a large pot that he had placed beneath the window. Then he called, "Come out, Señor Coyote; breakfast is ready."

The coyote jumped through the window and fell into the pot of boiling water. It was surely a miracle that saved his life, but the scalding water took the hair from his body and several toe nails from his feet.

"*Ay, ay*," said 'Mano Coyote, as he crept with flinching feet and sore hide through the thicket. "'Mana Zorra will pay for this. If I ever see her again I will kill her and eat her up."

Thus went 'Mano Coyote through the brush whining and swearing revenge until he reached a *laguna*. There, before him, lay the fox gazing at something in the water.

"Now I have you," cried the coyote. "Now you are to pay for your smart trick."

"Don't kill me, 'Mano Coyotito," pleaded the fox. "Look! I was placed here to watch this cheese."

"What cheese?" asked the coyote.

The moon was full and the reflection lay at the bottom of the *laguna*.

"There," said the fox, pointing at the reflection. "If you will watch it for me I will get us a chicken. However, be on guard lest the cheese slip beneath the bank."

"I'll watch it for you," said the coyote, "but don't be long. I'm dying for a chicken to eat."

'Mano Coyote had waited and watched several hours when he discovered the cheese slipping beneath the western bank of the *laguna*.

"Hey, Señor Cheese, don't go away," he called. "If you run away, I'll catch you and eat you up."

While 'Mano Coyote talked, the cheese continued to slip away. The coyote, fearing it would escape, sprang into the *laguna* and was soaked and chilled to the marrow before he reached the bank again.

"'Mana Zorra will pay for this," he howled. "Wherever I find her I shall kill her and eat her up."

The coyote had hunted the fox several days when at last he found her lying on her back in a small cave beneath a cropping of boulders. She was sound asleep.

"A' 'Mana Zorrita," hissed the coyote, "now I shall eat you up."

"Don't eat me, 'Mano Coyotito," begged the fox. "Look! When I went to get a hen, the *caporal* asked me to lie here and hold the world on my feet to keep it from falling down. He has gone to get more help and will be back soon to fix it. *Ay de mí*, 'Mano Coyote, I'm hungry. I know where there is a hen, but she will likely be gone when the *caporal* returns. *Ay de mí*, 'Mano Coyote, I'm hungry."

"I'm hungry, too," said the coyote. "Look, 'Mana Zorra;

move over to one side. I'll hold the world on my feet if you will hurry and fetch us a hen."

"Good," said the fox, "but take care that the world doesn't fall and come to an end."

"I'll hold it," said the coyote, lying on his back and pushing up with all the strength of his four feet. "However, hurry; I'm hungry."

The fox escaped, and the coyote remained beneath the rock for several hours until he was almost paralyzed by the increasing weight of the world.

At last, being unable longer to stand the pain of his cramped position, he said, "If it is going to fall, then let it fall. I'm quitting this job."

He sprang from beneath the ledge and ran into the clearing. The rock didn't fall and the world showed no signs of coming to an end.

"*Ay, ay,*" said he, "'Mana Zorra shall pay for this. If I ever catch her I shall kill her and eat her up."

At last the fox was found beneath a large bush near a *gicotera.*[4]

"A', 'Mana Zorra," he cried, "you have played your last trick, for now I'm going to eat you up."

"Don't eat me, 'Mano Coyotito," begged the fox. "Look! I was on my way to get the chicken when a school teacher offered me pay to watch a class of boys."

"Where are the boys?" asked the coyote.

"There, before us; it is their schoolroom."

"Where is the money?" asked the coyote further.

"In my pocket," said the fox, as she rattled some broken pieces of porcelain.

"*Pos,* that's good," said the coyote. "What are you going to do with it?"

"I'm going to buy you a pair of trousers and a skirt for myself."

---

[4]*Gicotera,* a rat's nest at the roots of a bush, but Santiago Garza told me that a kind of bee makes its nest in a *gicotera.*

"Your idea is good," observed the coyote. "However, you must leave some money with which to purchase food."

"Certainly," said the fox. "I shall buy us a chicken apiece. But why did you mention food, 'Mano Coyote? *Ay, ay de mí,* I'm dying of hunger."

"I'm hungry, too," said the coyote.

"Look!" said the fox. "Watch these boys for me and I'll fetch the hen right away."

"*Cómo no?*" said the coyote; "only hurry, 'Mana Zorra."

The fox saved her hide again and the coyote was left with the devil to pay, for the schoolroom was a hornets' nest and the boys weren't pupils but a lively lot of hornets.

The coyote sat listening to the hum of pupils reading their lessons when he noticed that the sound had ceased. "They are loafing on me," he said. "I'll shake them up a bit."

He shook them up and this would have been his last adventure had he not found a *laguna* into which to dive and escape the swarm of hornets.

"*Ay, ay,*" wailed the coyote. "'Mana Zorra shall pay for this. Wherever it is that I find her I shall eat her up, hide and hair."

At last 'Mana Zorra was found in a *carrizal*—a reed swamp. 'Mano Coyote had not forgotten the hornets' sting, the moon cheese, the world trick, and the wax man.

"Now there shall be no more foolishness," said he. "'Mana Zorra must die."

"Don't eat me," pleaded the fox. "Don't eat me, 'Mano Coyotito. Look! I was on my way to get the hens when I met a bridegroom. He invited me to be godmother at his wedding. I felt it would look bad to refuse, and now that you are here you and I shall be *padrino* and *madrina.* You know how it is at these weddings. There is always plenty to eat and drink, and when it comes to chicken, there is none better in the world than that served at a wedding feast. *Ay, ay,* I'm hungry, 'Mano Coyotito."

"*Pos, sí,*" said the coyote; "I'm hungry, too. But where is the wedding party?"

"They are to pass at any time now," said the fox. "You stay

here and I'll see if they are coming. If you hear popping and cracking you will know it is the fireworks shot by the friends of the couple. I shall be back soon."

'Mana Zorra slipped around the cane brake and set fire to it in first one place and then another. 'Mano Coyote heard the popping and cracking and began to dance with joy.

"*Taco Talaco*," said he, "here they come. *Taco Talaco*, *ay*, *Taco Talaco*, what a hot time there will be."

He discovered his mistake too late. The fire had trapped him completely, and so ended the career of 'Mano Coyote the dupe, shouting "*Taco Talaco*" and dancing at his own funeral.

El Pájaro Cú

It was when God made the world. When He created the birds, He first made them and then feathered them. This would have been wise except that a scarcity of feathers left one little creature completely unclothed. This was Pájaro Cú. Yet he, Pájaro Cú, didn't mind in the least, and went about from day to day as innocent as the dawn and as naked as the palm of your hand.

"What is to be done with him?" asked the owl.

"Poor thing," said the dove.

"Shocking," screamed the peafowl. And everyone agreed that it was shocking, a pity, and that something should be done.

"I move," said the owl, "that we each chip in a feather. None will miss so little, and yet all together will make him a splendid coat."

All agreed to this and were at the point of contributing when the peafowl began to wail. "No—, no—, no—," she screamed, "he would then be so vain we could never manage him; think of what you are doing; think of how beautiful he would be. His coat would contain red from the redbird, green from the parrot, black from the crow, white from the swan, gold from the canary, and silver from the guinea. No, no, it will never do, for he will burst with pride."

"We can't leave him this way," said the jackdaw. "He would disgrace the whole republic of birds."

"Yes," said the owl, "he must be clothed. If it is agreed, we will all give a feather, and I will go bond for him."

All the birds from the most common to the rarest contributed, and presently the Pájaro Cú was dressed beyond all description.

He walked to the fountain, gave one look at his magnificent self, and said, "Why do I associate with such birds? I will leave."

Thereupon he flew straight up into the blue of the heavens. Señor Owl followed but to no avail. He was too heavy, and Pájaro Cú was too light. He returned completely exhausted only to face an angry mob.

"So you were to go bond," said the rooster. "You have betrayed us."

"What do you plan to do, Mr. Owl?" asked the crow.

"What do I propose to do? What can be done? May I ask?"

Thereupon the birds flew at him, and it was with many wounds he escaped to a small hole in the side of a hill.

Three days passed, and it seemed he would die of hunger. Then a visitor called at the cave.

"Crut, crut," said he.

"Come in, Señor Roadrunner," said the owl.

"I have brought you a lizard, Señor Owl."

"*Muchas gracias,* Señor Paisano. I am indeed glad that I have at least one friend. Tell me, Señor Paisano, what am I to do?"

"Stay here; don't leave. Señor Cuervo has sworn to kill you."

"But I can't stay here," said the owl. "I must leave this hole in the ground. Tonight, while Señor Crow is asleep, I shall go to the swamps, and I will never cease hunting until I shall have found the Pájaro Cú."

"I will help," said the paisano. "While you search the woods and swamps by night I will watch the roads by day."

And thus it has been ever since, that Señor Roadrunner keeps an eye on the roads and calls, "Cu-rut, cu-rut."

And in the woods at night the owl calls, "Cú, Cú, Cú, Cú, Cú."

MEXICAN TALES

The Parrot Tale-Teller

A rich merchant and a student while drinking one day at an inn began to quarrel. The student said that women were fickle and the merchant contended that they were as trustworthy as men.

"My wife would never disobey me," said the merchant.

"Any man's wife will disobey," said the student.

The argument continued until bets were placed. The student, having no cash at hand, was to serve the merchant three years without salary in case he lost, but, if he won, he was to receive double the amount of a clerk's salary.

Pretending a few days' trip away on business, the merchant, after having exacted a promise from his young wife that she would pray for him each morning at mass during his absence and after having ordered the servant woman to keep the doors closed and locked, packed his saddle bags and left.

Then the student, in accordance with the agreement they had reached, knocked at the door and asked to speak to the merchant's wife.

He was told that under no conditions were strangers to enter the house while the husband was away.

Immediately he went to a magician friend—a relative of the devil—and explained the affair from beginning to end, the result being that he was changed into a parrot. Now as a parrot he entered the merchant's home through a small opening near the door.

"Look!" said the young woman the next morning when she discovered him. "Behold what a beautiful pet!"

"It is time for mass," said the old woman. "We must hurry."

"Don't go to mass," said the parrot. "Don't go to mass, and I shall tell you a story."

"What kind of a story?" asked the young woman.

"I will tell you," said the parrot, "if you will promise to remain and listen to it."

Although the church bells were ringing and the old woman insisted upon going immediately to mass, the merchant's wife

21

promised the parrot that she would stay and hear the story through.

"Once upon a time," said the parrot, "while the king and queen of Spain with their little daughter were traveling through a forest some distance from their palace, the princess lost her favorite doll. They had returned home before the toy was missed. Immediately after the loss was discovered, the little girl, without the permission of her father and mother, left the castle and wandered away into the woods.

"Before long she was lost. After wandering for a night and day, she came to a city. The people took her to their king, who, seeing that she was very beautiful, concluded that surely she was a princess and so gave her a home within his palace. Soon she had become a favorite with the ruler and the object of jealousy and spite on the part of his relatives.

"One morning, tiring of her toys, the little princess asked the king if she might go to the gardens and play with the other girls of the place.

" 'No,' said the king, 'you are a princess and must live like a princess.'

" 'Ask,' said a girl who had stood near the door and heard the king's answer—'ask in this order: "By the soul of your daughter, may I go play?" '

"The princess had not heard of a daughter and felt that the request in this form was a reference to herself. Also, she did not know that the king had forbidden any reference to his daughter.

" 'By the soul of your daughter, may I go play?' asked the princess.

"She was thrown into a dungeon and wandered through dark halls and passages until she came to a room where lay a beautiful girl asleep.

" 'Wake up, please, and tell me where I am,' said she, touching the sleeping girl's cheek.

" 'This girl is enchanted,' thought the princess. 'She is like the sleeping beauty of a story the nurse used to tell. I shall try the magic words of the story and see what happens.'

"The girl awoke, said she was the king's daughter, and shortly the two of them had found their way from the dungeon and had come before the king.

" 'My daughter,' said he, 'is it really true? Can it be true that you have broken the enchanted sleep?'

" 'She is no longer asleep,' said the princess of Spain. 'The spell has been broken.'

"The king was overjoyed. 'I shall adopt you,' he said. 'You shall be my second daughter and shall inherit half my kingdom.'

" 'It was nothing to awake her,' said the princess. 'I need no reward, for I am the princess of Spain.'

" 'Why didn't you tell me before?' asked the king.

" 'Because,' said the princess, 'as you now see, the time for that had not arrived.'

"The princess of Spain returned to her parents and a great celebration was declared at her homecoming.

"Now, *Mamacita*," concluded the parrot to the merchant's wife, "did you like the story?"

"Yes, indeed," said the latter.

The women did not attend mass that day, but spent the time making a perch for the parrot.

"It is time for mass," said the servant the following morning. "Hurry, *señora*, or else we shall be late."

The merchant's wife hurriedly dressed and was preparing to leave when the parrot called, "*Mamacita, mamacita,* I have a new story."

"New story! May God bless me, *señora*, we must go to mass," said the servant.

"No, *Mamacita*," cried the parrot. "There will be another mass, but after today there will never be a story like this."

"You know the promise you made your husband," continued the servant. "You promised to pray every day for his safe return."

"I can pray here," said the young woman. "I must hear the story. Go ahead, *periquito*, tell me the story."

"Well, once upon a time," said the parrot, "in the Land of Far Away there was a princess who had been afflicted with a strange disease. She could not talk, and, once she fell asleep, days would pass before she awoke again. The king, her father, called the wise men of his kingdom, and it was their opinion that the princess of Spain should be requested to come to the bedside of their princess.

"A ship set sail and within a few weeks returned. The princess of Spain was aboard, and as soon as she reached the castle, she was taken to see the afflicted girl.

" 'Lock us within this room tonight,' said the princess. 'I shall sleep in the same bed with your daughter and tomorrow she will be cured.'

"At twelve o'clock that night a dim light entered the room.

"A Turk took from beneath the bed a hidden key and with it loosened the tongue of the girl afflicted. Then while the princess of Spain pretended to sleep, the two talked at length and disclosed that the girl had refused to marry the Turk and that he in turn had brought a spell upon her to the effect that she could speak only when her tongue was loosed with a magic key.

"It was a simple cure for the princess of Spain. She made a sign of the cross and the Turk dropped his key and fled, and the sick princess was made well again.

"When the king offered half his kingdom in payment for the cure, the princess of Spain refused it, saying: 'It was nothing that I did. Thank the Virgin Mary.'

"*Mamacita*," concluded the parrot, "did you like the story?"

The women did not go to church that day; instead they amused themselves talking to the parrot.

The following morning the servant called, "Up, *señora*, up; it is time for mass."

"*Mamacita*," called the parrot, "I have another story."

"Remember the promise to your husband," said the old servant. "You must go to mass and pray for his safe return."

"*Mamacita*," said the parrot, "stay and hear my story or I shall leave and never return."

"My husband won't know the difference," said the young woman. "I will stay."

"Once upon a time," said the parrot, "a prince in a land not far away was with a party hunting in the woods when by chance he found a doll. 'What a beautiful doll!' said he. 'I must meet the girl who owned it.'

"His men called to him and begged that he continue the hunt, but his only answer was, 'What a beautiful doll! I must meet the girl who owned it.'

"The chase was abandoned. The prince returned to the palace and lay down to rest.

" 'Are you tired?' asked the queen.

"The answer was, 'What a beautiful doll! I must meet the girl who owned it.'

"The prince was put to bed, ill with brain fever, and day and night he repeated, over and over again, 'What a beautiful doll! I must meet the girl who owned it.'

"The fame of the princess of Spain had reached the ears of the king of this foreign land and he sent for her. Weeks passed, the ship returned, and the princess entered the palace. She was shown to the prince's room. Upon entering, the first thing she saw was the doll.

" 'My doll!' she cried. 'How strange!'

" 'Your doll?' asked the prince.

" 'Yes,' said the princess. 'I lost it in a forest seven years ago.'

" 'I am no longer ill,' said the prince, 'for I have found the girl who owns the doll.'

"The two were married. They became the king and queen of Spain and ruled that land for many years.

"*Mamacita*," said the parrot to the merchant's wife, "did you like the story?"

"Yes, indeed," she said, "but there is knocking at the door."

The door was opened and, as the husband entered, the parrot disappeared.

"What is wrong?" asked the husband. "Aren't you happy that I am home again?"

"It isn't that," said the young wife. "My pet, a talking parrot, has this moment flown away and I feel that he will never return."

"Strange," mused the husband; "strange that you should

regret the loss of a parrot at a time like this. Tell me, how came the bird here?"

The wife told how it was found in the house the morning after the husband's departure, spoke of the stories, and in a forgetful moment in her narrative admitted that she had not gone to mass and had not prayed for the safe return of her husband. Realizing that he had lost the bet, the man gave way to his wrath and the two argued and quarreled all that day, the next, and the next, and some say they would be quarreling still if it weren't that the devil came and took them away.

The Faithful Lion

Once a hunter captured a lion cub and gave it as a pet to his only daughter. With foreboding and regret the father watched the rapid growth of the beast.

"Take care," said a neighbor, "lest some day he yield to his inborn instincts of a killer. It is dangerous to allow your daughter to feed and caress him."

"Henriqueta," said the father, "our neighbor is right. We must destroy your pet."

"No, father," said the girl, "he must not be killed."

The father yielded on condition that the animal be chained to a tree. Sometime thereafter Henriqueta began to meet secretly near a *laguna* one of several lovers. Four bandits learned of this, and it was agreed among them to wait for her in ambush near the trysting place and kidnap her for ransom.

So it happened one evening while the father was away that they captured the girl, gagged her, tied her hands and feet, and placed her on a horse ridden by the leader. Then all rode at break-neck speed for their camp in the mountains.

Each time upon her return from the *laguna,* it was Henriqueta's custom to stop at the large tree at the rear of the house and pet the lion. On this occasion when she did not return to the tree, the lion grew restless. He would walk to and fro, lie down, yawn, look with head lifted high down the dark path to the *laguna.* Then he would whine and resume his restless yawning and pacing to and fro. At last either the suspense or a premonition of danger so aroused him that he screamed and sprang and ran on his chain with such fury that the collar broke; then a large shadow slipped through the brush to the banks of the *laguna*. There was a brief pause and the animal disappeared into the night.

The bandits had gone some five leagues when their horses began to show signs of fear. It was only with much quirting and spurring that they were kept to the *sendero* (breach).

The cause of alarm apparently vanished. Then, while the bandits were trailing along the banks of a ravine beneath large overhanging trees, the lion dropped from a limb upon the neck of the horse carrying the girl. Mount and riders were thrown to the ground. The bandit leader was killed, and with great haste the others took to their heels.

When Henriqueta's father returned to the ranch, he missed his daughter and ran to the large tree. The missing lion to him meant only one thing. Henriqueta had been slain and carried away.

He called his men, armed them and began a hunt that lasted into the following day. At last, with all hopes gone, they returned home, where they found Henriqueta lying exhausted on the porch and the lion near by watching over her.

Truthful John

El pan para los muchachos,   Bread for children,
El salvado para los machos,   Bran for mules,
Y el vino para los borrachos.   And wine for drunkards.

In a certain *granja* there was a cowherd whose name was Juan. Since he never lied, he was called Juan Verdadero. Afternoons when he returned from the fields with the stock one would hear the following conversation between him and the *patrón*.

"Juan Verdadero, how is the herd?"
"Some fat, some poor, upon my word."
"And the white and greenish-colored bull?"
"*Señor*, quite green and beautiful."

One day the owner of the adjoining farm visited Juan's *patrón*.

"Our neighbor," said he, "is a great liar. He tells me he received forty pesos a head for his cows. What a liar! Doesn't it seem that way to you?"

"But, *compadre*," said the *patrón*, "it may be true."

"No," said the neighbor, "any man under the urge of necessity will lie."

"Not true," said the *patrón*; "I have a *vaquero* on the place who never lies."

"So I have heard. I'll bet you my *granja* against your *granja* that your boy Juan Verdadero can be induced to lie," said the neighbor.

"I'll bet he can't," said the *patrón*.

Next day the neighbor sent his beautiful daughter with a diamond ring to the fields in search of Juan Verdadero. She found him, placed the ring in his hand, and asked, "Juan, do you like this ring?"

Juan, who had never before seen a thing so valuable, was quite carried away.

"I shall present it to you," said the girl, "if in return you will give me the heart of the green bull."

"No," said Juan, "for then what should I tell the *patrón?*"

"Oh, you can tell him a wild beast ate the bull. . . . You are honest; the *patrón* will believe you."

Juan struggled with himself, but the desire to possess the ring overcame him.

The bull was killed and its heart was given to the girl, who, overjoyed, departed immediately for her *granja*.

Now Juan had never lied before and he found it hard to invent a credible falsehood. No sooner would he choose a story than it seemed unbelievable. He removed his coat, hung it on a post, and, placing his hat atop, kneeled before it as if it were the *patrón*. Then he said:

"Juan Verdadero, how is the herd?"

"Some fat, some poor, upon my word."

"And the white and greenish-colored bull?"

Here he paused. Three times he repeated this without finding it possible to lie.

The evening shadows lengthened toward the east, and the diamond lost its luster. Juan, now weeping in despair, must return with his cows to the ranch house, and, without the green bull, must face the *patrón*.

The two men waited at the corral gate. The neighbor smiled with condescending patience as the *patrón* began:

"Juan Verdadero, how is the herd?"
"Some fat, some poor, upon my word."
"And the white and greenish-colored bull?"

There was no answer.

Again the *patrón* repeated:

"Juan Verdadero, how is the herd?"
"Some fat, some poor, upon my word."
"And the white and greenish-colored bull?"
"Dead, *señor*, dead."

"What?" shouted the *patrón*, pretending anger.

Juan, kneeling before him, told how a girl as pretty as the summer's dawn had given him a diamond ring for the heart of the bull, and how, in a moment of weakness, he had yielded.

The *patrón* was overjoyed.

"Juan Verdadero," he said, "from now on you are the *administrador* of my *granja*."

The neighbor was compelled to give over his entire estate, for he had lost the bet.

Quieres que te lo cuente otra vez?	Shall I tell you again?
Este era un gato,	This was a cat,
Con los pies de trapo,	With feet of tatters
Y los ojos al revés.	And eyes turned back.

The Two Compadres

These were two *compadres*. One was rich and the other poor. The rich man was very genial, and never a day passed that he didn't make it a point to greet his *compadre* and *comadre*. But further than an exchange of *buenos días* he gave nothing, and since his *compadre* was very poor, his niggardliness was resented.

"*Vieja,*" said the poor man to his *señora,* "I've thought of a scheme. We must get money from our *compadre.* Go to the place where you grind *masa* and ask the family to lend us twenty cents; then buy a pen, ink and paper. I shall go into the chaparral and catch two jack rabbits."

Within two hours rabbits, paper, ink and pen were at hand.

"Now, old woman," the poor *compadre* said, "sit just outside the door and call to me when you see our *compadre.*"

Presently the *señora* said, "Here he comes."

The poor *compadre* seated himself quickly at the table and with pen in hand pretended to be very busy writing a letter.

"*Buenos días, comadre,*" greeted the rich man. "*Cómo le amaneció?* (How did you get up this morning?)"

"Very well, thanks, *compadre.* Only we have little to eat."

"And my *compadre,* where is he?" asked the rich man, ignoring the hint.

"*Ai 'ta dentro,*" responded the *comadre.* "He is inside writing a letter to a friend in the city."

"*Buenos días, compadre,*" greeted the poor man. "You will pardon the delay in speaking to you. I am in a hurry to get a letter off to a friend in the city."

"Then I will not detain you since surely you will need hurry to the post office."

"No, *señor compadre,*" responded the poor man. "I don't mail my letters. I have a rabbit that is trained to run errands. He does the job quicker and saves me stamps."

Thereupon the poor *compadre* tied the letter to the rabbit's neck and turned him loose. The rich *compadre* was surprised at the speed with which the pet took off down the flat.

"When will he return from the city?" he asked.

"Not later than tomorrow," said the poor *compadre.* "You see how he runs. Neither hound nor hawk will stop him."

"Marvelous," said the rich man. "I shall return tomorrow to

learn more about this wonderful rabbit. If he's as good as you say, I must buy him."

The following day the poor *compadre* said to his *señora*, "Look, *vieja*, sit just outside the door and call to me when you see our *compadre*."

She sat and presently said, "There comes our *compadre*."

Then the poor *compadre* brought in the other rabbit and ran him about the room until he was almost winded and was panting like a horse with the thumps.

"*Buenos días, comadre*," greeted the rich man. "Has my *compadre*'s pet returned yet with the mail?"

"*Sí, señor*. Come in; it has just this instant arrived. Your *compadre* is reading the letter now."

"*Quiubo, compadre*," called the poor man. "*Pase, hombre*. Only look at this! Good time, don't you think?"

He handed the rich man a letter addressed to himself that he had just that morning faked.

"And look how winded my rabbit is! Once on the flat he travels like the wind."

"*Pues sí*," said the rich man, "it is all very good. However, you don't need him as I do. Sell him to me, *compadre*. How much will you take—one hundred dollars?"

"You know, *compadre*, I would sooner sell him to you than anyone else; yet it is impossible. First, he's a pet and, second, I need him."

"But I need him worse," said the rich man. "I will give you five hundred dollars for him."

"No, *compadre*, I am sorry, but . . ."

The rich *compadre* stooped quickly, picked up the rabbit, and said, "*Adiós, compadre*. I'm taking him with me. If you want a thousand dollars, come to my house."

The deal was made and the rich *compadre* began writing letters.

His *señora*, too, wrote many letters and after a bit she said, "*Mira, hijo*, I must return these jewels to our friend in the city. Will our rabbit take them?"

"*Cómo no?*" said the man. "He's perfectly safe. He travels

like the wind across the flat. Neither hound nor hawk will stop him."

They made a package of the jewels and the letters and tied it to the rabbit's neck. He took off with a speed that amazed them both and the man said, "You will see; tomorrow morning early he will be back with the answers."

However, the morrow came and went and so did the day following without the rabbit's returning. The third day a cruel suspicion dawned upon the rich *compadre* and he swore to get revenge.

In the meantime the poor *compadre* had been busy cooking another pie for his friend.

"*Vieja,*" he said to his wife, "take this peso to the market square and buy a beef's bladder and a quart of blood, and on the way home find some kind of rare flower. Bring these to me and sit just outside the door and call to me when you see our *compadre.*"

The flower, blood, and bladder were brought, and the man explained that the rich *compadre* would be very angry when he arrived and would likely want to fight.

"You," he said, "you put the bladder filled with blood beneath your waist on the left side and when we become noisy come to me and say, 'Look, *viejo,* you musn't quarrel with my *compadre.* You two will end by becoming angry.' Then I will jump to my feet and stab the bladder and say, 'Woman of the devil, attend to your own business.' Then you fall as if dead, and our *compadre* will feel compromised. I will then take the flower and pass it before your face. You must sit up. I will do this again and you will stand. And on the third pass of the flower you will smile and say, 'I feel well again.' "

All being arranged to the finest detail, the *comadre* sat just outside the door. Presently she said, "*A-a-a viene mi compadre.*"

The man pretended to be busy.

"*Buenos días, comadre,*" said the rich man. "Is my *compadre* here? I must speak with him."

"*Pase, compadre,*" said the poor man.

The quarrel began immediately. One accused the other of fraud and the other denied the accusation.

"Look, *viejo*," said the woman, "you musn't quarrel with my *compadre*. You two will end by being angry."

Thereupon the poor man sprang to his feet, and stabbed her. She fell to the floor and the blood ran from the wound.

"*Dios mío!*" said the rich man. "What have you done, *compadre?* They will hang us for this."

"Don't worry," said the poor man. "I have a magic flower of life. Behold."

He took the flower from his pocket and with the first pass before the wounded woman's face she sat up, with the second she stood, and with the third she said she was well again.

"Sell me that flower," said the rich *compadre*.

"No, *compadre*, I can't; I expect to go to the city, and, once there, I shall get rich curing people of all kinds of ills."

"I will give you one thousand dollars for your magic flower."

"No, *compadre*. Something will go wrong, and then you will blame me."

"Blame you for what, *compadre?*" said the rich man.

He snatched the flower from the poor man and said, "If you want twenty-five thousand dollars, come to my house."

The bargain was made.

"I saw our *compadre* leaving here," said the rich man's wife upon returning from mass. "You must have nothing to do with him. Remember the rabbit."

"Remember nothing," said the rich man. "Listen! woman of the devil, attend to your own business."

Thereupon he stabbed her, and she fell to the floor.

The daughter and the servants began to weep.

"Shut up, you," said the man. "It is nothing. I have a magic flower of life. Behold, and you will see her come alive."

He passed the flower before the dead one's face, but she did not sit up. He repeated this, and she did not stand. He repeated it once more and she did not speak. She was dead *de veras*.

"*Ay, ay, ay,*" wailed the man. "So soon as I shall have buried

33

my *señora*, I shall go immediately and kill my *compadre*."

In the meantime the poor man was setting another trap for his *compadre*.

"*Vieja*," he said, "get four candles and a large white cloth. Your *compadre* will be here soon, and I must play dead."

Candles and cloth were brought. The man laid himself flat on the floor and crossed his hands over his chest. The woman covered him with the sheet and put two lighted candles at the head and two at the feet. Then she sat just outside the door and presently said, "*A-a-a viene mi compadre*." And the man lay as still as death.

"*Buenos días, comadre*," said the rich man.

The woman began weeping bitterly and did not return the greeting.

"What is the matter, *comadre*?" said the rich man.

"Your—your—*compadre* is dead," said she.

The rich man removed his hat and entered the room.

"Too bad, *comadre*. What killed my *compadre*?"

"Too—too—toothache," wept the woman.

"Ha!" said the rich man. "Strange that he should die of toothache. Living or dead, however, I think I shall take him with me."

Thereupon he unfolded a large sack and slipped it over the body of his *compadre* and tied it securely.

Just then he heard a burro passing by and he called to the two *arrieros* driving it to help with the sack and its contents. They placed the load on the animal and made off *calle arriba* (up the street) for the rich man's home.

Upon arriving there he told the *arrieros* to wait until he saddled his horse. He entered his corral and left them at the gate.

"I wonder what is in this sack," whispered an *arriero*.

"*Ay, ay*," came a voice from within, "take me down and I'll tell."

They removed the sack from the burro.

"*Ay, ay*," came the voice, "untie the sack and I'll tell."

They untied the sack.

"*Ay, ay,*" said the man, "lift me to my feet and I'll tell."

They lifted him and he said, "My *compadre* is trying to compel me to marry a rich girl. Though I explained that I have a family, he wouldn't listen, and for that you see me here."

"I'm not married," said an *arriero.* "I will marry the rich girl for you, *con mucho gusto.*"

They placed the *arriero* in the sack, and before the poor man escaped *calle abaja* (down the street) he had them promise to say nothing to the rich *compadre* about the change.

Presently the rich man returned all booted and spurred and ready to ride.

"Where is your friend?" he asked the *arriero.*

"He had some business to attend to and asked me to stay and help you."

"Here is ten dollars," said the rich man. "I won't need you now. Leave the burro to me."

He drove to the sea, removed the load, and dumped it into the water. Then he returned to town and sat out in front of his house to read a newspaper. Presently he saw seated against the wall just across the street another man.

"For the life of me," he said, "it is my *compadre. Oiga,* you, listen, *compadre;* come over here. How did you make out, *compadre?*"

"I'm provoked," said the poor man. "You dumped me into the sea but not far enough out. Look!"

When released from the sack at the corral gate, the poor *compadre* had gone home and thence to the thickets. While there, fate so had it that he found the jewels the rabbit had lost.

"Look at these pearls," said he. "The ocean bed is covered with them and the people of the sea gave me these before I came away."

"What?" said the rich man. "I must have some jewels like that. *Compadre,* do me the favor to tie me in a sack and dump me into the ocean at the very place where you fell."

"No, *compadre,*" said the poor man. "Something will go wrong and you will blame me."

35

"By no means, friend. Look, I will put my hacienda in trust for you. Do me this one great favor, *compadre*."

"Very well," said the poor man.

The trust was made; the rich *compadre* was duly sacked and dumped into the sea in accordance with his own wishes, and the poor *compadre* is now rich. He is held in great esteem by the people of his town for his many innocent little pranks.

A Boom in Guarache Leather

These were two men who lived in Coyame. One was rich and the other poor. The rich man counted his cows on an adding machine, while the poor man needed only one finger of one hand to keep track of his. Yet, Don Pedro Carrasco, the man of wealth and importance, was envious of the poor man José Días, for the latter's cow was large, fat, and never dry.

"José," said Don Pedro, "I will give you one hundred pesos for your cow."

"*Pos, señor*," said the *peladito*, "she is my only possession, and if she were sold my family and I would starve *sin remedio*."

"I will give you ten cows in exchange for yours," said Don Pedro.

"Pardon, *señor*," said José, "my one cow is never dry and she gives ten times more milk than your ten cows would give."

Don Pedro walked away without further comment, but those who saw the anger in his face felt that José would ere long have much cause for regret.

Three days later the two men met on the *plazuela*.

"*Buenos días*, José," said Señor Carrasco with such a show of courtesy that the *peladito* was thrown completely off his guard. "Are your *asaderos* selling well?"

"*Sí, señor*," said the poor man, "with God's help I sell enough cheese to furnish my family with food and clothing. I have no cause for complaint, *gracias á Dios*."

"It seems a pity to spend one's life barely living, José. With *guarache* leather selling in Aldama at ten pesos a pair, inside two days you could be a man of wealth. You know, *amigo*, that beyond the mountains the people have only this week learned to wear sandals. Your cow would make one hundred pairs of *guaraches* and ten times one hundred would bring one thousand pesos. You see," continued Don Pedro, "you see, a good friend to tip one off and a bit of figuring and a bit of common sense are all one needs these days to make money out of no money at all."

"Is it really true," asked José, "that in Aldama *guaraches* are ten pesos a pair?"

"*Hombre,* would I say so if they were not?" responded Don Pedro. "Go ask Lupe Aguilar, the brother-in-law of Cuca Ramírez. It was only this morning that he told me, and this very day I shall kill some cows and sell their hides for *guaraches.*"

The trick worked. Within an hour José Días was no longer content with the even trend of things. "One thousand pesos," he mused. "Just fancy, the *vieja* could have fine clothes, the daughters the many things they need, and I would no longer have to work. A thousand pesos, *figúrese no más!* Just figure that to yourself!" The *peladito* became such a victim of illusions that before nightfall he had killed his cow, skinned her, and cut the hide into small strips the size of the sole of a man's foot. Without caring for the meat in any manner, he left that very night for Aldama.

Bright and early the following morning on a street in Aldama two policemen were startled by a strange vendor's call.

"*Guaraches!*" was the cry. "*Guaraches!* Ten pesos a pair."

"Is he drunk or crazy?" asked one of the policemen.

"We will take him to the *presidente municipal* and soon find out," said the other.

José told his story, and everyone except the *presidente* laughed.

"Carrasco has caused you to make a fool of yourself, my friend," said he. "Your rawhide isn't worth three pesos, much less a thousand. Here, take this coin, buy yourself a *taco*—sandwich—or two and leave Aldama."

Mechanically José accepted the gift and, without bothering to shoulder his bundle of *guarache* leather, took to the street.

"Now there will be no clothes for the *vieja*," said he, "no gifts for the daughters, and now of all times there will be no rest for myself. What a fool I've been!"

Just then a street vendor called: "*Máscaras! Máscaras del diablo!*"

José turned, saw a cartload of masks, and on the very top a devil's face so red-eyed, sharp-eared, wolfish, and weird that he decided to buy it. He gave the *presidente's* coin to the vendor, took the mask and, placing it beneath his shirt, proceeded on his way out of town.

Night overtook him on the mountain slopes west of Coyame. With night came a cold north wind and the poor man was at the point of freezing when to the left of the road he saw a camp fire. He approached it and found ten men seated on ten leather bags around the blaze.

"May I warm?" asked José.

A minute passed before a word was spoken. At last, however, one of the men told him to come near the fire and make himself comfortable.

José was too cold just then to care who his hosts might be. Later, however, while warming his hands in the blaze, he studied them one by one and concluded that they were bandits.

Suddenly a noise was heard. The men jumped to their feet.

"What is it?" asked José.

"One of the saddle horses staked in the brush," said the captain. "We thought it might be Indians. A tribe has been on our trail since sunrise."

José figured it would be well to leave, but the warmth of the fire and the rushing of the bitter norther through the catsclaw brush, plus the fact that he was very tired, caused him to delay and finally to abandon any intention of leaving the fire for the night.

One after the other the bandits spread their sarapes side by side near the fire, lay down, and went to sleep. The night grew colder and the wind stronger. José was too busy keeping warm to think of sleep. For an hour he spent the time turning first his face and then his back to the fire. He got more wood from the brush, built a larger blaze, and still he thought that surely his nose would freeze.

He was warming his back and wondering just how he could make himself more comfortable when suddenly he remembered the mask. He placed it over his face. His nose, ears and cheeks soon were warm again but his hands were cold. He turned to the fire, reached into the blaze and was rubbing his hands and groaning when the bandit nearest the blaze awoke.

Now, this fellow hadn't been a good man and what he saw looking at him through the flames and smoke paralyzed him with fear. Presently he eased over to the nearest bandit and touched him with his elbow. This fellow also, like the first, was scared stiff and could hardly breathe. One by one the bandits awoke until the last man, the captain, was nudged by his neighbor.

The captain had had a bad dream. He dreamed he was dead and the devil had come to get him. When he awoke to find himself free to run, run he did, calling to the men as he went, *"Córranle, muchachos!* Run for your lives!"

José was unaware that they were awake until he saw them running away and heard the captain screaming at the top of his voice for his men to run. "Indians!" he thought and followed hot on the heels of the bandits. One of them saw him coming and yelled, "He's coming, *muchachos!* Run for your lives!"

José ran so fast the mask slipped over his eyes and he stumbled and fell to the ground. He lost no time in getting to his feet again, but he had lost his sense of direction for the moment. He listened. There was no sound anywhere.

"Strange," said he as he fumbled the mask. "Strange. I wonder. Válgame Dios! It must have been the mask. I must call these fellows back and explain."

He followed in the direction they had fled until he came to a large precipice, and there a hundred feet below he heard a bandit groaning. They had all fallen over the cliff and were dead or dying.

José returned to the fire and picked up one of the ten leather pouches. Greatly to his surprise it was full of gold pieces. He opened another. It, too, was full of gold; and so it was with the rest of them—all full of gold. He tied the pouches in pairs *mancornado*—yoked together—fashion and put them on five of the saddle horses that had been staked by the bandits. Then mounting another horse, he set out for his hut and, with the ten sacks of gold all safe, reached it before dawn.

At ten o'clock that morning the one he-gossip of the *villa* came nosing around.

"*Buenos días,* José," he said.

"*Buenos días, señor.*"

"They tell me you killed your cow, *amigo.*"

"*Sí, señor!* I killed her."

"They tell me, José, that you tried to sell her hide for *guarache* leather at ten pesos a pair," added the gossip with a hint of honeyed derision.

"*Mire, amigo,*" said José. "Don Pedro Carrasco did me a great injustice."

"Don't tell me that," said the man.

"Yes," continued José, "he told me to sell the hide at ten pesos a pair, but fortunately I met a friend in Aldama who tipped me off to the fact that *guarache* leather was selling at twenty pesos a pair. Look."

He took a handful of gold from his right pocket. "What do you think of that?" he said with a wee small hint of boasting. "And if that isn't convincing, look."

He drew another handful of gold from his left pocket.

"Look, *amigo,*" he went on, "this is yours. Take it. Certainly, all of it, my friend. Only do me one little favor. Don't tell Don Pedro Carrasco about it. I am going to buy his cows, kill them all and sell their hides. *Figúrese, hombre* (consider, man); at twenty pesos a pair for *guaraches,* with all those cows I shall soon be the richest man in the whole republic. But remember, not a word to Don Pedro Carrasco."

What were promises to the town's he-gossip? Within thirty minutes Don Pedro knew the whole story. By nightfall he had killed all his cows and at dawn the following morning he was in Aldama with the first wagonload of *guarache* leather.

"*Guaraches!*" he cried, "*Guaraches!* Twenty pesos a pair."

"Listen," said one of the policemen to the other. "He's back again."

"No," responded the other officer, "it's someone else."

"Is he drunk or crazy?" asked the first.

"Crazy, likely, and twice as crazy as the other. Let's take him to the *presidente municipal.*"

Don Pedro told his story and everyone laughed, including the *presidente.* In fact the *presidente* laughed himself into a fit of coughing and it was some time before he could regain enough composure and dignity to speak as an impartial judge. "*Todos andamos cogeando del propio pie,*[5] Don Pedro, and you have limped into bad business on account of avarice. *En su mismo pecado lleva Vd. la penetencia* (your sin carries its own penitence). And since justice was so prompt in this case I feel there is nothing for me to do except to give you your liberty and a bit of good advice. Remember this: *Para pagar es corresponder* (the way to pay is to return the favor). Give my regards to your friend José Días, and on your way out, *hombre, cante por no ponerse a llorar* (sing to keep from crying)."

José and his family are wealthy now and they have given much money to the *santitos* and the poor.

Charge This to the Cap

These were two *compadres.* One was rich and the other poor.

"*Vieja,*" said the latter to his wife one day, "it isn't right that we should starve. I'm going to ask our rich *compadre* to help us."

Upon reaching the rich man's home, the poor *compadre* was received badly. He asked for food but received not so much as sympathy. In fact, the rich *compadre* was discourteous to the extent of laughing at the poor man, his attitude, and clothing, and his hat in particular.

"You need no help, *compadre,*" said he. "Go sell your cap. As a curiosity it is worth a fortune; and it is so full of holes,

---

[5]"We all go limping, each on his own foot." This is a proverb meaning that each person reacts according to his own defects.

it is at least a good riddle to set people guessing just when it will decide to be no cap at all."

Three years passed and the poor *compadre's* luck, which could not have been worse, was now somewhat better.

"*Vieja*," said he, "I'm going to take the little money we have and get even with our rich *compadre*."

First he bought himself a gray cap with a blue band; then he went to a watchmaker's shop and bought a cheap watch.

"*Amigo*," he said to the watchmaker, "I need your help. My *compadre*, a very rich man, has insulted me and you can help me get revenge. After we have changed the price tag to indicate a very valuable timepiece, I shall leave the watch with you and call for it later. When I return you are to act as if you have never seen me before and I shall pretend to be buying the watch for the first time. I shall take it, point to my gray cap and say, '*Debo de gorra*' (charge this to the cap), and you are to respond, 'You owe nothing; take it.' "

Being assured of the watchmaker's help, the poor *compadre* went to a jeweler, bought a string of imitation pearls, and made the same arrangements with him that he had made with the watchmaker. "When I take the pearls and say, '*Debo de gorra*,' you are to say, 'You owe me nothing; take it.' "

From the jewelry store our poor *compadre* went next to a dry goods store and bought a suit, and then to an inn, where he paid for two meals. In each case it was understood that on his return he was to point to his gray cap and say, "*Debo de gorra*," instead of paying for his purchase.

With the trap well set, he visited his rich *compadre*, and, being well-dressed, was received with excess courtesy.

"*Compadre*," said the rich man, "what a fine new cap! What kind is it?"

"Oh! it isn't so much," said the poor man; "yet it has proved valuable upon more than one occasion. However, *compadre*, I've come to town to make some purchases. If you don't mind, I should be pleased to have you go with me. After this business is attended to, you shall be my guest at dinner."

"*Con mucho gusto*," said the rich *compadre*, who was much

in favor of getting something for nothing. "It will be a great pleasure to accept your invitation."

They went first to the watchmaker's shop.

"Let me see a good watch," said the poor man.

"A good watch will cost a lot of money," said the merchant.

"It isn't the price; it's the watch that counts," said the customer. "I'll take that one marked three hundred dollars."

The watch was handed to the poor *compadre*.

"*Debo de gorra*," said he, pointing to his gray cap.

"You owe me nothing; take it," said the merchant.

The rich *compadre* was amazed but held his peace.

The two went immediately to the jewelry store. Here the imitation pearls had been marked up to one thousand dollars. The poor *compadre* took them and instead of paying for them said, "*Debo de gorra*."

"You owe me nothing; take them," said the jeweler.

Next they entered the dry goods store and the suit was bought and paid for with a point to the cap and the words, "*Debo de gorra*."

The two *compadres* went to an inn and had dinner and from all appearances this too, like the suit, pearls, and watch, was paid for with a salute with the right hand to the gray hat and the words, "*Debo de gorra*."

"What a marvelous cap!" said the rich *compadre*. "Sell it to me."

"No, *compadre*," said the poor man. "I could hardly live without my gray cap with the blue ribbon."

"I will give you thirty thousand dollars for it," said the rich man.

After a bit of hesitancy on the part of the poor man the deal was closed and the rich *compadre* rushed home to tell his wife.

"*Hija*," said he, "this is to be the day of days. Come, we will buy whatever you want."

"How?" exclaimed the wife. "You will buy the diamond necklace I asked for a year ago?"

"Certainly, woman," boasted the rich man, "and even more."

They went to the best jewelry store in town and bought a diamond necklace. Then instead of paying for it the rich *compadre* pointed to his gray cap and said, "*Debo de gorra.*"

"What does that mean?" said the clerk.

"It means, stupid, that I don't have to pay for the necklace."

Evidently the clerk thought otherwise, for he had the rich *compadre* arrested.

To-day, the poor *compadre* lives in luxury while the rich *compadre* is in a madhouse.

"It worked," says the rich *compadre* over and over again. "It worked; I saw it with my eyes. It is a magic cap, I tell you. The one who wears it never pays for a thing; all one needs to say is, '*Debo de gorra.*'"

Treason in Saints

In an Indian *ranchería* at the foot of a *sierra* lived two *compadres*, Juan and Tomás.

Juan was gentle and kind, and by the sweat of his brow earned an honest living, while Tomás, on the other hand, was lazy and lived by his wits.

Compadre Juan had been plowing his field in preparation for the planting of corn and beans. One morning upon entering the corral he found that one of his oxen was gone. He stood for a moment thinking, and then he said: "Perhaps it is my *compadre* Tomás; perhaps it is he who stole the ox. I will go to his house and look for evidence."

Before reaching the home of his *compadre*, he met the latter's little son.

"Good morning, *hijito*," he said. "Where is your *tata?*"

"At home," replied the child. "He has killed an ox and is stripping the flesh to dry. The hide is up there under the cliffs."

Juan was calm.

"That is good," he said. "That is indeed very good, *hijito*. Maybe your *tata* will divide the meat with me."

Upon reaching the house, Juan greeted both his *compadre* and *comadre* and said: "Compadre Tomás, I have come to ask permission to consult your San Antonio.[6] I am in trouble and need a revelation, and since your saint is so famous for his miracles, I feel he may help me."

"Yes, of course," said Tomás. "Why not? It will be a pleasure to lend you my San Antonio."

Thereupon he took a statuette from a shelf and handed it to Juan. It was Saint Anthony holding the child Jesus. Juan walked to one side and pretended to converse with the image. At last he crossed himself, placed the saint back on the shelf and turned to Tomás.

"Compadre Tomás," he said abruptly, "be it known that last night an ox was stolen from my corral. Your San Antonio here says that you are the thief, and that you are stripping the flesh to dry and have hid the hide under the cliffs. Now, since I was planning to kill that very ox and since you have so kindly done the work for me, I will say nothing to the authorities about the matter, on condition, of course, that you produce both meat and hide immediately."

Reluctantly Tomás admitted his guilt, brought forth the meat and hide and sacked them for his neighbor. The latter, with many thanks, bade his *compadre* good day and disappeared down the trail.

Helpless, Tomás watched the reward of his cunning slip from his grasp. As he stared down the trail, his face became gradually that of a demon. He walked across the room to the little shelf, and with the very first blow of his *machete*, he knocked Saint Anthony from his place. The child Jesus, unharmed, rolled beneath the feet of the woman.

"Baby, no; baby, no," she begged, trying to save the little image from her husband's rage. "*Nene*, no; *nene*, no!"

"And why not? *Nene*, too, I tell you; *nene*, too; lest he grow up and become a traitor like his *tata*."

---

[6]In a book just off the press, *Three Dollars a Year*, an informal and anecdotal exposition of the Zapotec Indian village of San Pablo Cuatro Venados in the State of Oaxaca, Mexico, (The Delphic Studios, New York), by G. Russell Steininger and Paul Van de Velde, a diverting version of this tale of San Antonio is told as pertaining to an actual occurrence in the village.—*Editor.*

PURO MEXICANO

And thus it was that San Antonio and the Niño Jesús were destroyed for knowing and saying too much.

Baldheads

A fellow sent his son to town to purchase food. Wishing to walk the streets a while and yet fearing to go about with money on his person, the youth decided to deposit his purse somewhere for safekeeping. He entered a house bearing the sign *Casa de Encargos*.

"Yes, *joven*," said a clerk, "you may, with all confidence, leave your money with us."

After four hours of sight-seeing, the youth was back for his money.

"What? Who are you? You deposited nothing here," said the clerk.

It was evident that this was not a bank, but a place where country folk were skinned.

The youth returned home and told his father what had happened.

The father asked, "Can you describe the man who took your deposit?"

"*Señor*," said the son, "he was a bald-headed man."

"Not so good," said the father, "not so good."

"Tell me, son," continued the father, "is he balder than I?"

"No," responded the son, "not so bald by far."

"Then don't worry; just leave him to me. Come. Let's go to town."

The father provided himself with a small buckskin bag. This he filled with buttons and rusty washers. Having told his son what to do, he entered the house bearing the sign *Casa de Encargos*, and placed the bag on the counter.

He asked the clerk, "*Señor*, is this a bank? I should like to deposit some money here."

"*Sí, señor*," answered the clerk, "you may, with all confidence, leave your money with us."

At this moment, as prearranged, the son entered and asked

the clerk for his money. The latter, fearing to lose a larger sum, said, "Yes, *joven*; here is your money."

After counting out to him peso for peso, the clerk turned to the man and said, "This boy, *señor*, is my regular customer."

"I am glad to know that," said the father. "I wanted to be sure my son had left his money with you. You won't need this bag of buttons and rusty washers. *Con su permiso, señor*, I shall not deposit it. With your permission."

And, bowing politely, he left.

"Keep an eye on baldheads, son," said the father.

Juan Pelón

This was a hardheaded boy. Once his mother left the baby in his care. Juan Pelón, curious to know how children were put together, cracked his little brother's skull and took out his brains. When the mother returned, Juan said, "Look! The baby's head was full of worms."

On another occasion the mother left him at the house while she went for water. Juan Pelón made a nest, put eggs in it and sat on them. When the mother returned she found the door locked.

"*Ábreme la puerta*, Juan," she called.

"I can't open the door," answered Juan. "*Estoy cuelco*" (I am setting).

The mother called a priest, who, after much argument with the boy, convinced him that it was a hen's business to set.

At the mother's request the *padrecito* took Juan Pelón away in order to cure him of his absurd tricks.

Some days later the priest said to Juan, "Go buy a sack of grapes."

The boy bought the grapes and on his way back to the priest ate more than half of them. He emptied the remainder on the ground, filled the bottom of the sack with prickly pear leaves and placed the grapes on top of them. He gave the sack to the priest, who, without offering any of the fruit to Juan, began to eat, and each time he put his hand into the sack for a grape he said, "*Ay*, Juan Pelón."

PURO MEXICANO

"Hay,"[7] said Juan. "Yes, Little Father, *hay muchas* (there are many), but on top no; down below *hay*."

The priest plunged deep into the sack and got his hand full of thorns.

"Ay, ay, ay!" he shouted. *"Ay, Dios mío!"*

"Didn't I tell you, *padrecito*?" laughed Juan. "Of a truth *hay*."

The boy's sharp wit was repaid with a flogging.

Later the priest put eggs on the fire to cook and told Juan to sit near the door and watch them. The *padrecito* walked back and forth before the door, let wind each time he passed Juan Pelón, and said, "Eat *ese huevo*, Pelón."

Presently Juan went into the house and ate all the eggs.

The priest, at last having acquired a good appetite, entered, found the eggs gone, and asked, "Where are the eggs, Juanito?"

"I ate them," said the boy. "Didn't you tell me to eat the eggs?"

Juan Pelón was flogged again.

The priest lay down to rest, and when he had gone to sleep Juan stole two *talegas*[8] of money and hit for a *resaca* in the desert. He hung the coins on a tree in a way to suggest that they had grown there. Two mule drivers came along and bought the tree for four *talegas* of money.

Juan Pelón stole a ride on a wagon to the city. The law there was strict and *coyoteando*[9] was forbidden. He was arrested and placed in the *chirona*. No one was ever known to leave that particular prison alive. All the first night Juan heard the voices of two dead men.

"Caigo ó no caigo?" each kept saying. "Do I fall or do I not fall? Do I fall or do I not fall?"

"Why can't they fall?" thought Juan to himself.

"Buried in one corner of the jail is a jar of money," said one

---

[7]The joke here is dependent on a play of words. *Ay* and *hay* are pronounced alike; *ay* is an exclamation; *hay* means either *there is* or *there are*.

[8]*Talega*, a bag of 1,000 dollars or pesos.

[9]Sniping, pick-pocketing. A number of uncomplimentary slang words in use in Mexico are derived from *coyote*.

48

of the dead men, "and in the opposite corner is another. One is for you and one is for the poor."

Juan dug both jars of money up and awaited the coming of the executioner. Soon a jailor entered the door, and Juan killed him. Then came the executioner, and Juan killed him. The priest followed the executioner, and Juan killed him.

Juan Pelón left the jail and since then has not been seen.

Pedro de Urdemalas

Pedro de Urdemalas lives by his wits. In a way he is a liar but, different from Don Cacahuate, Tío Aurelio, and Compadre Doroteo, he does not lie for the glory of lying. His *mentiras* are a means to an end, and the most desirable end to him is to skin the fellow who is out to get the other man's hide. However, he often tricks the innocently gullible. Also, being a man of chance, he is a plaything of fate; one day he is rich and the next poor.

Once when considerably the worse for his manner of living and while wandering along a highway tired, hungry, and without money, he came to a hog ranch. It was the first of its kind he had ever seen and, despite his low spirits, he was greatly amused by the great array of swine tails.

"There are many tails," said he, "and wherever there is a tail there is a hog. This gives me an idea, and if it works I shall have money to spend."

He took his knife and cut the tails from the hogs and continued on his way until he came to a *resaca*, or swamp. There he busied himself sticking the hog-end of the tail stumps in the mud. Then, after tramping around and digging up the earth about each, he sat beneath a willow and began to weep.

Presently a man rode up horseback.

"Why are you weeping?" he asked.

Pedro wept louder than ever and said, "Why shouldn't I weep? I have lost a fortune in this bog hole. Those tails you see are all that is left to show for hogs that were."

"Poor fellow," said the stranger, "weep no more. I shall buy your herd and have my servants come and dig them out of this *atascadero*. How much do you want for them?"

"*Señor*," said Pedro de Urdemalas, "it is not my wish to sell them, for life is wrapped up in my hogs, but you see how hopeless things are. Rather than lose them, I will sell them to you for one thousand dollars."

The trade was made. Pedro went away weeping until he was out of sight and then took to his heels.

The stranger brought his servants, and he wasn't long finding out how well he had been swindled. Frantic, he directed a search for Pedro but all to no avail. He gave up the hunt and did the only thing left for him to do, and that was to swear revenge in case he should ever again meet Pedro de Urdemalas.

Well, sir, true to form, there came a day when again Pedro was broke and hungry. Immediately he began devising a new lie with which to snare some sucker.

"I need twenty cents worth of *frijoles*, a pot, an underground furnace, and a little time," said he to himself.

He bought beans and pot, dug a furnace, and, after having burned some wood to coals, he put the pot over them and hid all traces of the fire. Presently the pot began to boil, and Pedro, with a long thorn, speared those frijoles that boiled to the top and ate them. He was amusing himself in this manner when a traveler approached.

"*Buenas tardes, buen amigo* (good-day, good friend)," he said. "What are you doing?"

"No, nothing," said Pedro de Urdemalas, "just waiting for those who are to arise and observing those who go."

"Pardon," said the traveler, pointing at the pot, "what makes that thing boil?"

"Nothing; it is a magic pot," Pedro informed him. "In the preparation of my meals I never have to bother with fire. So soon as the food is in it and it is placed on the ground it begins to boil."

Now, the stranger was a traveling man and figured that he needed just such a pot.

"How much do you want for it?" he asked.

"I don't care to sell it," said Pedro.

"I will give you a thousand dollars," bartered the traveler.

"See here, *amigo*," said Pedro de Urdemalas, "I am badly in need of money; otherwise I would not think of disposing of such a rare pot. It is a bargain, but we will have to take care lest it discover the change in masters and refuse to boil. Sit down very quietly and give me the money. Don't speak or move until I am out of hearing."

It was with the utmost caution that the trade was made. The stranger, almost afraid to breathe, sat by the boiling pot and Pedro tiptoed away. After an hour of patient watching the new owner of the magic vessel noticed that the beans and water were not boiling. He picked up the pot and immediately realized that he had been skinned. At first he swore revenge, but after a second thought he was so humiliated by his gullibility that he was glad to forget about it.

It was late in the afternoon when Pedro de Urdemalas decided it would be safe to rest his weary legs. Tired out by the haste with which he left his last victim, he sat beneath a mesquite not far from the road and wondered how he might add another thousand dollars to his ill-gotten gain. Presently, he began by boring holes in the coin he carried, and, when this was done, he hung it to the branches of the tree in such a manner that it appeared to have grown there.

The following morning two wagon masters on their way up the road were amazed by what they saw. They went to the mesquite and were at the point of plucking the rare fruit when Pedro saw them.

"*Eit, eit!*" he shouted. "Leave my tree alone."

They asked the name of the tree.

"This is the only one in existence," said Pedro de Urdemalas. "It bears twice a year and it is time to gather this season's crop."

"How much do you want for this plant?" they asked.

"Don't insult me," said Pedro. "Why should I want to sell a tree like this? It would be foolish."

"We can pay your price," they insisted. "Besides, it isn't our intention to leave here before you agree to sell."

"Oh, well," said Pedro, "give me a thousand dollars and the present crop and the bargain is closed."

They agreed. Pedro gathered the coin from the tree, collected the purchase money, and left for parts unknown.

The wagon masters built homes near the mesquite, pruned it, watered it, and did all in their power to aid in a rich crop of coin the following season.

It being only a mesquite, their reward was mesquite beans.

These poor fools, like the others, had been beaten, but were thankful to have come off no worse.

Pedro, in the meantime, was, as an old *corrido* says, *"siempre caminando,"* always traveling.

One day, however, much to his surprise and great concern, he met a giant.

"Ay, Chihuahua!" said he, "this is an ugly business. How am I to manage now?"

Quickly, before the giant had seen him he took a *guarache* from his foot and threw it into the air.

"What do you say?" said the giant. "If you feel strong, let's see if you can whip me."

Just then the *guarache* fell.

"What's this?" asked the giant.

Then Pedro de Urdemalas explained that three days previous he had thrown a man into the air and this *guarache* was the first he had seen of him since.

The giant was frightened and figured that if that were the case it might be advisable to go easy with Pedro. However, gathering new courage, he said, "I'll bet you my life against yours you can't beat me at three stunts I know."

"What do you mean?" asked Pedro.

"First," said the giant, "let's see you ram your arm through the heart of this tree."

Pedro asked that he be given a day to prepare for the feat, and the giant agreed to the request and went away.

Pedro de Urdemalas thought for a long time. Then carefully he removed the bark from a large tree; after hollowing out a place in the trunk the size of his fist and the length of his arm, he placed its bark back again.

The next day the giant returned and asked if Pedro were ready to attempt the first feat. Upon being assured that he was, the giant said, "Choose your tree."

"I'll take this one," said Pedro, "and, since I accepted the challenge, I'll hit first."

He walked to the tree and with an easy jab sent his fist an arm's length into the trunk.

The giant admitted he was beaten and chose not to hit.

"The second feat," said he, "is to see who can throw a stone the farther."

Having been granted a day for preparation and the giant having gone away, Pedro de Urdemalas caught a quail, and on the following morning hid it beneath his blouse.

The giant returned, chose to throw first, and sent a stone a quarter of a league before it came to earth.

"Stand away," said Pedro. "I must wind up."

And while the giant was not looking, Pedro pretended to throw and turned the quail loose.

"There it goes," said he.

The bird passed out of sight while still rising into the air. The giant admitted that Pedro's stone had gone the farther.

"To-morrow we will wrestle," he said.

Pedro de Urdemalas spent the night tearing up the soil and breaking down the chaparral. He tore his clothes and scratched his hands.

The next morning when the giant asked the meaning of the strange disorder Pedro replied, "No, nothing; I've been fighting a man larger than you."

"Where is he?" asked the giant.

"I threw him into the air and he hasn't come down yet," said Pedro.

"*Caraay!*" said the giant. "I'm glad to admit you are the better man. However, before you take my life come be my guest tonight in my home."

In the guest's room immediately above the bed there hung

by a trigger a large iron bar released by a rope back of the door. After supper Pedro de Urdemalas was shown to bed. But not for nothing had Pedro lived by his wits, and before long he discovered the trap. He arranged the covers so as to suggest a body beneath them and hid behind the door.

At midnight the giant quietly entered the room and crept to the bedside to see just how the sleeper lay. When he leaned over the bed, Pedro released the iron bar and the giant was killed.

Pedro left this place. Three days later, while walking along the road, he came face to face with the man who had bought the swine tails.

"Now you are going to pay," said the man, catching Pedro by the arm. "You have had a lot of fun during your life, but now that is all over."

"It is all very true," said Pedro. "Dispose of me whenever you please."

Pedro de Urdemalas was taken to the hacienda and there was placed in a large barrel. The lid was fastened on the barrel, and one little hole was bored in the side.

"We will eat dinner," said the man to the servants, "and then we will take him to the river and drown him."

Pedro remained quiet until they were out of hearing and then began rocking the barrel. This had been left near a slope, and when at last it turned over it began rolling away from the house and came to a halt in a meadow near a herd of sheep.

"*Buen amigo, buen amigo!*" called Pedro.

A herder came to the barrel and asked, "What's the matter?"

"Nothing at all except that they are trying to compel me to marry the king's only daughter," said Pedro. "If you care to, you may take my place."

"*De veras?*" asked the herder.

"Yes," said Pedro, "it's true; only get me out of here and you get in."

The change was made and the barrel was rolled back to the top of the slope and placed where the man and his servants had left it. Then Pedro gathered the sheep and drove them away.

In due time the barrel and contents were thrown into the river, and, as it sank from sight, there came the gurgling sound of *gori-gori-gori-gori.*

Some days later the man and his servants were hunting.

"Isn't that the man we drowned?" said one of them, pointing to a herder some distance away.

"I'll swear it is," said the man.

They approached and spoke to Pedro de Urdemalas.

"I thought you were drowned," said the man.

"Didn't you hear the *gori-gori-gori* when the barrel sank?" asked Pedro. "Well, each *gori* was a sheep. Once the barrel was on the bottom of the river, the underwater people opened it and let me go."

"What shall we do with him, boys?" said the man.

"He's had enough," said the servants. "Let him go."

Pedro Urdemalas sold his sheep and entered the king's service. The ruler was a great tease and made life miserable for his servants. However, Pedro turned the trick on him so often the king was offended.

"Take this rascal and hang him," said he.

"Grant me a last request," pleaded Pedro.

"Very well," said the king.

"Let me choose the tree upon which I'm to be hanged."

"Granted," said the king. "Soldiers, go hang him and never let me see his face or hear of him again."

Pedro de Urdemalas chose to be hanged to a sunflower plant. The soldiers were perplexed. They had heard the last wish granted and also they were afraid to bring the matter again to the king's attention. Consequently, they released Pedro de Urdemalas on condition that he never show his face again.

Keeping the Shirt-Tail In

Two men, famous in the art of lying, met one day at the crossroads.

"Where have you been, *amigo?*" asked one.

"*Amigo,*" responded the other, "I've been afar and have seen miracles and wonders."

"Yes?" responded the first. "Listen to me if you should care to learn about miracles and wonders. Just listen to me."

"Very well, what have you to say?" asked the first.

"Well, for instance, I saw a pumpkin that was so large a shepherd used its hollow in which to bed a thousand sheep at night."

"Wait," interrupted the first; "that reminds me. I, while traveling through Italy, saw an oven so large it took a thousand men to fire it."

"Why," gasped the other, "why such large ovens?"

"To cook your pumpkins in," answered the friend.

"You are good, *amigo*," said the victim. "In fact, if truth weren't distasteful to me I'd swear you were my master. Let's combine our virtues and earn our living lying. You tell 'em and I'll swear to 'em. Yet, I warn you, if your exaggerations get top-heavy, I may find it hard to coöperate. Let's say, in such a case, I give your shirt-tail a jerk. That will be the sign to cut down a bit."

Having reached an agreement in all matters pertaining to their procedure, they continued on their way. Presently they came to a town and approached a group of men on the plaza.

"In my country," began the master, "rattlesnakes are a mile long."

His companion, fearing such audacity, jerked the other gently by the shirt-tail.

"They may not be a mile long at that," retracted the first, "but they are easily a half-mile in length."

The modest companion continued to tug at the shirt-tail.

"Of course, they could be shorter, but I'd swear that if their shirt-tails were out, they would be two yards long."

The people could stand no more.

"Kill the cowards," they cried. "Run them out of town."

"You see," said the master as he looked back upon the place, "people prefer lies straight. A diluted lie is a sin against art. Follow my advice: keep your own shirt-tail in and leave mine alone."

They chose to travel separately. The master was to lead and the friend was to follow.

Presently the first man entered a wretched little village. He told the people that in the last town he had passed through there was a newly-born baby with seven heads. This news caused much interest and the informant was given all the food he could eat.

Presently the next man arrived.

"*Señor*," the people asked, "is it true that in a town up the way a child was born with seven heads?"

"Why, *señores*," gasped the late arrival, "I . . . I couldn't exactly swear to that, but . . . but . . ."—he stuck his shirt-tail in and continued—"but on a *mecate* (a rope line) I saw hanging out to dry a little white shirt with seven collars on it."

This fellow, too, like the first, was treated with much consideration.

These liars are still lying, and you may be sure they both keep their shirt-tails in.

El Borracho del Bahía

Chano Calanche was a *borracho*. He was seldom sober, for there was nothing he disliked more than to look upon this cold and prosaic world through eyes uninspired by liquor. *Por eso, señor*, he was drunk most of the time. However, now and then, lacking the *conque* (with-which) to purchase drinks—for, be it known, *señor*, that Chano Calanche, like myself, was miserably poor—and, fearing sobriety as if it were a plague, he begged, borrowed, stole and even worked for his *mescal*.

Upon this occasion, being broke and nearly sober and having been followed by bad luck from one *cantina* to another, he had decided to try the only chance left him, the Cantina del Aguililla, which was located near the outskirts of the *villa*.

It was a dark and stormy night. Bandits, after having murdered three priests, had made themselves at home at the Cantina del Aguililla. The bodies of two of the unfortunates had been dragged back of the bar and the third lay near a table around which the outlaws sat when Calanche entered. *"Buenas noches, caballeros,"* said he. "Is there one of you who would favor me with a drink?"

"Who are you?" asked the bandit captain.

"I am," responded Chano, "the most miserable man in the world. Some are born happy; that is to say, in the good graces of God; some sing and are happy, but I, *caballeros,* am happy only when I have taken a little, and just now I am suffering the torments of being broke and dry."

"Ah," said the captain, who had quickly guessed Chano's financial rating, "so my good man would be tight and happy and yet hasn't the price of a drink. I know of only one solution to your problem, *amigo*: earn your happiness; whether by the point of a pistol or by labor, earn it. Here," continued the captain, "is a dead *padrecito* who should not be found in this disreputable place. If you will take him to the thickets and lose him I will see to it that you are given the finest quart of wine in this *cantina.*"

Chano had not seen the corpse near the table. But now, with the prospects of good cheer so near at hand, he could hardly be expected to bother about the whys and the wherefores of a dead priest. "That is a bargain," said he, "only that you give me one little glass of *mescal* to start me off."

The *mescal* was poured for him. Then with the corpse over his shoulder, the drunkard left the *villa* by way of a small trail. Upon reaching the chaparral, he made straight for a mining shaft and with little feeling and formality threw the corpse into the abandoned hole.

In the meantime the outlaws had thought up a good prank. Betting on the drunkard as an easy mark, they dragged one of the two corpses from behind the bar and laid it near the table in the very same position occupied by the one just carried away.

"Here I am back," greeted Chano upon reëntering the saloon. *"Mi capitán,* I did as you commanded; I lost the *padrecito.*"

The captain, laughing like a demon, coughed and choked with laughter. "What do you say to that, boys?" said he. "A curious sense of the ridiculous, no? Our friend leaves the room but the *padrecito* does not go with him. Perhaps we were to send the *padrecito* to you, *amigo*, and so? *Bueno*, it's our fault. But now, see here," he said, "pick up this priest, hold him tight and don't let him go until you have lost him in the thickets. You understand?"

Juan was too confused for understanding. *"Señores,"* he said, hesitating to touch the corpse that lay at his feet. *"Señores,* am I dreaming? I've had weird illusions when drunk, but this . . ."

"Pick him up," interrupted the captain. "Are you afraid?"

This was too much. Chano would not be called a coward. He walked to the bar, drank a glass of *mescal,* and with never a word, lifted the corpse from the floor to his back and made off down the trail to the river. Here, he tied a large stone to the *padrecito's* neck, and, pushing the body into the stream, remained to watch it sink.

"Now," he said, "Chano Calanche, let yourself not forget what your eyes have seen."

The bandits, having arranged the third corpse as they had the second, awaited the return of the drunkard.

"Caballeros, I remember well what my eyes have seen."

"Oiga," said the captain, "it is getting late into the night and it is no time for pranks."

"But I lost the *padrecito* and have returned for the best quart of wine in this *cantina.*"

An outlaw who at that moment was standing between Chano and the corpse stepped aside. A bitter expression of disgust came over the drunkard's face as he looked down upon the corpse at his feet. He poured and drank two glasses of *mescal,* picked up the body and said, *"Caballeros,* give me an axe. This *padrecito* has annoyed me sorely. No dead man shall stand between José Chano Calanche and the best quart of wine in this *cantina.*"

You like this story, yes? No, no, this isn't all. *Ahora verás.* (Now you will see.) Wait, you must hear the part *más graciosa.*

Bueno, Chano Calanche carried the *padrecito* three miles into the chaparral. Finding a small thicket of dead mesquites, he placed his burden upon the ground, cut wood, and built a large fire. When the blaze had begun to crack and roar with heat, the corpse was thrown in and covered with dry wood.

"You shall never return," said Calanche. "I will see you to ashes and dust before I leave you." He sat himself down upon the ground just out of heat range and watched the burning *padrecito*.

It was daybreak. A priest who was returning to the *villa* from a visit in the country saw the fire and decided to dismount from his mule and warm up a cup of *atole* (corn gruel). He was seated near the small blaze when our drunkard, Chano Calanche, awoke.

"You shameless wretch," screamed Chano. "I put you there to burn, and there you sit preparing a meal over your own funeral fire. I shall teach you a trick. *Ahora verás!*"

The *padrecito* had not seen Chano when he dismounted and was so badly frightened by the latter's shouts and curses he sprang to the back of his mule and fled.

The best quart of wine was never claimed by José Chano Calanche, and to this day it occupies a place of esteem in the Cantina del Aguililla and is not to be had at any price.

Wine and the Devil

The world had been made and God was preparing to plant the vineyard when the devil asked, "What are you doing?"

"I'm planting some grapes," said God. "There will be times in the life of man when he will need wine to cheer him up."

"Would you mind if I help?" asked the devil.

God meditated for a bit. "What is he up to now?" thought He. At last, feeling no harm could be done, he said, "All right, you may help."

"You will be surprised at my efficiency," said the devil.

He went to work immediately. First, he killed a mockingbird and sprinkled the blood along the rows. Then he killed a lion, and then a swine and sprinkled their blood, too, from one end of the vineyard to the other.

"A' 'sta listo," said he. "Now we are ready and we shall see what happens."

We are all well aware what happened. When a man first begins drinking he feels the effects of the bird's blood and sings. He continues to drink until fired by the lion's blood; then he fights. His thirst increases until he has drunk as deep as the swine's blood, and the next thing we know he is in the gutter.

Ay, qué mala suerte! What ill fate!

Blanca Flor

Juan was a gambler and had lost everything he possessed. One day of so many he strolled from the town grumbling to the effect that for some money and a bit of luck he would sell himself to the devil. Immediately there reined up before him a man on a large black mount.

"I am the devil," said he; "state your contract."

"Some money to start and five years of unbroken luck," said Juan.

"Granted," replied the devil. "Within five years you are to come to me and perform three commands. You will find me on the Plains of Berlín at the Hacienda of Qui-quiri-qui."

Juan began gambling again, and his devil's luck performed miracles for him. He won money, land, houses, and stock until there was nothing else to be won.

At the end of the *plazo* of five years he set out for the Plains of Berlín and the Hacienda of Qui-quiri-qui, and within a month reached a hermitage. The hermit greeted him and said, "What are you doing in these parts, good man?"

"I'm looking for the Plains of Berlín and the Hacienda of Qui-quiri-qui," said Juan.

"I have lived hereabouts for one hundred years," said the hermit, "and I have never heard of the place. However, I am the ruler of the fishes of the sea. I shall call them and ask them the way to the Plains of Berlín and the Hacienda of Qui-quiri-qui."

Thereupon he whistled three times and the fishes from all depths came to the shore.

"Where are the Plains of Berlín and the Hacienda of Qui-quiri-qui?" asked the hermit.

Not a living form from beneath the waves could make reply.

"Twenty days from here there is a brother older than I," said he. "Surely he will be able to direct you."

Juan traveled twenty days and reached the second hermitage.

"What are you doing in these regions?" asked the hermit.

"I'm seeking direction to the Plains of Berlín and the Hacienda of Qui-quiri-qui," said Juan.

"I have lived here over one hundred years," said the hermit, "and I have never heard of the place. However, since I rule the animals of the earth, I shall call them and ask them the way to the Plains of Berlín and the Hacienda of Qui-quiri-qui."

Thereupon he whistled three times and the animals from the forests and the plains and the mountains gathered before his door, but none could make reply.

On the following day the hermit commanded the lion to conduct Juan twenty days to the third and last hermitage.

"Oh, good man," greeted the oldest hermit, "what seekest thou in this desert land?"

"I'm looking for the Plains of Berlín and the Hacienda of Qui-quiri-qui," said Juan.

"I have lived here for two hundred years," said the hermit, "and have never heard of the place. However, since I rule the birds of the air, I shall call them and ask them to direct thee wherever thou wilt go."

He whistled three times. Birds of every description gathered before him, and he counted them and found the eagle was not there. He whistled again and again, and at the fourth call the large bird lit before the ruler.

"I heard your calling," said he, "but I was far, far away on the Plains of Berlín near the Hacienda of Qui-quiri-qui."

"This eagle knows," said the hermit to Juan. "Tomorrow thou shalt kill six lambs and with the meat well packed mount the back of this king of birds."

The following morning the eagle left the earth for the clouds of high heaven, carrying Juan and the pack of six lambs upon his back. From time to time he called for food and Juan fed him, and in the afternoon of that very day he settled down upon the Plains of Berlín not far from the Hacienda of Qui-quiri-qui.

"Look to your right," said the bird. "Go to those baths and wait. Three doves will come there to bathe. They are three beautiful girls. First, two will arrive. You are not to disturb them. They will go away and another will come to bathe. She is the prettiest of the devil's three daughters. Her name is Blanca Flor (White Flower). As soon as she shall have assumed human form and shall have removed her clothes and entered the bath, you will possess her clothes and refuse to return them until she has agreed to marry you."

Juan did as commanded. He did not bother the first two doves. However, when the third had changed from dove to maiden and had entered the bath, he sat down near her clothes and refused to allow her to leave the water until she had consented to marry him.

Then Juan told his bride why he had come to the Hacienda of Qui-quiri-qui.

"Very well," said Blanca Flor. "However, when you are asked into the devil's mansion, you must refuse, saying you prefer a dirty little hut near the corral; and when you are asked to partake of food, you are to refuse that also, saying you prefer *tortillas* that are hard, old and moulded."

"Come in, friend Juan," greeted the devil.

"No, *gracias*," said Juan. "I had rather be at home in a dirty little hut near the corral."

"Come dine with me," said the devil.

"No, *gracias*, I am not used to fine foods," said Juan. I prefer *tortillas* that are hard and old and moulded."

"Very well," said the devil, "within three days I shall make the first of the three demands. Rest well, for it will require strength."

At the end of three days the devil came to the dirty little hut and said, "Juan, tonight you are to fulfill my first demand.

Behold that mountain. At midnight pick it up and place it on the other side of the hacienda."

Juan was confused beyond all powers of description. He went to Blanca Flor, and explained what was expected of him.

"Don't worry, my love," said she. "I shall shift the mountain for you."

At dawn the devil was asked to view the work. *"Vieja,"* said he to his wife, "he has changed the mountain."

"I would say," said the *diabla,* "that our daughter Blanca Flor did that. However, she is locked in her room with seven keys."

Then the devil returned to Juan and commanded him to go the following night and plant an orchard bearing fruit down near the Laguna of Death.

Juan was confused by such a demand and told his troubles to Blanca Flor.

"Don't worry, my love," said she. "I shall plant the orchard for you."

Next morning the devil was asked to view the orchard.

"Vieja," he called to his wife, "he has planted the orchard and the trees are laden with fruit."

"If it weren't for my faith in the lock of seven keys," said the *diabla,* "I would say that Blanca Flor had planted the orchard."

The devil's third demand was that Juan ride a horse that had never known bit, saddle, or spur.

"The horse," said Blanca Flor, "will be the devil himself. Be careful how you enter the corral. Master him with a club. Keep him down as you would a locoed horse, beat him between the ears. Under the shed you will find saddle, spurs, and the bridle. Kick the spurs aside; they are my sisters. Do not touch the saddle, for it is my mother. Be careful with the bridle, however, for it is myself. Bridle, mount bareback, and use the club.

The horse did every trick known to demon, but Juan was not to be thrown. At the end of three hours a panting, sweating and bleeding horse was led into the corral and Juan went to the large house and asked that the devil come down to the lot and see how well the horse was broken.

"My master is sick in bed with fatigue and a battered head," said a servant. "He says to tell you that he will see you later."

"That must never be," said Blanca Flor. "We must leave tonight."

At twelve o'clock that night, in some manner known only to the devil's prettiest daughter, Blanca Flor picked the lock of seven keys after having spat four times in her room. Then she and Juan, on the poorest horse in the *remuda*, escaped from the Hacienda of Qui-quiri-qui.

The *diabla*, suspicious of Blanca Flor, came to her door and called, "Blanca Flor!"

"*Mande!*"[10] answered the first spittle.

Later the *diabla* called again. "*Mande!*" answered the second spittle but rather faint, for it was nearly dry.

Later, along toward dawn, the *diabla* called again, "Blanca Flor!"

"*Mande!*" said the third spittle, but scarcely above a whisper.

Just as day was breaking over the Llanos of Berlín the *diabla* called again, "Blanca Flor!"

There was no answer. The seven keys, used one after the other, opened the door. Blanca Flor was gone.

The devil gave chase and soon overtook the runaways.

Among the many things that Blanca Flor took with her were a brush and a looking-glass. When it had begun to look as if the devil was sure to catch them, she threw the brush over her shoulder, and when it struck the earth there sprang from the soil a thicket of thorns. After much delay the devil found his way through the brush and had all but caught Juan and Blanca Flor when the latter threw to the earth a looking-glass. Immediately it formed a large lake. The devil quit the chase, but the *diabla* continued to follow until she came to a little hut.

"Have you seen a man and a girl pass this way?" she asked the owner of the place.

---

[10]*Mande!* Literally, *command. What is it?*

"*Sandías y melones,*" said the man.

She asked three times, but "Watermelons and cantaloupes" was the only answer she got.

"I shall leave you at this pool until I have made arrangements for our wedding," said Juan to Blanca Flor.

"When you reach your home, embrace no one," said Blanca Flor, "for if you do you will forget me."

Juan reached home and declined to embrace all until, at last, forgetting his promise, he put his arms about an aunt who was ill in bed. He forgot Blanca Flor.

Three days later he arranged to marry another girl. The day of the wedding arrived and everyone for miles around attended. Among the many friends were an old man and an old woman, bringing with them a young woman who just that day had come to their home to live. This girl was very beautiful and on a green bough she carried were two doves.

"Talk for them, little dove," said the girl. "Tell them about the Hacienda of Qui-quiri-qui and the Llanos of Berlín. Tell them of Blanca Flor and a promise that was forgot."

The little dove told the story I have just told you.

"Ay," said Juan, "I remember now. I am Juan the gambler. I sought the Llanos of Berlín, the Hacienda of Qui-quiri-qui. With the aid of Blanca Flor, I changed the mountain, planted the orchard and rode the demon horse. It was Blanca Flor who showed me from those infernal lands to my home and my former self, and this is my wife to be, for this is Blanca Flor."

Juan and Blanca Flor were married. Juan no longer gambles, and they live on a ranch not far from here.

The Tooth of Gold

Once upon a time there was an old woman who had a vain daughter.

And since the woman was old and poor, she said to the daughter one day, "*Hijita,* I believe it would be well for you to get married."

"The idea!" laughed the proud young lady. "Just as if there were a man in the whole world fit for me."

The little old woman made no reply.

"*Mamacita,*" added the girl, "we shall make a bargain, you and I. Since it is your wish, I will marry, but it must be to a man with a golden tooth."

Now where there are vanity and pride there is a devil not far in the offing. A young man knocked at the door.

"My object here will not please you, *señora,*" said the handsome youth. "I have come to ask for the right hand of your daughter."

"Her happiness is my happiness," said the mother. "*Hija,* you have heard."

"Yes, mother," whispered the girl, "and also have seen a golden tooth. I will marry him."

Immediately after the wedding, a most unusual thing happened. The groom, with not so much as a good-bye kiss, left, saying he would return within three days.

"Mother," said the girl, "what manner of man is this?"

"A strange one, daughter, a very strange one. Perhaps that comes from the fact that he has a golden tooth."

"What shall I do?" asked the daughter.

"Listen, *hijita,*" said the mother. "Your *santitos* have been long forgotten. Bring them forth from the closets and trunks; dust them well; put them on the tables, and hang them on the walls; then pray to them, *hijita.* Thus the saints may help."

The girl did as she was told to do.

Three days later the husband came home. "What is this?" he shouted, "what is this? Tear these images down, break them, sweep them into the patio, and burn them. I can't bear the sight of them."

The young wife was forced to do as told. She took down her *santitos* from the tables and the walls, broke them, swept them into the patio, and burned them.

"Here," said her husband, removing the golden tooth from his mouth. "Here is something better. Now see to it that no *santitos* are brought here again. Also here is some money. I am leaving you again. In three days I shall return."

"Stay with me," pleaded the girl. "It isn't *santitos* or golden teeth or money that I want. It is you; I want you."

"You want me?" laughed the man. "You want me? Women have gone to hell for that. *Adiós.*"

"Mother, what can this mean?" asked the girl. "He will not lie with me and has left me again. What can it mean?"

"God knows, *hijita*," answered the little old woman. "I will ask the *padrecito.*"

"*Padrecito,*" said the woman to the priest the following morning after mass, "I have come to you for help. My vain and thoughtless daughter married a man with a golden tooth. In addition to refusing to lie with her, he has compelled her to burn her *santitos*, saying he cannot bear the sight of them. What manner of man is he?"

"Woman," said the *padrecito*, "your son-in-law is the devil."

"God's mercy," exclaimed the little old woman, "and now, how am I to rid myself of him?"

"Listen to me," said the *padrecito*. "Here is a crucifix. Go to the plaza and buy a mule-whip and a jug with a tight-fitting stopper. Take these to your daughter's room, nail a nail in the door, unstop the jug and place it beneath the bed, and then with the mule-whip, stopper and crucifix handy await the return of the devil. When he arrives and enters the room, shut the door, hang the crucifix on the nail, and then with the mule-whip beat him without mercy. He will wither to the size of a dog and will hide beneath the bed, but don't let up. Lay on the whip until he has withered to the size of a wasp and for safety has crawled within the jug. Then drop the whip, and plug the mouth of the jug with the tight-fitting stopper. With this well done, place the jug and its contents in a sack and have it buried six feet underground one league from the village."

The little old mother hastened to the plaza and did as she was told. Having arranged the jug, stopper, whip and crucifix in convenient order, she seated herself and awaited the return of the devil.

On the third day, as he had promised, the latter returned

and entered the room. The *madrecita* closed the door quickly, hung the crucifix on the nail, and turned upon the poor devil with fury. She flogged her bewildered victim until, wailing and screaming, he withered to the size of a dog and fled beneath the bed. She laid on the whip with increased fire until the unfortunate devil shrank to the size of a wasp and crawled into the jug for safety. Then she dropped her whip, snatched up the stopper and pressed it hard and tight into the mouth of the jug.

Just then she heard someone singing a doleful drunkard's song. It was the village toper on his way down-street to the *cantina*.

"Listen, man," called the *madrecita*, clapping her hands, "listen; where are you going?"

"I am seeking a Christian who may wish me a happy morning," answered the toper.

"I have an errand for you," said the little old woman. "I will give you thirty pesos if you will take this sack and its contents one league from this village and bury it six feet beneath the ground."

"That is not an errand," said the toper; "that is work. However, just wait a little minute until I find someone to wish me a happy morning. I will return and do this work."

"You need go no farther," said the *viejita*. "Here is a pint of wine. Drink it with my wishes for many happy mornings."

Having drunk the wine, the toper took to the street with shovel, pick and sack. "I am still thirsty," he thought. "When a man is *crudo* his health is easily impaired. I shall spend one of my thirty pesos for a quart of *mescal*."

He entered a *cantina*, called for *mescal*, drank a quart of it, and left.

Presently a weird, buzzing voice called, "*Valecito!*"

"Ha," said the drunk, "only when a man has money does he get such greetings. I'll show them that they are of small import to me."

"*Valecito*," called the weird voice again.

69

"This grinds me to the marrow," said the toper. "Who's calling *Valecito?*"

"It is I, *Valecito*," said the voice; "it is I, here on your back. I'm your old friend the devil. Let me go."

"Ah, my old friend the devil, is it? And I am to let you go. Ha, ha, ha, how original you are. Listen, I was to bury you six feet underground; now that I know you, I will make it twelve."

"No, *Valecito*," whined the devil, "you can't do that. Besides, I'm going to make you a master in the art of magic healing. Cures will be simple for you. Merely place your left hand on the affected part and call, '*Valecito!*' The patient will arise and go his way hale and hearty. Now, come, *Valecito*; let me go."

"That's a trap," said the toper; "you are trying to trick me."

"Trick you!" laughed the little wasp, "trick you! Why should I waste my precious time tricking fellows who are constantly deceiving themselves? Be it known that my word is good, *Valecito*, and my contracts are always valid. Let me go."

The toper agreed to the pact; the jug came open with a puff, and a cloud of sulphur smoke mixed with the morning breeze.

The newly-made healer returned the pick and shovel to the little old woman and assured her that the job was well done.

Upon reaching his *jacalito*, the toper nailed a sign above the door. It read, "*El Curandero Maravilloso*. He cures all ills."

In a certain quarter of the village was a dying man. All doctors who had seen him said there was no cure for him, and now, with hope gone, he was slowly giving way to death.

The relatives heard of The Wonderful Healer. They said: "No harm can come from calling him in. Besides, he may cure our brother here. Who knows?"

The Healer was called. After studying the patient attentively, he agreed to effect a cure for one thousand pesos. The family agreed to the price and left the room.

"*Valecito*," called The Wonderful Healer, placing his left hand on the patient's forehead. "*Valecito!*"

"Give him a life pill and he is cured," whispered the devil.

The life pill was given. Immediately the man arose, called to his brothers and assured them he was no longer sick. The Wonderful Healer was paid.

"*India*," called the toper upon reaching his home. "*India vieja*," he called to his wife, "it works. I am indeed The Wonderful Healer. In a few days now, if God will help, we shall be rich and at ease for the rest of our lives."

In the meantime, *señores*, the devil, with the caution of a cat had observed every move of his mother-in-law. Thirsting for revenge, he spied upon her constantly.

One day the *viejita* was cleansing the patio with a short brush broom. As she bent forward to sweep the ground, her skirts were slightly lifted in the rear.

"Now," said the devil, "this is my chance."

The little old woman fell to the ground with cramps in her abdomen. The girl rushed to The Wonderful Healer and begged him to come quick, that her mother was dying.

The toper took his satchel and hat and went to the home of the patient. "She is very sick," said he. "Leave the room, close the door, and I will cure her."

He approached the sick woman, laid his left hand upon her abdomen and called, "*Valecito!*"

"What do you want, *Valecito?*" answered the devil.

"What? Are you in there? Come, *Valecito,* let me cure the woman; I need the money," said The Wonderful Healer.

"No more than I need revenge," answered the devil. "You know how she locked me in a room and beat me without mercy. You know well how she stopped me within a jug and offered you thirty pesos to bury me alive. She deserves no mercy. I will kill her and take her to eternal torment."

"No, *Valecito,*" said the toper, "you can't do that. Remember the contract; there was to be no tricking."

"Very well," said the devil, "stand aside and I will leave her, but from you I will take the power that is rightly mine. From this day on you are no longer The Wonderful Healer." The devil departed.

The *viejita* was cured of her mortal ailment and the toper is drinking again. His only request is that we fill our glasses, lift them high, and wish him a happy morning.

The Dog that Ran to the Moon

This was a married man. The only members of his family were his wife, his dog, and himself. He took good care of his dog. Once when he had no work, he said to his wife, "I'm going across the mountains to see my *compadre*. It may be possible that he will give me work or a bit of corn for *tortillas*. Prepare me a lunch."

That evening the *señora* said to him, "In this *morral* is your lunch."

And he said to her, "Hang it up on a peg in the wall. I am am going to leave very early tomorrow morning."

The next morning the *compadre* saddled his dog and traveled until the fall of night. Where night fell he pitched camp, and, after eating lunch, he fed his dog. The following morning he was on his way, and at nine o'clock he arrived at his *compadre's* hacienda.

"What a miracle!" said the other *compadre*. "We were not expecting you here."

"Since I had no work, *compadre*," said the new arrival, "I thought I would run over to see if there were some way you could help me. My *señora* has very little food in the house."

Then the wealthy *compadre* said, "It is all very well, *compadre*. I have provisions enough for all of us. You need look for no work. You may spend the night with me."

"Very well," said the visitor.

They entered the house and the rich *compadre* said, "We are to have a race here next week, *compadre*. A stranger has just arrived in town with a *misionero* horse, and they say this horse is very fast. There is a man in town who owns a fast horse also. There is a bet of five thousand pesos and they are going to run five hundred *varas*. In addition to this bet, the one who loses is to give a dance and pay for the music, and the dance is to last for three days. I should like for you to come and attend this race and festival."

"Yes, I shall come," said the poor *compadre*.

So on the following day the rich *compadre* prepared two *fanegas* of corn, two *fanegas* of *frijoles*, two *fanegas* of red chile, and a box of bacon. "Here are some provisions," said he. "Out there in the corral you will find an *atajo* of burros. You will need them to take this food home."

"It will not be necessary, *compadre*," responded the poor man. "Already I have a way to pack these provisions."

"What do you mean?" asked the rich *compadre*.

"Oh, I will pack them on my dog," said the other.

"You don't mean that," said the rich man.

"Oh, yes, I do," said the poor man. "The only thing I shall need further is that you lend me four ropes."

"There in the corral you will find all you need," said the rich *compadre*.

Then the poor man took the four ropes, and in *mancornado* fashion, he tied the two *fanegas* of corn, the two of *frijoles*, the two of chile, and the box of bacon to the back of the dog. Then he said to the rich man, "*Compadre*, I am going now."

The rich *compadre* replied, "I shall expect you next week."

"Yes," said the poor *compadre*, "*con el favor de Dios*, I shall return." He left.

Away down the road at nightfall he unloaded his dog and gave her plenty to eat. She was very tired. The next day he packed her again and continued on his journey. As he was going along about six o'clock that morning, a deer ran across the road ahead of him. The dog gave one wild bark and took after the deer. The man followed the dog, and, fearing that she would lose the pack, he called. But the dog did not return. The man finally went on and arrived at home very sad.

His *señora* asked, "Well, how did you make out?"

"Very badly," was his response.

"And why?" asked she.

Then continued the *compadre*, "Because the dog packed with all the provisions ran off after a deer. I fear she will lose them. It will be hard getting them all together again."

The *compadre* passed the day waiting and worrying and at

nightfall the dog had not returned. Then said the *compadre* to the *señora*, "Put me down a pallet out here by the door. I shall listen during the night. Possibly I shall hear the dog barking."

At midnight the dog returned. *"Vieja, vieja,"* the man called, "my dog has returned. She is still packed. Quick! Bring a light."

When the light was brought, they discovered in addition to the pack of corn, *frijoles,* red chile, and bacon, a deer atop the load.

"Start a fire," said the man. "The dog is very tired; we must cook some of this meat for her." Presently she was fed.

"This is fine," said the man. "Now I shall be able to attend the races."

"I will go also," said the woman.

"Why not?" asked the man.

Early the following morning the dog was saddled, and the man and the woman mounted and were on their way. A good distance down the road night fell and they camped. The following day at nine o'clock they reached their destination. The following day they attended the race. There they saw the *cabestro* (hair rope) stretched across the track, the choosing of the *vedoros* (judges), and the horses rearing and fighting to be on the mark.

At last the *santiaguero*[11] was appointed; the horses were placed side by side touching the *cabestro.* Then the *santiaguero* called, "Santiago"; in a second he repeated, "Santiago"; and then a third time he called "Santiago." Now the horses were off. At about two hundred fifty *varas* the *caballo misionero* was reaching his forelegs out ahead of the other horse; at the end he was fifty *varas* ahead. There were *vivas,* explosions of firecrackers, and music. The dance began and lasted three days and nights.

When the celebration was over, the owner of the dog said to the other *compadre,* "Go over and tell the winner I have an animal I would like to race."

---

[11]The *santiaguero,* starter, properly calls "Santiago" three times; at the third call the horses should start.

"What do you mean?" asked the *compadre*. "You have no horse."

Then with a wink, the friend replied, "I didn't say *horse*; I said *animal*; tell the winner I have an animal I would like to race."

When the owner of the missionary horse—a horse taken about the country to match against anything put up—heard the proposition, he said, "I will race anything. What are your stakes?"

"Ten thousand pesos," was the reply.

"Then let it be box stakes so that everyone will have a chance to bet one way or the other, and we will race tomorrow."

The following day people arrived on horseback, in ox carts, and afoot. They bet on the *caballo misionero*. Eight hundred *varas* was to be the distance. The challenger placed three vaqueros twenty-five yards from the end of the track with instructions that they were to wait with ropes down. Said the owner of the dog, "My animal has a hard mouth, and you will have to rope her to stop her."

Soon all was set. The starting line was approached at a trot and the *santiaguero* called, "Santiago!"

The dog won the race, ran past the three cowboys, jerked their steeds from under them, and broke the ropes. She would have been running still had there been no end to the earth.

It was now late. The jockey dismounted, unsaddled, and hung his bridle and spurs to a golden hook in the blue wall that had stopped them, lay down, and went to sleep. The next morning, much to his surprise, his bridle and spurs were not to be found and the golden hook was gone. He looked everywhere. It was a casual glance into the sky that revealed them. He had hung his bridle and spurs to the horn of the moon and there they have hung ever since.

The *compadre* and *comadre* are now very rich. And they are still living just over the mountains somewhere this side of the end of the earth.

75

PURO MEXICANO

La Madrina Muerte

Not far from a certain city lived a poor man. He had a large family and the youngest child, a boy, was yet to be christened.

One morning the man said to his wife, "I shall not work today; instead I shall seek a godparent for our son."

He had walked only a little way when he met a poor man.

"I know that you are looking for a *padrino* for your child," the poor man said. "I will be his godparent."

Not knowing it was God to whom he spoke, the man said, "No, you are too poor; you have nothing to give your *ahijado*."

Farther down the road he met a man of wealth. "I know," said he, "that you are looking for a *padrino*. I will be godfather for your son."

"No," said the father.

Next he met a woman. It was Death.

"I know," said she, "that you are looking for a godparent. I will be godmother for your son."

"Good," said the man. "Since you are not partial to youth, age, wealth, or poverty, you may be godmother to my son."

It was Death who baptized the child.

Some years later she returned and asked that her godson be allowed to walk with her into the forest.

In the forest Madrina Muerte plucked a flower and presented it to her *ahijado*, telling him that it would bring him happiness in accordance as to how it was used.

"This plant will cure all ills," said she, "and from now on you will be known as the Famous Healer. However, if, upon attending a patient, you see me at the foot of the bed, you are to leave him to me."

The Famous Healer had cured many people when he was called to the bedside of the king.

"Cure me," said the monarch, "and my daughter and kingdom are yours."

Though Madrina Muerte stood at the foot of the bed and forbade the cure, the Famous Healer disobeyed her.

76

Being a good *madrina,* she forgave her *ahijado* this, his first offense.

A few days later the princess took seriously ill and the Famous Healer was called. Madrina Muerte was there and forbade the cure, but the godson disobeyed her again. The princess, like the king, was cured; and the following day was set for the wedding. But Madrina Muerte called for her *ahijado* and took him to a dark abode where burned candles representing the souls of dying mortals.

"This," said Madrina Muerte, pointing to a new candle, "is your soul. When it is burned down, you are to die."

The *ahijado* asked for more life, and Madrina Muerte placed a small candle on top of the one representing his dying body.

"You have disobeyed," said she, "and you must pay with life."

So it was that Death's only godson died, and never since has she served as *madrina* or revealed the name of the life-giving plant.

Juan Oso

Once upon a time there lived near a town in the mountains of the west a man and his daughter. Back of his house was a large garden, wherein Aurora, the daughter, spent many hours daily caring for the flowers. Often in the full of the moon she would remain in this garden late into the night. One night while she was seated on a stone bench beneath a tree she fell asleep. A large bear came and took her away.

When she awoke, she was in a cave and a bear sat near the entrance. Presently he went away. Before leaving, he rolled a large boulder against the mouth of the cave.

The father, who was a very rich man, offered a large reward for the return of his daughter. Hunters from far and wide went in every direction in search of the girl. One morning about five years later, she was discovered near the cave cutting flowers. A large bear lay asleep near by.

The hunter who found her called to her and said, "Don't

77

be afraid. I shall not harm you. I've come to take you to your father."

The girl was afraid and ran to the cave. However, before entering, she called to the man, "You had better leave, because this animal may see and kill you."

The man responded, "I'm not afraid. I have a gun. I have come to take you home to your father."

The bear awoke and rushed upon the man, but was shot and killed. The girl was taken to her father's home.

The father was happy and paid the hunter the reward.

After some time the girl gave birth, and they named the child Juan Oso (John Bear). This child grew to be a large and uncontrollable boy.

One day the father of the girl said, "I believe it would be well to send Juan to school."

After a few weeks, Juan became well acquainted with all the pupils and, being no longer timid, he tried to play with them. However, he was too rough. He hurt the other children.

He was a very disobedient boy. He respected only his mother. One day while fighting a man, he was shot. Despite his wound, he broke the man's neck with one blow of his powerful fist. His mother put him to bed and before long he was cured. "You see," said his mother, "it doesn't pay to be rude. From now on be a good boy." Juan did not improve in disposition, and before long he ran away from home.

Soon he began drinking and hanging out at saloons. One day while he was drunk, a number of men tried to kill him. The police came and Juan, feeling that he was involved, fled with the others to the mountains. Here he fell in with two who were to be his friends thereafter. One was Aplastaceras (Flattens-out-wax), and the other was Tumbapuertas (Knocks-down-doors). Wherever these three went, they found it easy to rob; for no door could withstand the strength of Tumbapuertas, and Aplastaceras could flatten out any wall as if it were wax. One day while hidden back of an inn, they were surrounded by officers and a great crowd of citizens. When they were taken into the street, a fight began. Police and citizens were thrown right and left. Some were killed and others were crippled. There were no human powers that could withstand Aplastaceras, Tumbapuertas, and Juan Oso.

They went to the mountains again and camped by a river. One of them had stolen a violin, and while he was seated near the river, he began to play. He drew the bow across a string, and behold, there stood before him a soldier. Then he drew the bow across the string four more times and four soldiers appeared.

The five of them stood at attention and asked, "What do you want?"

And the bandit said, "We are hungry. We want something to eat."

The soldiers went off and presently returned with all kinds of food.

"Attention!" said the musician, and the five soldiers stood at attention. Then the musician took up his violin and played and played until he had created a whole regiment. Then the three, Aplastaceras, Tumbapuertas and Juan Oso, with their army, returned to the city, laid siege to it, and took it.

They are living there now in great wealth and esteem.

The Son of Tata Juan Pescador

Not far from a large city, once upon a time, lived a fisherman and his family. Though there were only three of them and the father worked hard, they were very poor.

One evening at sunset a carriage drawn by six white horses stopped at Tata Juan's door. A blond young woman, as pretty as a princess, stepped from the carriage and asked for lodging.

"It would be a great honor," said Tata Juan, "but we are very poor, and have only this one little hut with its one little room."

The young woman insisted, and the poor family felt compelled to take her in.

Upon leaving the following morning, the young woman announced that she was going to the *centro* of the city and attend the fair. "I shall return."

Upon her return to the hut that evening she met the third

member of the fisherman's family. It was Juanito, the little son. His clothes were torn and in patches, his hair was long, and his face and hands were dirty.

"Give me this boy," said the young woman.

"We can't do that," said Tata Juan, "for he is our only child and some day will be our only support."

"Look, Tata Juan," said the beautiful young woman, "I am a fairy from the fairy town of Canela. Give me Juanito, and you will never regret. Tomorrow evening when I return from the fair, I shall expect your answer."

The following day there was much argument in the little family between father and mother. By nightfall, however, they had agreed to give their son Juanito to the Fairy of Canela.

"I am greatly indebted to you," said the fairy upon learning their decision. "In partial recompense I will present you with this magic vase. When you need money, say only the words, *'Componte, jarrito!'*[12] and it will be filled with coins immediately."

The next morning the fairy took Juanito to a bath and cleaned him up. Then she called in a barber and tailor and within less time than it takes to say *zape*[13] Juanito was transformed into a little prince.

"We shall go now," said the fairy.

The six white horses and the carriage returned. Tata Juan and the *pescadora* (fisher-woman) were told good-bye and soon Juanito and the fairy had gone.

The way to Canela was long and led through a desert. Midday was warm and Juanito began to drowse.

"Don't fall asleep," said the fairy.

Juanito, however, was no match for slumber and soon was sound asleep.

At sunset he awoke; he was no longer in the carriage, but alone on the desert. He was no longer a little prince, but the dirty street urchin of yesterday.

"What shall I do?" thought he. "Which way shall I go?"

---

[12]Something like "Do your stuff, little vase!"

[13]A common exclamation.

He sat down and removed a *guarache* from his foot.

"I have heard," said he, "that it is well to throw a hide into the air and follow the direction it points. Since I have no hide, I shall throw my *guarache*, which is made of hide."

The sandal was thrown, flip-coin fashion, and landed with toe pointing north. Juanito slipped his bare foot back into it and set out walking north.

He had gone but a little way when he heard sounds that chilled his blood. Being unable to make out what they were, he crept cautiously forward through the brush. At last he came to a small opening and immediately before him in the center of the clearing were a lion, an eagle, and an ant fighting over a dead cow.

The lion saw Juanito and called to him.

"Come here, boy. We must have someone to divide this kill for us; for otherwise we shall never reach an agreement."[14]

Juanito was afraid, but he dared not disobey. He gave the head to the ant, the loins to the eagle and the remainder to the lion.

"You have divided well," said the lion. "Now you must have your fee. Come, pull a hair from my mane."

"There is one of my feet," said the ant.

"What are you going to give?" said the lion to the eagle.

The latter did not answer but flew away.

"What shall I do with this hair and foot?" asked Juanito.

"If you are in trouble," said the lion, "and need my help, hold the hair between your forefinger and thumb and say, '*Dios y mi buen león* (God and my good lion). If it is the ant you need, say, '*Dios y mi buena hormiga*' (God and my good ant).

"*Bueno*," said Juanito, "then I shall start with you, Señor León."

Thereupon he held the mane hair between the thumb and forefinger and said, "*Dios y mi buen león!*"

"At your service," said the lion.

---

[14]For a variant of this manner of division, see account of the division of a deer by the boy in "The Metamorphosis of a Folk-Tale," by Elizabeth W. DeHuff, this volume.—*Editor*.

"Take me to the town of Canela," said the boy.

They walked toward the north until late and pitched camp for the night near a tree.

Presently a voice came from the branches overhead. "It is I, the eagle," said the voice. "Don't leave camp tomorrow morning until a cow is driven here. I shall take you to the town of Canela, but we must have meat."

At dawn a beef was driven into camp. The ant stung its foot and during the pause the lion sprang on it and killed it.

The meat that was not consumed by the four was jerked and bagged, and at noon Juanito, with the meat, climbed on the eagle's back.

"When I call, 'Carne,'" said the eagle, "you must give me meat. That way I shall not have to come to earth. Hold tight; here we go."

The eagle had called "Carne" seven times and had eaten the entire supply when it lit on the bank of a lagoon.

"Sh—, quiet," said he. "A monster lives in the mud beneath this lagoon. We must kill him before we can continue our journey. Call the lion and the ant."

The boy first took the lion hair and said, "Dios y mi buen león," and then with the little foot of the ant held between the thumb and forefinger he said, "Dios y mi buena hormiga."

Both lion and ant came immediately, but not a second too soon, for a large wave was already rolling shoreward from the lagoon. Puerco Espín, the monster, made for the boy, but was attacked by the lion. The battle was fierce and both were badly wounded. The lion was forced to quit the fight to rest and pull poisonous barbs from his paws, but the Puerco Espín crawled back to the lagoon, rolled in the mud, and was cured of his wounds immediately.

For the second time he prepared to attack the boy, but before he reached him one foot was so paralyzed by the ant's sting he could not move a limb. Before the lion and eagle killed him, the latter said, "When we open him a snake will escape. Kill it quickly. A dove will come from the snake. I shall catch it and bring it to earth. Within the dove is an egg. We must kill the dove to get the egg. Then, boy, you are to carry the egg in your hand to the palace door at Canela, where you will find the guard distracted by the ant's sting. Break the egg on his head, and you will be received into the palace. If, however, by accident or otherwise the egg is broken beforehand we shall all find ourselves by the carcass of the first beef in the center of the desert and the whole business will needs be repeated again."[15]

The boy was careful with the egg, and after a flight of a few hours the eagle placed him at the palace door in the town of Canela. The ant had preceded them and had done his job well, for the guard was swearing and scratching his ankle. Juanito came near with the caution of a cat, broke the egg on the guard's head and was received into the castle, given a good supper, and shown to his bed. He removed his clothes and crawled beneath the cover.

"You are now within the castle of Canela, Juanito," said a voice from beneath the bed. "It is I, the fairy of Canela who speaks."

"I am homesick," said Juanito. "Take me to my father and mother."

"No, Juanito, they have been so busy with the *jarrito* they have forgotten you."

Juanito's heart could stand no more. "All the same, I am homesick. Take me back."

"Very well," said the fairy.

Next day the coach, drawn by the six white horses, stopped at the castle door. Juanito and the fairy took their seats and soon were on their way through the desert.

"Don't fall asleep," said the fairy.

However, Juan was no match for slumber and awoke that evening all alone in the middle of the desert. He lost no time in getting his directions and before dawn had reached the city of his birth.

In the absence of his son Tata Juan Pescador had worked the magic vase day and night, had become fabulously rich, and had

---

[15]For variant accounts of the lethal egg in the dove see "The Metamorphosis of a Folk-Tale," by Elizabeth W. DeHuff, this volume.—*Editor.*

been elected governor. Pride got the better of him, and he decreed that no one was ever under the penalty of death to refer to him as Tata Juan Pescador.

Juan knew nothing of this, and, not finding his parents at home, asked an old woman the whereabouts of Tata Juan Pescador.

"*Ay, hijito,*" said she, "if you go about asking for Tata Juan Pescador you will be shot. Call at the city home of the *gobernador* and ask to see *el Señor Gobernador.*"

Juanito did this and said he was the governor's son. Tata Juan Pescador said he had no son and had the boy arrested as an impostor. He spent the night in a cell within the governor's mansion.

At early dawn a voice spoke through the bars of the windows, "The fairy of Canela sends you food that you may eat, a prince's suit that you may dress, and a *talega* of *reales*[16] that you may attend the fair. Go with the governor and spend the whole bag of *reales.* At twilight return to this cell."

Juanito dressed quickly and ate. An old woman came to his door with prison food, but when she saw a prince instead of a street urchin, she ran to the governor and asked him to go to the cell in person.

Tata Juan Pescador was frightened, released Juanito, and fell to his knees with apologies.

"That is all very well, Señor Gobernador," said Juanito; "we shall go to the fair."

They passed the day in the *centro,* spent all the *reales* and returned at twilight to the mansion. It was against the governor's wish that the prince should sleep that night in the cell, but he insisted on having his bed there.

At early dawn the voice spoke again through the bars of the window.

"The fairy of Canela sends you food that you may eat, a king's robe that you may dress, and a *talega* of *reales* that you may attend the fair. Go with the governor and spend the whole bag of money. At twilight, return to this cell."

---

[16]One thousand dollars; a *real* is 12½ cents.

Juanito, as he had done the day before, dressed quickly and ate. Again came the old woman to the door, saw the king, and fled to the governor.

"I'm not so sure but that you'll be shot for this," said she. "A king is in the cell."

Tata Juan Pescador, in even more anxiety than the day before, hastened to release the king and apologize.

"That is all very well, Señor Gobernador," said Juanito. "Come, we shall go to the fair again."

The day was passed in the *centro*, the *reales* were all spent and at twilight Juanito was in his cell again.

As on the two previous occasions, the voice spoke again through the bars of the window.

"The fairy of Canela sends you food that you may eat, an emperor's robe that you may dress, and a *talega* of *reales* that you may attend the fair. Go with the governor and spend the whole bag of money. At twilight do not return to the cell but make yourself known to your father, Tata Juan Pescador. Then at dawn on the day following, return to the town of Canela."

When the old woman came to the prison door, she fled to the governor and said, "Now I'm sure you'll be shot, for it is the emperor you have in prison."

Tata Juan Pescador was so frightened he could hardly stand. He apologized and released the emperor.

"That is all very well, Señor Gobernador," said Juanito. "Come, we shall attend the bull fight at the fair."

That evening Juanito did not return to the cell. Instead he fell on his knees before his father and mother and revealed his name.

Tata Juan and the *pescadora* were hardly equal to the great joy that was theirs. The three of them, Tata Juan, the mother, and son, sat up all night, and a little mouse heard Juanito tell them the story I have just told you.

Juanito left his parents in a sea of tears when he set out for

Canela, but the little mouse doesn't know whether he fell asleep in the desert or not.

Colorín colorado;	*Colorín colorado;*
Que este cuento	That this tale
Se ha acabado.	Is ended.

Ua-pa-chi (Kickapoo Tales)

It was when God made the world. Everybody was happy. The hawk and the sparrow, they danced. Also the bear and the rabbit; and the butterfly and the thundercloud danced together, too. All people were happy, but it was all the time dark.

"I don't like the dark," said the rabbit. "I want it to be light, always."

"*A-kui,*" said the bear, "no, I must have the dark; I kill people in the dark."

"Then I want a little light," said the rabbit.

"*A-kui, me-sue-aé;* dark all the time."

God awoke.

"Too much talk; I want to sleep," said God.

"I want light," said the rabbit.

"*A-kui,*" said the bear; "*a-kui, a-kui.*"

"*Na-hi,*" said God, "we must settle this. You two talk. The one who talks most, he wins."

Now, Ma-kua was large and fat. He talks slow. Me-sue-a was small and scared. She talks fast.

"*Me-si-me-pe-ko-te,*" said Ma-kua, "*Me-si-me-pe-ko-te;* let it be always dark."

"*Ua-pa-chi, ua-pa-chi, ua-pa-chi;* daylight, daylight, daylight," said the rabbit.

She won. That's why we have light.

The bear loses and will fight. He catches rabbit by the rump and by the nose. Rabbit ran away, but scars show where the bear caught him. They are near his eyes and tail. Have you seen them?

The goose and sparrow-hawk dance and then fight. Hawk wants most food. God says, "Too much talk; I want to sleep."

Hawk and goose are talking all the time.

"*Na-hi*," said God, "you two run race."

The goose is slow, and the hawk is fast. The hawk laughs at goose. They fly to the sea. Hawk flies fast a while, then rests, then eats a rabbit, then flies again. Goose flies high, goes with the clouds, all the time flying, no stopping to eat and sleep.

When the hawk reaches sea, goose is there.

That's why goose doesn't work for food, and that is why the hawk must always work.

Thundercloud and butterfly dance and then fight. Thundercloud will have all the flowers and runs butterfly out of his garden. They fight and talk.

God says, "You two, too much talk. Thundercloud too much noise. I want to sleep."

Butterfly and thundercloud talk all the time.

"*Na-hi*," said God, "you two run race to sea."

Thundercloud laugh so loud boulders roll from mountain, and Me-me-ke hides beneath a leaf.

"You two run race," said God.

Wind, thundercloud's friend, no longer friend; now helps butterfly. He loves butterfly. He takes butterfly to sea.

That's why butterfly owns all the flowers, and that's why thundercloud roars with anger.

Goat herder herding goats. Rain falls and creeks and rivers run over banks.

"*Ku-u*," says goat herder, "*neh-pe nah-ne*, water falls everywhere all the time. Goats must go high on hills."

He drives goats high and water comes high up the hill. Lions, bears, wolves, cats, all there. Deer, goats, cows all there. Lions, bears, wolves, and cats learn to eat deer, goats, and cows.

Water goes down to creeks and rivers again.

The Wonderful
CHIRRIONERA

By Dan Storm

AH, *señor*, you laugh. Why? *Válgame Dios*, much more strange to me appears the style of fighting you gringos use, each combatant throwing into the face of the other his hands, the fingers shut and not gripping so much as a stick of wood, to say nothing of the handle of a *machete* or a knife. With these eyes I have seen such a fight. And you, *señor*, you well know yourself how when anger strikes between two Frenchmen they commence dealing each other blows with their feet like two horses. *Ah, Chihuahua*, what a shameless thing! Then why, my friend, I ask you another time, do you have on your face the look of someone listening to a poor man whose horse has run away and left him to wander alone and on foot for days in the wilderness—why do you look at me in this way when I tell you of *la chirrionera*, that snake who stands upon his head and whips his enemy to death with his tail?

"Let it be the truth, *señor*, what is said of me by my friends, that when much *pulque* or *buen mescal* has climbed up to my head, my brains become excited and my thoughts jump and dance about gleefully, so that my tongue, working many times more rapidly than that of any old woman, says things that the next morning I cannot remember. But look. How could my tongue be crazy already? The gourd is yet almost half full. And the moon is only just now beginning to show her face so red over that mountain yonder."

The old vaquero shook his 8-shaped gourd until the *mescal* inside sloshed promisingly; then he removed the corn-cob stopper. A sudden flicker of the mesquite campfire lighted up

THE WONDERFUL CHIRRIONERA

his shiny Indian face as he tilted back his head. It was hard to tell which gurgled louder, the gourd or the old vaquero's throat. As he set the gourd down with a hollow sound, ten thousand wrinkles came into his face. "Aaaeeehaa!" He compressed from his sinewy throat a wild Indian yell, which startled the horses picketed near by and went echoing up to the stars and off through the desert to the distant mountains. Wiping the back of his hand across his black mustache, he shoved back his old straw *sombrero*, which crowned him the king of story-tellers.

"*Bien, señor*, if you do not believe that there are *chirrioneras*, all you have to do is to ask old Mariano Quizando, *un viejito* who can be seen seated every day in front of his little *jacal* in the little town of Venaditos, in the state of San Luis Potosí. This old, old man, Mariano, once tamed a *chirrionera* for a purpose very strange. And there happened a thing very curious. Now all you have to do is just only to speak the word "*chirrionera*" to this *viejito* and his brows will come down over his eyes so he cannot see, and his mustache will droop over his mouth to shut in the words. Up around his ears he will pull his *sarape*; and you may shout at him and wave your hands in front of his face all day if you like and he will remain so, like those ancient Indian *estatuas* that I have seen in the plaza of La Capital."

And then he told this story:

Old Mariano had next to his house a garden and an orchard, the most beautiful and luxuriant imaginable, surrounded by a high adobe wall. Above the wall could be seen the *duraznos* (peaches) shining in the sun, and the *ciruelas* (plums) red and sparkling like rubies, and so many of them. Many! Many! You could not see the branches. The same of grapes, mangoes, *chirimoyas*, and oranges. Such fruits! The people passing by would stop and stare and swallow as if they were eating. Ah, so delicious and so plentiful, it makes me hungry to think of them now.

And Mariano, quick-tempered, irritable old bachelor that he was, smiled never so broadly as when people would stop to gaze in hunger at his fruits. The few times he was known to laugh were when three little boys who lived near by would come to gaze up pitifully at the ripe fruits. Juan, José, and Daniel, the boys were called; and when they went over to old Mariano's house, he would point up to his fruits and say: "Ah, you admire my *fruitas,* boys! And well you might. *Seguro.* They are even more delicious than they look. Ah, see how the blackbirds and doves eat them greedily! Is this not proof enough that the fruits are most delicious? Ah, and see how that biggest blackbird goes from mango to plum just tasting, tasting daintily."

And the three little brothers, Juan, José and Daniel, from down below on the ground, looking up, would say one to the other, "*Ah, mire no más* (only look at) the peaches, the plums, the *manguitos,* and the little grapes! Why can not we taste of that mango that the blackbird has just knocked to the ground inside?"

But old Mariano would show his wolf teeth and laugh.

No, never would old Mariano give even a partly rotten fruit to anyone. Of truth, if a blackbird should alight on an overhanging branch and peck a fruit outside to the ground so that the three brothers could pick it up, devouring it among themselves as they ran, the old man would get his rifle, shoot at the guilty blackbird, and then spend the rest of the day talking angrily to himself. Yet he knew that the three brothers were the sons of Juan Santos, a poor *arriero* who worked hard every day, only oftentimes to spend all his hard-earned and scanty wages on *tequila* Saturday night, so that some days there were neither *tortillas* nor *frijoles* in the house.

But as time passed, the three boys grew taller and their bones harder, while old Mariano began to stoop more as he lifted his feet more slowly from one step to the next. Time is just.

At last one day the three brothers tasted of the jealously-guarded fruits of old Mariano. Early one morning before the dawn Juan, José, and Daniel went down the hill to the *arroyo;* and here, working like ants with their *machetes,* they cut a long pole and made little steps in it so that soon they had a chicken-ladder like those you see going from one landing to the other in mines. After much stopping to rest, the three carried the ladder up the hill and slowly, slowly over to old Mariano's orchard. Grunting and panting, they managed to place the small end of their ladder upon the top of the high adobe wall. The youngest brother, Daniel, who did not wear *guaraches,* went quietly, quietly, his bare feet making no more noise on the ground than those of a coyote, up to Old Mariano's door and peeked in. Back he came with the word that the *viejo miserable* was taking his afternoon siesta and was trumpeting snores so loud that surely he would not be awakened if two burros were suddenly to bray into each of his ears.

Like a squirrel, Juan, the eldest brother, went up the ladder. From the wall top he climbed into a peach tree. His hands working as rapidly as those of a young monkey, he snatched fruits in every direction and let them fall over the outside of the wall to José and Daniel, who threw them into *morrales* slung about their necks in readiness.

When their bags were nearly full of fruit, the boys began to relax their caution and to laugh. In this moment old Mariano appeared in his doorway. Yelling insanely a malediction, he threw his hands at the sky and broke running toward the boys. Daniel and José with their *morrales* turned and raced into the chaparral and took straight up the mountainside like two young goats who know that the wolf is behind them. Juan hardly had time to scramble down the ladder. Just as he reached the ground, old Mariano, rushing up like a bull, made a grab at the boy and took hold of the one suspender to his *pantalones.* Juan jerked away, leaving the old man holding the strip of blue cloth in his hand. Then old Mariano gave chase; but Juan, even though he had to hold up his pants as he ran, soon left the puffing *viejo* behind.

Bellowing maledictions into the unoffending air and stamping the innocent ground, old Mariano went, not to his own house, but, as do all his kind in cases like this, to the house of the boys' parents. Here he awaited Juan Santos and asked him indignantly what kind of vicious creatures he had raised for sons, that they must rob an old man. In the jail, the jail, was where they belonged. They would be executed upon reaching majority, all of them.

"I am sorry," said Juan Santos, "but, *señor*, before the dawn I put the *aparejos* on my mules, and when the sun comes up I am driving the animals over the trails through the mountains. Already darkness has come when I arrive here at the house. How can I know what my sons are doing during the day? I cannot tie them as I would dogs, for they know how to untie the knots. Neither can I put them in a corral as I would goats, for they would very quickly climb over and be out. But this I tell you: every time they steal your fruit, I shall let you whip them, as punishment."

"Very well," said old Mariano. "It is good."

Juan Santos told his boys what he had said to their enemy. *"Pues,"* he added, "that old man is too weak. He cannot hurt you. He will only drive some of the dust out of your clothes."

So the next time the boys stole fruit from old Mariano's orchard, Juan Santos took his boys over to the old man's house. With a small stick, the *viejo* first worked on Juan, the eldest, who shouted, *"Ay! ay!"* at each blow as if his end had come. By the time the old man was ready for José, the strength was gone from his arm. But José yelled mightily. When finally it came Daniel's turn, his cries were plainly artificial ones, for the old man could hardly lift his arm for the blow.

Little did the *viejo* Mariano realize how many years had stolen into his bones, stiffening his joints and weakening his muscles. Daily came the boys to his orchard, and reported faithfully for their punishment, crying loudly, loudly.

Old Mariano was desperate.

"Ay, ay, Dios," Mariano said, "at first I chopped to pieces the ladders of the little devils; but they make new ones. *Chihuahua!* I cannot keep up with them. They are three and I am one. Oh, yes, they still come to be whipped. But, *caramba!* It is with them a playful game and with me hard work beyond my years. Loudly they shout and cry when I whip them; but I know that in truth, even while they yell so loudly, they are at me laughing. *Ay de mí! ay de mí!* I do not know what to do. For

me, what recourse? Must I continue suffering injustice from three young fiends? Ah, if only again I had my youth, my strength. *Ay de mí! Qué suerte tan mala me toca!* (What ill luck has befallen me!)"

His bad luck caused old Mariano to arise very early one morning. The night before, much *tequila* had made him fall asleep early; and as he had not cursed all he desired that day, he arose early this morning so as to spend every bit of the day in the thing that now was his only pastime and consolation.

He had not been seated outside his doorway long, when suddenly, becoming alert, he did something he never before had been known to do. He became suddenly silent in the very middle of an eloquent malediction, leaving half the curse to float uncompleted in the air.

With open mouth, he stared out in front of his house at the road where an ox-cart was passing. The driver lay in the cart sleeping peacefully; but the two oxen went on at a very good pace. Why? A whip would strike out from time to time, hitting the oxen a smart blow. Mariano blinked his old eyes. Surely he couldn't be still drunk from the *tequila* of last night! A whip striking the oxen! Yet no one holding the handle! Thus it was.

"*Hola!*" Leaping up from his chair like a man truly inspired with the devil, Mariano went running, stumbling, yelling, and waving his arms for the driver to stop. As the old man approached, the driver sat up and rubbed his eyes.

"But that strange whip you have, sir!" the *viejo* panted.

"Think you so?" answered the driver, smiling.

"No handle, and no hand ahold of it; yet it strikes the oxen. Are you, *señor*, perhaps a magician . . . ?"

As the cart came to a halt, the whip curled up like a snake. Mariano's eyes almost left their sockets. The whip *was* a snake! For a moment the old man was speechless.

"Yes," said the driver calmly, "many wonder at my Chapo. He is a *chirrionera,* one of those snakes who stand upon their heads and whip their enemies. I have trained him to keep the oxen going at a steady pace."

By this time Mariano had managed to loosen his tongue. Now his eyes shone with a new fire—like those of a fox who has suddenly thought of a new and better way to catch chickens.

"*Señor*," he said excitedly, "*señor*, tell me. Can you tell me where I could find such a snake as your Chapo?"

"Yes," said the driver. "Go into the desert at the foot of the mountain called Sierra de Nopal Colorado (Mountain of Red Cactus). Make sure that you go directly after a rain. As you approach the mountain, you may become frightened, thinking that someone is shooting at you with a powerful rifle. But do not be alarmed: it will be merely the *chirrioneras* popping their tails in an effort to dry themselves after their bath in the rain, which falls only once a year in that region."

So, when the first rain fell, old Mariano made haste into the desert and towards the Sierra de Nopal Colorado. Before long he stopped and listened. There came through the desert the sound as of many guns firing off. As was predicted, the ancient thought of running. Surely, he thought, the *revolucionarios* and the *federales* were having a terrific battle. But he remembered what the ox-cart driver had told him, and went cautiously on again, approaching the foot of the mountain whence came the loud sounds of popping and cracking.

As he crept through the tall *nopales* and the brushy mesquite of the desert, old Mariano clasped in one hand a long pole, on the end of which was a small loop of reata made to snare with.

Slowly, slowly, he crept closer, closer to the little clearing at the foot of the mountains. Hiding behind a large stone, he watched a strange sight. Here were more than one hundred dark purple snakes, most of them popping their tails and sending little sprays of water into the air. From behind his rock Mariano arose stealthily with his long pole. But the wary snakes saw him and went squirming and bouncing as fast as deer through the chaparral. All except one. A large, handsome *chirrionera* stayed. Not yet had he popped himself dry. He was so laden with rain water that he could move but slowly.

94

THE WONDERFUL CHIRRIONERA

Upon this helpless one old Mariano pounced. Soon he had the snake's head secure in the loop at the end of the long pole. Struggle and squirm as he would, the snake could not work himself free. With a great smile on his face, the old man manoeuvered the captured snake on the end of the pole through the chaparral toward the little town of Venaditos.

Old Mariano turned loose the captive *chirrionera* in his orchard and set out for him every day a big bowl full of the finest fruit. At first the snake, on seeing the old man approach, would crawl rapidly away and cringe, coiled tightly, in the darkest corner of the orchard; but in a little time he became more tame, until soon he would eat fruit not only from the big bowl, but even out of the old man's hand.

As time passed, the creature came to feel very much at home around Mariano's house, and grew to believe, like a dog, that he was watchman of the place. Whenever a stranger came into view, the snake would stand upon his head and snap his tail so that it cracked loudly in warning. And if the old man wanted the stranger driven away, he had simply to say to the snake, *"Pégalo!"* (Hit him!) Then the *chirrionera* would race like a dark purple streak along the ground toward the one at whom his master was pointing. Standing upon his head, he would bounce around and around the victim, striking him with his tail from every direction, so that the one being beaten could only think that there were a dozen magic whips surrounding him, beating him whichever way he turned to escape.

So pleased was old Mariano with his *chirrionera* that he named him Angelito.

Now, careful, careful, was the sly old Mariano to keep secret to the three boys the fact that he had this Little Angel snake in his possession. The old fox waited until he had his pet trained perfectly. And then what a lashing the three fruit-stealers would get!

Luego, luego, after some little time, one day the three boys, Juan, José, and Daniel, came carrying their ladder to old Mariano's house. Laughing and joking they came now, for they had grown to regard the old man's whippings as great sport.

They were even a little disappointed that they had received no beatings for three weeks. Working leisurely, they placed their ladder in position against the wall; and Juan raised his foot to climb up.

"*Pégalos!*"

The boys turned quickly and looked. In his door stood old Mariano, a strange smile on his face, pointing at them. At the same time, the boys caught a glimpse of a dark purple shining snake streaking toward them faster than a galloping horse. Before they could move, Angelito had circled twice around them and had dealt them each a smart blow with his tail.

Crying in surprise and pain, the three boys scattered in different directions. Angelito followed Juan and whipped him several blows. Then, streaking rapidly, rapidly, after José, the snake caught up and slapped him with his tail as he ran. The same for Daniel.

And all the while old Mariano, standing in his doorway, roared like a bear with laughter and shouted: "*Eso es, mi Angelito precioso!* (That's it, my precious little angel!) *Ándale, Angelito. Zas! Dale otro al diablito.* (Give the little devil another.) Do not let him get away, Angelito. Ah, how does it feel? Boys, do you like this game? Very good sport, no? *Ay, Dios. Válgame Cielo Santo.* My stomach! I shall die of laughing."

After the dutiful Angelito had driven the three boys to their house, he came back to his violently laughing master. And late into that night, old Mariano and his *chirrionera* sat up, celebrating their victory. For Angelito there was a very big heap of fruit; and for the old man a bottle, some of the contents of which he poured from time to time into the gaping mouth of Angelito, who seemed greatly to relish a little stimulating drink with his meal. "*Mi Angeli-ti-ti-to,*" old Mariano was saying in the voice of one who is talking to a little baby. "What eyes you have so beautiful! Eat much that you may have much strength to whip the little fiends hard, hard. *Sí,* and drink another time, *mi Angeli-ti-ti-to.*"

And Angelito would drink and smack his lips and say, "Ah," shaking his head, and resume eating his peaches, plums, oranges, grapes, and mangoes. "Ah, ah, smart, smart you are, *mi Angelito*," the old man would say, stroking the snake's head fondly. "Everything I say you understand. Drink another time, Angelito. *Eso es.* A reward for your good work today. The thieving boys so without shame, how their hides must even now be smarting from the stinging blows you gave them. Ha! Ha! They will not visit again soon. No, no, not while you, my little angel, are here. Ah, how I love you, my little sweetheart, Angeli-ti-ti-to. Here, I give you a kiss."

For several days the three boys did not come near old Mariano's house. Very different from the feeble taps of the old man were the stout blows from Angelito's tail. Some way they must get rid of that whipping snake. How?

After thinking much, Juan, the eldest boy, got together in his head a plan—a plan which made him smile.

One night very dark when the moon had hid her face behind the clouds, Juan, Daniel, and José came and placed their ladder quietly against old Mariano's orchard wall. Angelito and his master were inside the house sleeping heavily after much drinking of *mescal*. Juan, slinging a *morral* over his shoulder, ascended the ladder to the top of the wall, climbed into the top of a peach tree and came down through the branches to the ground.

Peering all about him through the darkness, Juan saw over by the house something big and round. Over towards it he went, slowly, slowly feeling with his foot on the ground every step. He felt of the object. It was Angelito's bowl. And full of fruit. So considerate of his snake was old Mariano that he had prepared the night before his breakfast. Very good, thought Juan to himself. So much the better.

With his knife Juan cut open each mango, peach and plum, and took out the seeds. Then, reaching into his *morral*, he got handfuls of salt, chile and gunpowder and put a mixture of all these into the fruits where the seeds had been. When he had thus seasoned the last fruit, Juan stepped to the peach tree, climbed it to the wall, and came down the ladder.

The next morning before the sun had appeared, and while

old Mariano still slumbered, out of the door toward the big bowl of fruit crawled Angelito.

In his fiery eyes was smouldering a slight ill temper—which might well be expected after such a night of drinking. Much, much hunger had Angelito. Straight to his bowl he went and began eating the fruit greedily.

Now, *señor*, you know as well as I that in order for food to be savory it must be seasoned. And I can always win against the strongest garlic, chile or onion. But *válgame Dios*, anyone knows that enough is plenty. Bad enough it is to overdose food with too much of even one seasoning. But *Chihuahua!* Such a combination! Salt, chile, gunpowder! More dangerous this than war. One is likely to explode to all parts of the landscape, the right arm to be thrown and left hanging in a pine tree on the top of a mountain where the circling buzzards will perch and feed, the left arm to be sent sailing across the desert to land in some cactus bush about which will gather coyotes.

So greedily did Angelito begin eating that he devoured four fruits immediately. He coughed, strangled. His eyes flashed fire. Bounding into the air, he came down belching, choking, and squirming around like a lasso spinning, and cracking his tail.

Cursing in his own snake language, Angelito started toward the door. In he went and jumped upon the foot of old Mariano's bed. Wrapping his neck about the foot rail, the enraged *chirrionera* raised his tail quivering in the air. Old Mariano lay on his face, snoring into his pillow. Down came the tail like a black flash. *Zas!* Old Mariano bounced up off his bed with a great yell. Sitting up, he stared with large eyes at Angelito. Down came the tail again. *Zas!* "*Ay!*" Old Mariano rubbed his eyes. Was he dreaming? Another blow from the tail assured him that he was not, and out of bed he jumped. Angelito followed and struck him a blow. Another. Another. "*Ay*, Angelito, have you gone crazy from so much drink last night? No, no, Angelito! This is Don Mariano, your master and friend who every day feeds you. *Ay, ay, ay, Dios!* Angelito, stop! You will kill me. Angelito! Angelito! Do you not recognize . . . *Ay, Dios, Dios!*"

THE WONDERFUL CHIRRIONERA

Around and round the room went the old man, Angelito following him like a shadow and showering blows about his head and shoulders without intermission. Dropping to all fours, the old man crawled under the bed more rapidly than an armadillo. But there Angelito followed him. Out on the other side scrambled the old man, crying for help. From his bed he managed to grasp one of the rafters of his house and pulled himself up. Popping his tail on the ground, Angelito gave a great leap and wound himself around the rafter and beat the old man several blows. Down dropped the old man, to run around the room again, shouting, desperation in his eyes. In the corner he saw an axe. This he seized. Standing in the corner, he held the weapon over his head and shouted to Angelito, "Do not approach nearer. I will chop your fiendish head from your cursed body." With one swift flash of his tail, Angelito knocked the axe spinning from the old man's grasp.

For a moment the old man cowered trembling like a cornered rabbit. Then madly he dashed past Angelito out the door. Out sprang Angelito also, bounding along on his head behind the old man and whipping him every step with his tail. And at every blow the old man would cry out, jump, and run the faster.

Outside, near the door, stood Juan, José, and Daniel. "Look only," they called out one to the other, laughing. "*Mira no más.* How playful are the old man and his whipping snake. A game they are playing. Yes, a race. *Pues, válgame Dios,* the *viejo* has recaptured his youth! See how lightly his feet touch the ground! See how he leaps the stones and bushes! *Ándale, ándale, viejito!* Little precious Angelito is catching you. *Zas!* Ah, the game must be tag. *Zas!* Another love tap! Ah, it must be that the old man also has eaten of the highly seasoned food. Look, look how playful is the little snake!"

For the greater part of a league Angelito chased old Mariano into the desert, beating the dust from his clothes at every step. Over cactus they leaped; around mesquite trees they circled; down and up the banks of arroyos they fell and scrambled madly. Before their path scattered coyotes, armadillos, paisanos, rabbits, and all the other creatures of the desert, running in wild fear and confusion.

Finally, Angelito grew tired of the chase, the high seasoning having made it hard for him to fetch his breath. Back to old Mariano's house he went, and here he stayed until he and the three boys had eaten all the fruit from old Mariano's orchard. Then back he went to his home in the desert at the foot of Sierra de Nopal Colorado. And not until then did old Mariano return to his house.

"Shake your head, *señor*," said the story-teller when he had done, "until your teeth loosen and drop one by one to the ground like hailstones from the sky; but what has happened has happened. Go to the little town of Venaditos and there you will find old Mariano. 'Is he not dead?' you ask. Ah—no, yes, if you do find the old man there, look near by on the hill and about the city for an old grey burro. For old men of selfish and mean disposition do not die but turn into grey burros, which, it is well known, die never. This old burro will have no mustache to droop over his mouth, no brows to frown down over his eyes, and no *sarape* to pull up over his ears; so you might get from him the whole story of his life as man. That is, *señor*, if it is true what has been told to me since my childhood: that the burros, very wise and astute *animales* that they are, know how to speak the language of you gringos."

BR'ER COYOTE

By SARAH S. MCKELLAR

EUDELIO ÁLVAREZ, our ranch cook at Hacienda La Mariposa, in northern Coahuila, may be just a simple-minded, happy Mexican Indian; nevertheless he is one of the most engaging personalities and truest friends I have ever known, and to him I owe not a little of the interest and pleasure that a residence of years in Mexico has brought me. Eudelio's parents have lived their lives on the ranch. He was born there; it is his *tierra*—he belongs to us as we belong to him. When scarcely more than a child, he was lured away to fight through the revolution, but to this day he can not tell which side he was on. If asked, he will look rather puzzled and reply, "*Pues,* it was first for one general and then another, but I can not remember their names." He was promised riches, he says, and invariably laughs at the good joke on himself when he adds, "But all I got was my wounds and this crooked arm."

Our children are devoted to Eudelio. Many a guest, too, has come under his spell. In his spare time Eudelio makes ropes, quirts, and other gifts for his friends. And the yarns he can tell! Finding the children were becoming more and more fascinated by Eudelio's stories, I decided to investigate. What should I discover but that they were nothing more or less than the same old Uncle Remus animal yarns that had been such a delightful part of my own childhood in the Old South. After all, my children were getting their full share of Uncle Remus, and more.

In vain, though, did I try to make Eudelio tell me his stories. He was polite, did not refuse exactly, but I never got a single one. He was plainly embarrassed. The ranch cook telling the *señora cuentos*? It just wasn't done, that's all. The atmos-

101

phere of a kitchen was not conducive to story-telling, anyway. I should have known better.

So, late one evening when darkness was creeping over La Mariposa, I followed my small son to Eudelio's *jacal*. My strategy worked, for however poor a Mexican home may be, its hospitality is always perfect; a guest may not be refused anything. Several dogs and an over-sociable pig were disposed of, and I was welcomed into the family circle gathered about the embers of the supper fire out in front of the thatched *jacal*. With pardonable pride, Antonia, Eudelio's wife, brought forth a brand new chair. I settled myself as far back in the shadows as possible, my presence a false note the sooner forgotten the better for story-telling. One child was already fast asleep on the ground. Another, whimpering in its mother's arms, was admonished, "Be quiet, Lelito, or the coyote will get you," and immediately it cuddled closer and was silent. All the others drew near with expectant smiles at the mention of *cuentos*, while an uncle, Tío Luis, declined a box with thanks and seated himself comfortably against a post, remarking, "The old sit best on the ground." And then Eudelio began.

The *cuento* I have chosen is one he calls *El Señor León y El Señor Coyote*, though throughout the story the "br'er" of the Negro stories is used, becoming *hermano*, Spanish for *brother*. We meet our old friend, Br'er Rabbit, but he is in Mexico and is now Hermano Conejo, though the same delightful hero, always being saved by his wits. Taking the place of Br'er Fox, however, is Hermano Coyote.[1] The Mexicans are not so familiar with foxes. It is the coyote who is their natural and constant enemy in the ranch country, the coyote who must get the worst of it in every story. Eudelio used very few words in telling his *cuentos*; the simplicity of their style was marked. At the high points, however, he became dramatic, imitating the animals very cleverly, to the great delight of little Juan, Sapopa, Ramón and all the rest of the children with whom the

[1]Compare with "Sister Fox and Brother Coyote," by Riley Aiken, in this volume; also with the fable of the coon and the coyote in "Ranchero Sayings of the Border," by Howard D. Wesley, page 214, this volume.—*Editor*.

BR'ER COYOTE

ever-generous Mexican stork had blessed him and his Antonia.
Notice the strong local color, the ranch flavour, throughout
El Señor León y El Señor Coyote.

It was a coyote. He was hunting for something to eat and
came upon a rabbit nibbling grass. The coyote asked, "What
are you eating, Hermano Conejo?"

The rabbit answered, "I am eating tender young grass."

"But, Hermanito Conejito," the coyote said, "I do not know
how to eat grass. I have hunger for meat."

The poor little rabbit trembled with fear. But also he was
thinking, for he had a very good head. There was an ant hill
near by. The rabbit showed it to the coyote and said to him,
"Here you can have some good honey that is better than meat.
Keep digging and you will find it."

The coyote began scratching in the ant bed and the rabbit
ran away. The large red ants swarmed out. They bit the coyote
here, they bit him there; and he found no honey. He yelped
with the pain. *"Ay! ay! ay!"* He rolled over and over to rid
himself of the ants, and the more he suffered the angrier he
became with the rabbit for fooling him. So he ran after
Hermano Conejo, and when he caught up with him he said,
"Now, you tricky rabbit, I'm going to eat you."

"No, do not eat me, Hermano Coyote," said the rabbit, and
quickly he began knocking ripe prickly pears from a *nopal.*
"Eat these *tunas* instead; they are very sweet this year and
much more *sabrosas* than rabbit meat."

While the greedy coyote stopped to taste the *tunas,* the
rabbit got away. He ran far, but at last he had to stop at a
water hole because he was tired and had much thirst. He was
still drinking when a mountain lion, or panther, came.

"Don't waste time drinking water, little brother rabbit," the
lion warned him, "a coyote is coming close behind me. Run
quickly before he gets here and eats you up. Leave the coyote
to me; I'll attend to him. Hurry! *Ándale! Córrele!"*

So the little rabbit ran on, and in this way he escaped. When the coyote reached the water hole, the lion alone was there to greet him.

"Good morning, Hermano Coyote, where are you going so fast?"

"I am chasing a rabbit because he would not give me meat."

"Wait a little while," said the lion, "and I shall get you all the meat you wish. What kind of meat do you know how to eat?"

The coyote answered, "I know how to eat field mice and rabbits and goats and sheep. I know how to eat little calves and chickens and all such things."

"But I do not kill that kind of meat," said the lion. "I like young mules and horses. In all the world there is no meat *tan sabrosa* as that of a colt."

"Just get me any kind of meat," said the coyote. "For the love of God, hurry, Hermano León, for I am almost dead of hunger."

"All right," said the lion, "I shall climb up this tree. You hide below and make yourself ready. I see a cloud of dust."

"What is it?"

"A *manada* of mares and colts coming to water. Keep quiet; do not move, Hermano Coyote."

The lion and the coyote kept very still. The mares and their colts stopped to drink. A yearling colt came close, and the lion sprang from the tree to its back. The surprised colt bucked and pitched.

"Hold on, Hermano León," cried the coyote, full of delight. *"No te flojes, compadre!* Hang on, pardner! *Pícale con las espuelas!* Scrape him with the spurs! Ride him, cowboy!"

The lion rode the colt well, just like a vaquero, and in no time had it by the throat and killed it. "Here is your meat, Hermano Coyote," he said, "and now you see how one kills a colt."

"Yes, but you have spurs to hold on with," said the coyote.

"And you, also, have spurs," said the lion. "Have you not *uñas* on your toes as well as I? Now I have taught you how to get meat, I shall leave. *Adiós,* Hermano Coyote."

BR'ER COYOTE

The lion left, and the coyote ate until he could eat no more. But another day came when he had hunger. So he said to himself, "I see a cloud of dust in the distance. It must be the *manada*. Perhaps there may be another fat colt in the bunch, and I can kill it as Hermano León showed me."

The *manada* drew closer, and, sure enough, there was a young mule that was fine and fat. While it was drinking at the water hole, the coyote sprang upon its back. But Hermano Coyote was not a vaquero; he did not know how to ride, and his spurs were no good. The mule bucked but once and off Hermano Coyote rolled to the rocky ground. The mule kicked him here, the mule kicked him there; he kicked him on the nose; he kicked him all over. "*Ay! ay!*" Hermano Coyote yelped and swore, limping away as fast as he could. Soon he met the lion.

"What's the matter with you, Hermano Coyote?" the lion asked, trying not to laugh. "You look rather ill."

The coyote was very angry. "What's the matter with me? Just look and you will see how bruised and near death I am from doing as you told me."

"Oh, but you do not know how to get on in the world." The lion laughed and laughed. "You will die of hunger yet. But here are many deer and antelope. See if you can get one of them. They do not buck like mules and horses. Look how they are passing. Put on your spurs well because these animals will run away with you if you are not careful."

"But how can I catch one?" asked the coyote. "Please, Hermano León, help me; show me how it is done."

"Which one do you want?"

"I want that young doe."

"Very well then, Hermano Coyote. I'll get in this tree and you start the bunch running this way. Then you come and help me here."

"Good," said the coyote. "Now I shall get my fill."

He cut out the doe he wanted and drove her directly under the tree where the lion waited. Hermano León sprang upon the doe's back; Hermano Coyote helped, and together they killed

105

her. The lion ate what he wanted first, as lions always do, and left all the rest for the greedy coyote.

Once more a day came when the coyote had great hunger, and this time he was all alone. He wished to kill another deer and he was sure he knew how it was done. Although coyotes do not climb well, he managed to get into a tree as the lion had taught him. There he waited and waited for a deer to come by. At last when he was almost dying from hunger, a foolish deer stopped to graze beneath the tree. The coyote leaped upon its back. But it was not a young doe. It was a very strong, old buck.

The coyote dug his spurs into the buck's flanks and tried to stop him, but the buck only ran faster and faster. As the coyote could not ride like a cowboy and as his spurs were too small, he soon rolled off the buck's back and over a bank into a deep hole in the river. The banks of the river were so slick and steep Hermano Coyote could not get out. Because he was greedy and not content with eating the food God wished him to eat, he was drowned.

The
BULLET-SWALLOWER

By Jovita González

H E was a wiry little man, a bundle of nerves in perpetual motion. Quicksilver might have run through his veins instead of blood. His right arm, partly paralyzed as result of a *machete* cut he had received in a saloon brawl, terminated in stiff, claw-like, dirty-nailed fingers. One eye was partly closed— a knife cut had done that—but the other, amber in color, had the alertness and the quickness of a hawk's. Chairs were not made for him. Squatting on the floor or sitting on one heel, he told interminable stories of border feuds, bandit raids and smuggler fights as he fingered a curved, murderous knife which ended in three inches of zigzag, jagged steel. "No one has ever escaped this," he would say, caressing it. "Sticking it into a man might not have finished him, but getting it out—ah, my friend, that did the work. It's a very old one, brought from Spain, I guess," he would add in an unconcerned voice. "Here is the date, 1630."

A landowner by inheritance, a trail driver by necessity, and a smuggler and gambler by choice, he had given up the traditions of his family to be and do that which pleased him most. Through some freakish mistake he had been born three centuries too late. He might have been a fearless *conquistador,* or he might have been a chivalrous knight of the Rodrigo de Narváez type, fighting the infidels along the Moorish frontier. A tireless horseman, a man of *pelo en pecho* (hair on the chest), as he braggingly called himself, he was afraid of nothing.

"The men of my time were not lily-livered, white-gizzarded creatures," he would boast. "We fought for the thrill of it, and

107

the sight of blood maddened us as it does a bull. Did we receive a gash on the stomach? Did the guts come out? What of it? We tightened our sash and continued the fray. See this arm? Ah, could it but talk, it could tell you how many men it sent to the other world. To Hell perhaps, perhaps to Purgatory, but none I am sure to Heaven. The men I associated with were neither sissies nor saints. Often at night when I can not sleep because of the pain in these cursed wounds, I say a prayer, in my way, for their souls, in case my prayers should reach the good God.

"People call me Traga-Balas, Bullet-Swallower — Antonio Traga-Balas, to be more exact. *Ay*, were I as young as I was when the incident that gave me this name happened!

"We were bringing several cartloads of smuggled goods to be delivered at once and in safety to the owner. Oh, no, the freight was not ours but we would have fought for it with our life's blood. We had dodged the Mexican officials, and now we had to deal with the Texas Rangers. They must have been tipped, because they knew the exact hour we were to cross the river. We swam in safety. The pack mules, loaded with packages wrapped in tanned hides, we led by the bridle. We hid the mules in a clump of tules and were just beginning to dress when the Rangers fell upon us. Of course, we did not have a stitch of clothes on; did you think we swam fully dressed? Had we but had our guns in readiness, there might have been a different story to tell. We would have fought like wild-cats to keep the smuggled goods from falling into their hands. It was not ethical among smugglers to lose the property of a Mexican to Americans, and as to falling ourselves into their hands, we preferred death a thousand times. It's no disgrace and dishonor to die like a man, but it is to die like a rat. Only canaries sing; men never tell, however tortured they may be. I have seen the Rangers pumping water into the mouth of an innocent man because he would not confess to something he had not done. But that is another story.

"I ran to where the pack mules were to get my gun. Like a fool that I was, I kept yelling at the top of my voice, 'You so, so and so gringo cowards, why don't you attack men like men? Why do you wait until they are undressed and unarmed?' I must have said some very insulting things, for one of them shot at me right in the mouth. The bullet knocked all of my front teeth out, grazed my tongue and went right through the back of my neck. Didn't kill me, though. It takes more than bullets to kill Antonio Traga-Balas. The next thing I knew I found myself in a shepherd's hut. I had been left for dead, no doubt, and I had been found by the goatherd. The others were sent to the penitentiary. After I recovered, I remained in hiding for a year or so; and when I showed myself all thought it a miracle that I had lived through. That's how I was rechristened Traga-Balas. That confounded bullet did leave my neck a little stiff; I can't turn around as easily as I should, but outside of that I am as fit as though the accident—I like to call it that—had never happened. It takes a lot to kill a man, at least one who can swallow bullets.

"I've seen and done many strange things in my life and I can truthfully say that I have never been afraid but once. What are bullets and knife thrusts to seeing a corpse arise from its coffin? Bullets can be dodged and dagger cuts are harmless unless they hit a vital spot. But a dead man staring with lifeless, open eyes and gaping mouth is enough to make a man tremble in his boots. And, mind you, I am not a coward, never have been. Is there any one among you who thinks Antonio Traga-Balas is a coward?"

At a question like this, Traga-Balas would take the knife from its cover and finger it in a way that gave one a queer, empty spot in the stomach. Now he was launched upon a story.

"This thing happened," he went on, "years ago at Roma beside the Río Bravo. I was at home alone; my wife and children were visiting in another town. I remember it was a windy night in November. The evening was cool, and, not knowing what else to do, I decided to go to bed early. I was not asleep yet when someone began pounding at my door.

" 'Open the door, Don Antonio; please let me in,' said a woman's voice. I got up and recognized in the woman before me one of our new neighbors. They had just moved into a deserted *jacal* in the alley back of our house.

" 'My husband is very sick,' she explained. 'He is dying and wants to see you. He says he must speak to you before he dies.'

"I dressed and went out with her, wondering all the time what this unknown man wanted to see me about. I found him in a miserable hovel, on a more miserable pallet on the floor, and I could see by his sunken cheeks and the fire that burned in his eyes that he was really dying, and of consumption, too. With mumbled words he dismissed the woman from the room and, once she had gone, he asked me to help him sit up. I propped him on the pillows the best I could. He was seized with a fit of coughing followed by a hemorrhage and I was almost sure that he would die before he could say anything. I brought him some water and poured a little *tequila* from a half empty bottle that was at the head of the pallet. After drinking it, he gave a sigh of relief.

" 'I am much better now,' he whispered. His voice was already failing. 'My friend,' he went on, 'excuse my calling you, an utter stranger, but I have heard you are a man of courage and of honor and you will understand what I have to say to you. That woman you saw here is really not my wife; but I have lived with her in sin for the last twenty years. It weighs upon my conscience and I want to right the wrong I did her once.'

"As the man ended this confession, I could not help thinking what changes are brought about in the soul by the mere thought of facing eternity. I thought it very strange that after so long a time he should have qualms of conscience now. Yet I imagine death is a fearful thing, and, never having died myself nor been afraid to die, I could not judge what the dying man before me was feeling. So I decided to do what I would have expected others to do for me, and asked him if there was anything I might do for him.

" 'Call a priest. I want to marry her,' he whispered.

"I did as he commanded and went to the rectory. Father José María was still saying his prayers, and when I told him

that I had come to get him to marry a dying man, he looked
at me in a way he had of doing whenever he doubted anyone,
with one eye half closed and out of the corner of the other. As
I had played him many pranks in the past, no doubt he thought
I was now playing another. He hesitated at first but then got
up somewhat convinced.

" 'I'll take my chance with you again, you son of Barabbas,'
he said. 'I'll go. Some poor soul may want to reconcile himself
with his Creator.' He put on his black cape and took the little
bag he always carried on such occasions. The night was as
black as the mouth of a wolf and the wind was getting colder
and stronger.

" 'A bad time for any one to want a priest, eh, Father?' I said
in an effort to make conversation, not knowing what else to say.

" 'The hour of repentance is a blessed moment at whatever
time it comes,' he replied in a tone that I thought was
reprimanding.

"On entering the house, we found the man alone. The woman
was in the kitchen, he told us. I joined her there, and what do
you suppose the shameless creature was doing? Drinking *tequila*,
getting courage, she told me, for the ordeal ahead of her. After
about an hour, we were called into the sick room. The man
looked much better. Unburdening his soul had given him that
peaceful look you sometimes see on the face of the dead who
die while smiling. I was told that I was to be witness to the
Holy Sacrament of Matrimony. The woman was so drunk by
now she could hardly stand up; and between hiccoughs she
promised to honor and love the man who was more fit to be
food for the worms than for life in this valley of tears. I'd
never seen a man so strong for receiving sacraments as that
one was. He had received the Sacrament of Penance, then that
of Matrimony—and I could see no greater penance than marry-
ing such a woman—and now he was to receive Extreme
Unction, the Sacrament for the Dying.

"The drunken woman and I held candles as Father José
María anointed him with holy oil; and when we had to join
him in prayer, I was ashamed that I could not repeat even the

Lord's Prayer with him. That scene will always live in my mind, and when I die may I have as holy a man as Father José María to pray for me! He lingered a few moments; then, seeing there was nothing else to do, he said he would go back. I went with him under the pretext of getting something or other for the dying man, but in reality I wanted to see him safe at home. On the way back to the dying man I stopped at the saloon for another bottle of *tequila*. The dying man might need a few drops to give him courage to start on his journey to the Unknown, although from what I had seen I judged that Father José María had given him all he needed.

"When I returned, the death agony was upon him. The drunken woman was snoring in the kitchen. It was my responsibility to see that the man did not die like a dog. I wet his cracked lips with a piece of cloth moistened in *tequila*. I watched all night. The howling of the wind and the death rattle of the consumptive made the place the devil's kingdom. With the coming of dawn, the man's soul, now pure from sin, left the miserable carcass that had given it lodging during life. I folded his arms over his chest and covered his face with a cloth. There was no use in calling the woman; she lay on the dirt floor of the kitchen snoring like a trumpet. I closed the door and went out to see what could be done about arrangements for the funeral. I went home and got a little money—I did not have much—to buy some boards for the coffin, black calico for the covering and for a mourning dress for the bride, now a widow—although I felt she did not deserve it—and candles.

"I made the coffin, and when all was done and finished went back to the house. The woman was still snoring, her half-opened mouth filled with buzzing flies. The corpse was as I had left it. I called some of the neighbors to help me dress the dead man in my one black suit, but he was stiff already and we had to lay him in the coffin as he was, unwashed and dirty. If it is true that we wear white raiments in Heaven, I hope the good San Pedro gave him one at the entrance before the other blessed spirits got to see the pitiful things he wore. I watched the body all day; he was to be buried early the following morning. Father José María had told me he would say Mass for him. The old woman, curse her, had gotten hold of the other bottle of *tequila* and continued bottling up courage for the ordeal that she said she had to go through.

"The wind that had started the night before did not let down; in fact, it was getting stronger. Several times the candles had blown out, and the corpse and I had been left in utter darkness. To avoid the repetition of such a thing, I went to the kitchen and got some empty fruit cans very much prized by the old woman. In truth, she did not want to let me use them at first, because, she said, the fruit on the paper wrapping looked so natural and was the only fruit she had ever owned. I got them anyway, filled them with corn, and stuck the candles there.

"Early in the evening about nine, or thereabouts, I decided to get out again and ask some people to come and watch with me part of the night. Not that I was afraid to stay alone with the corpse. One might fear the spirits of those who die in sin, but certainly not this one who had left the world the way a Christian should leave it. I left somewhat regretfully, for I was beginning to have a kindly feeling towards the dead man. I felt towards that body as I would feel towards a friend, no doubt because I had helped it to transform itself from a human being to a nice Christian corpse.

"As I went from house to house asking people to watch with me that night, I was reminded of a story that the priest had told us once, and by the time I had gone half through the town I knew very well how the man who was inviting guests to the wedding feast must have felt. All had some good excuse to give but no one could come. To make a long story short, I returned alone, to spend the last watch with my friend the corpse.

"As I neared the house, I saw it was very well lighted, and I thought perhaps some people had finally taken pity upon the poor unfortunate and had gone there with more candles to light the place. But soon I realized what was really happening. The *jacal* was on fire.

"I ran inside. The sight that met my eyes was one I shall

ever see. I was nailed to the floor with terror. The corpse, its hair a flaming mass, was sitting up in the coffin where it had so peacefully lain all day. Its glassy, opaque eyes stared into space with a look that saw nothing and its mouth was convulsed into the most horrible grin. I stood there paralyzed by the horror of the scene. To make matters worse, the drunken woman reeled into the room, yelling, 'He is burning before he gets to Hell!'

"Two thoughts ran simultaneously through my mind: to get her out of the room and to extinguish the fire. I pushed the screaming woman out into the darkness and, arming myself with courage, reëntered the room. I was wearing cowboy boots, and my feet were the only part of my body well protected. Closing my eyes, I kicked the table, and I heard the thud of the burning body as it hit the floor. I became crazy then. With my booted feet I tramped upon and kicked the corpse until I thought the fire was extinguished. I dared not open my eyes for fear of what I might see, and with my eyes still closed I ran out of the house. I did not stop until I reached the rectory. Like mad I pounded upon the door, and when the priest opened it and saw me standing there looking more like a ghost than a living person, he could but cross himself. It was only after I had taken a drink or two—may God forgive me for having done so in his presence—that I could tell him what had happened.

"He went back with me and, with eyes still closed, I helped him place the poor dead man in his coffin. Father José María prayed all night. As for me, I sat staring at the wall, not daring once to look at the coffin, much less upon the charred corpse. That was the longest watch I ever kept.

"At five o'clock, with no one to help us, we carried the coffin to the church, where the promised mass was said. We hired a burro cart to take the dead man to the cemetery, and, as the sun was coming up, Father José María, that man of God, and I, an unpenitent sinner, laid him in his final resting place."

Tales from
SAN ELIZARIO

By Josefina Escajeda

TWENTY miles down the river from El Paso is San Elizario, a small Spanish-speaking community with few pretensions to importance other than that of the past. For nearly two centuries it maintained its dignity as one of the chief towns of the region; its legal and mercantile business was extensive; its old families maintained the Spanish tradition of courtesy and hospitality. A considerable folk-lore grew up before El Paso and Ciudad Juárez drained the town of inhabitants and prestige. For generations one particular family was regarded as possessed of supernatural powers, and many hair-raising stories concerning the doings of its members grew up.

The Witch of Cenecú

Eutiquio Holquín was a healthy young animal. No one in San Elizario could excel him in dancing the *fandango,* and he was always among the winners when on Sunday afternoon the young men gathered together to play *la chueca* and *la quemada.* But quite suddenly he was stricken with a strange malady. He lost the use of his limbs and had to lie in bed as helpless as a babe.

His mother tried every remedy she knew of, but Eutiquio did not improve. Soon he began to tell queer stories of a woman who came at night when everyone was asleep and forced him to take strange herbs and potions. Now it was clear why the remedies of his mother were of no avail. Eutiquio was bewitched.

One night his family were startled from their sleep by the cry, "Look! Look! Here I have her! Come quick! She takes me dragging!"

PURO MEXICANO

They hurried to his room. There a strange sight met their eyes. Eutiquio was being dragged toward the door—*but the person who dragged him was invisible.* Suddenly, near the door, he fell. His mother and his sisters rushed to him. With great effort they managed to get him back in bed. Eutiquio could not move.

"Didn't you see her?" he asked. "It was the *bruja*. When she leaned toward me to make me eat, I managed to catch her by the hands. Then I called you. She tried to get away, and, not being able to release herself, she dragged me toward the door. My strength left me, and she escaped. But I recognized her. She is a *bruja* from Cenecú.

After this episode Eutiquio began to improve. Gradually he recovered his strength and was soon able to walk around a little. When he was well enough to get on a horse again, he determined to go to Cenecú to punish the witch who had caused him so much suffering.

He arrived in Cenecú one afternoon and went straight to the house of the *bruja*. The girl who came to the door told him her mother was at the church helping to clean it for the *fiesta*. In spite of her protests, Eutiquio dismounted and walked into the house. After satisfying himself that the *bruja* was not there, he demanded that the girl show him where her mother kept her *monos*. She hesitated, but when Eutiquio threatened her with his quirt, she showed him an immense gourd under the bed.

Eutiquio took this gourd to the kitchen and began to examine its contents. There were rag dolls of every size. Some had a thorn in the head, others in an eye, others through the stomach, others through an arm or a leg. Each *mono,* or figurine, represented some victim of the *bruja's* evil powers.

Eutiquio stirred up the fire and threw all these *monos* into it. No sooner had he done this than the *bruja* was seen running toward her home, crying at the top of her voice. She rushed into the kitchen. Her dolls were ashes.

Overcome by the calamity that had befallen her precious *monos,* she fell to the floor in a faint. Never again could she be a *bruja*. With the destruction of her *monos* her powers had also been destroyed.

Doña Carolina Learns a Lesson

Nicolás and his *compadre* were jogging along in a rickety wagon on their way to the *bosque* to cut wood. They had left El Paso del Norte, now Ciudad Juárez, before daybreak, and were now near Cenecú. Nicolás looked up. He could not believe his eyes.

"Look, *compadre!* There comes a woman. She looks like Doña Carolina, the wife of our good friend Don Ricardo."

"It cannot be, *compadre*. What would a rich *señora* be doing out here in the *monte?*"

They hurried to meet her. It was Doña Carolina—a very much subdued and penitent Doña Carolina. This is the story she told them:

"My husband has gone to Chihuahua on business. He has been away longer than usual, and I began to wonder what could be keeping him so long. Yesterday morning I went to the house of Agapito, the *brujo,* and asked him to help me. He agreed to take me to a place where I could see what my husband was doing if I would promise to do just as he told me.

"Last night, at the appointed hour, Agapito presented himself at my house. '*Señora*,' he said, 'you must solemnly promise not to invoke God or the saints, no matter what happens.'

"*Dios me perdone*. I promised to do as I was told. Agapito blindfolded me and took me by the hand. I felt myself going up and up. We seemed to be flying through the air. At last I felt my feet on firm ground. Agapito uncovered my eyes. We were just outside a large cave. It was well lighted, but there seemed to be no one in it.

"Agapito spoke to me: 'If you are wearing a scapular, a medal, or a crucifix, take it off and hang it on that mesquite that you see near you. After you have done this, you may enter the cave and take the seat that you see there. Remember—do not invoke God or the saints no matter what happens.'

"I did as I was told and took my seat. I was alone in the

117

cave. Everything was so quiet that I could hear myself breathing. Suddenly I heard a great commotion, and a huge billy goat rushed toward me. His eyes were balls of fire, and the tips of his horns gave off sparks. I felt faint when he passed me, but, mustering all my courage, did not cry out.

"I had hardly recovered from this frightful scare when the largest snake I have ever seen came from the same direction from which the goat had come. It crawled closer and closer. Still I managed to control myself. Then, *señores*, this terrible creature came right up to me and began to wind itself around me. This was more than any mortal could stand. I cried out, '*Jesús, María y José, me favorezcan!*'

"At once the cave went dark. There was a terrible explosion. When I recovered consciousness, I was lying out here in the *monte*. I was beginning to despair of being rescued when I saw you coming. God must have sent you this way. May He have mercy on my sinful soul."

Nicolás and his *compadre* took Doña Carolina back to her home. Everyone noticed the great change in her. She was no longer the haughty, arrogant woman of former days. But only Nicolás and his *compadre* knew what had brought about this change, and they had promised never to tell.

La Casa de la Labor

Until some fifty years ago, the people of San Elizario made the sign of the cross whenever they passed a certain heap of ruins. There La Casa de la Labor, the largest and finest *rancho* in the vicinity, once stood. But the hand of God had fallen heavily upon it and destroyed it together with its mistress.

Doña Fidencia Ortega was the woman's name. Since the death of her husband she had managed her great *rancho*. Her servants feared and hated her, for many of them had felt the sting of her *cuarta*.

The previous year had been a dry one. The vineyards had borne but little fruit. It would soon be the feast of San Isidro, the patron of farmers; and there was no wine for the mass.

There was just one thing to do, for Doña Fidencia was the only one who had wine.

Father Pedro set out toward La Casa de la Labor. Surely Doña Fidencia would not refuse a little wine for the feast of San Isidro. Surely she must see how much the people needed the protection of this *santo*. Another dry year would cause untold suffering. Tired but full of hope, the good old priest arrived at La Casa de la Labor.

Doña Fidencia was relentless. Yes, she had wine. But it was barely enough for her own needs. Not one drop would she give. What did she owe to Father Pedro or his Church? Let him go about his business and leave her alone.

Slowly, disconsolately, Father Pedro returned to the *curato*. His eyes filled with tears and he shook his head. *"Dios que la perdone."* How could anyone refuse to give a little wine for the Holy Sacrifice of the Mass?

The next day La Casa de la Labor had disappeared. Not a sheep, not a horse was left. Only smouldering ruins remained to give testimony of the wrath of God.

What had become of Doña Fidencia? There were those who afterward said that they had seen her riding to the *laguna* on a bull that snorted fire, and that they had heard her laugh a diabolical laugh and cry, as she plunged into the water, never to be seen again, *"Hasta el infierno!"*

Agapito Brings a Treat

It was growing dark when *la conducta* from San Elizario stopped for the night. For days the men and their pack mules had been traveling from early morning until twilight. Many more days of hardship lay ahead of them before they should reach Chihuahua with their *carga* of salt and wine. The men were tired—tired of the road—tired of the food which they themselves were obliged to prepare while on *conducta*. Grumbling, they made ready to cook their scant fare.

Agapito Cercas spoke up: "Don't bother to cook anything. This very day a hog was slaughtered at my home. Just wait

119

a little moment. I am going to bring you *carne adobada, chile con asadura,* and *tortillas calientes!*"[1] The men only laughed and went on with their work. Agapito withdrew from the group. Clemente Durán followed him. One by one Agapito began to remove his garments and drop them to the right and to the left. When he had taken off all his clothes, he stood for a moment perfectly still. Then he vanished. Again and again Clemente called him. There was no answer.

Clemente gathered up Agapito's discarded clothing and returned to his companions to relate the strange things he had seen. The men about the camp fire were discussing these singular actions when Agapito's voice startled them into silence.

"Clemente, throw me my clothes. How do you expect me to come back without them?"

Clemente took the clothes and threw them in the direction from which the voice had come. In just a few minutes Agapito appeared. Before their astonished eyes he laid a *cazuela* (bowl) of *chile con asadura,* another of *carne adobada,* and a cloth full of piping hot *tortillas de maíz.*

At sight of such delicious food, a few of the men forgot all fear and ate it *con mucho gusto.* But the others refused it as tactfully as possible. For was it not clearly the work of a *brujo?*

A Hanged Man Sends Rain

Many of the old people of San Elizario remember the summer of 1868 for two reasons: it was unusually dry, and the first man to be executed in El Paso County was hanged there in August.

Bartolo Mendoza was convicted of the murder of his stepdaughter. He did not deny his guilt, but, as the time for his execution drew near, his remorse was great. He passed his days in prayer. As he paced back and forth in his cell, he would raise his voice in the prayers of the rosary and the litanies. For eight days before he was hanged, he attended mass and received communion daily. Bartolo was ready for death.

---

[1]Dressed meat, chile cooked with chitterlings, hot *tortillas* (corn cakes).

The night before the execution, the condemned man was saying his beads when one of the guards entered. "Bartolo," he said, "you will soon be face to face with God. Won't you please tell Him to send us a little rain? A few more days of this terrible drouth and all our crops will be ruined."

A look impossible to describe came over Bartolo's face. "Stop worrying," was all he said.

The next day dawned bright and clear. Not a cloud could be seen. The sun seemed to grow hotter with each moment that passed. At three o'clock it beat down mercilessly on the procession that was slowly making its way to the gallows.

Father Borrajo walked with the prisoner. As the priest intoned the prayers of the litany, the people joined in the responses. Slowly, praying as they went, the procession moved on.

At last they reached the gallows. With steady steps Bartolo mounted the platform, accompanied by Father Borrajo. He knelt to receive the priest's blessing. Then he got up, looked around him, and took his place. The noose was adjusted. In a second the trap had been sprung.

Hardly had he been pronounced dead when the sky began to cloud. By the time the procession with his body reached the church, a few drops of rain were falling. Before long it was raining hard, and the rain continued all through the night and all the next day.

Can anyone doubt that the soul of Bartolo Mendoza went straight to heaven?

The Metamorphosis of
A FOLK TALE

By Elizabeth Willis DeHuff

URING the fifteen years that I have been collecting New Mexico folk-tales, I have heard many versions of certain themes; but the most interesting variation was an old Spanish story, with its mass of detail, completely metamorphosed by the Indians to conform to their own apperceptive basis. Knowing nothing of kings, princesses, negresses and the ocean, the Indians had kept the plot and for the unknown substituted details of their own experience. Although I had long since learned not to confuse the natives of Spanish descent with the Indians if I wanted to keep in their good graces, I could not resist a question to the old man who told me the original Spanish story.

He looked at me confidentially and spoke in Spanish, for he knew no English. "All of these people around here say they are pure-blood Spanish, but they all have Indian blood—*sí, sí, todos!*"

"And what about yourself, *señor?*" I modestly asked, hoping that he understood my admiration for the culture of the Pueblo Indian.

Quickly his expression changed, as he stiffened and replied. "Me? No, I have no Indian blood. My great-great-grandfather came directly over from Spain." With difficulty I suppressed a smile—one Spanish ancestor, and what of the others?

His daughter was married to an Indian of the San Juan pueblo, and for several years we had been close friends, exchanging gifts, compliments and folk-tales. She did not know any Indian tales, she said, but she could tell me many

122

THE METAMORPHOSIS OF A FOLK TALE

Spanish stories that her father had told to her. And I found that her stories did have real Spanish origin, though most of them had been changed to suit Nuevo México.

Upon this day I sat with the old man in the small *sala* of a little mud ranch house just outside of the pueblo, waiting for Regina to finish a few household chores so that she could tell me a *"muy buen"* story *"y muy largo."* Finally she came in and settled herself stiffly in a straight chair, home-made and hand-carved in scanty, crude pattern; and the old man, having completed his duty as host, moved outside, crouched upon his haunches in the sunshine with his back against the adobe wall, and closed his eyes.

"It is the story of the three princesses," began Regina. And then she told me this story in Spanish, with the many adjectives of that extravagant language, spoken in the obsolete form of sixteenth century Spain.

A Spanish man and his wife had three beautiful daughters, but they were very poor. He had no other livelihood but the little money he gained by selling burro loads of firewood.

One day, while the man was in a thicket splitting a log, a lizard jumped out of the stump.

"How many daughters have you?" he asked the frightened man, who saw at once that the lizard was a magical prince.

"I have three daughters," he answered.

"Are they beautiful?" continued the lizard.

"Yes."

"Then tomorrow bring me the youngest one," demanded the lizard.

The man loaded his burro and went home. The next day he told his youngest daughter to put on her shawl and go with him to help load wood, as he felt ill. When they neared the spot where he had cut wood the day before, he turned and said to his daughter, "Be not afraid. A lizard will leap out. He is a prince."

But when the lizard jumped out, the girl was frightened and ran. The lizard pursued and caught her. "Be not afraid," he said to her. "Close your eyes. When you open them, you will

123

see a palace, which will be your new home." Then, handing the man two large bags of money, the lizard disappeared with the girl.

The man moved to another spot and began to cut down another tree. Out sprang another lizard, the brother of the first.

"Have you any daughters?" he asked.

"Yes, I have two."

"Are they beautiful?"

"Yes, very beautiful!"

"Then tomorrow you must bring me the younger one," commanded the lizard, "and I shall pay you well."

The man went home with his wood and his money and told his wife that he had lost his daughter in the woods and could not find her anywhere.

"As I looked for her, I found these two bags of money. Let the second daughter go with me tomorrow to help look again for the lost one."

Next day, the second daughter went with her father. When they came to the tree trunk where the man had been chopping, the lizard came out and grabbed the girl. Before she could scream, he told her to shut her eyes, and said that when she opened them, she would find herself in a palace, which would be her new home. The startled girl dared not disobey; so she closed her eyes. The lizard handed the man three bags of money and disappeared with the girl into the tree trunk.

Again the man moved to a fresh spot to cut his wood. Then a third lizard bounded out from the notch he had made in the tree trunk. This was the third brother.

"Have you any daughters?" he asked.

"Yes, I have one."

"Is she beautiful?"

"Yes."

"Then tomorrow you must bring her to me," commanded the lizard, "and I shall pay you well."

When the man returned home with his three bags of money and neither of his daughters, the wife would not believe that they had been lost. She suspected foul play and refused to let the oldest daughter go. But the girl, who had never been away from home, wanted to accompany her father. Sneaking her shawl out of the house next morning, she slipped away with him.

The same thing happened as before. Only this time the father received four sacks of money. Knowing that his wife would not believe that all three daughters were lost, he decided to tell her the truth and confess that he had sold them.

"Do not be sad, wife," he concluded; "your daughters are happy, for they are married to three princes."

But the poor mother was inconsolable over the loss of her daughters and every day she wept. She bore a baby boy and, as he grew to young manhood, he realized that his mother was accustomed to weeping almost every day, and he wondered why.

"Mama, why do you weep?" he asked one day.

She told him of what had happened to her daughters. "I feel that they are not happy, for their husbands are wizard princes and I want them back every day," she ended.

"Mama, I will bring them back," said the youth.

Immediately the young man set out in search of his sisters. As he journeyed, he met the four sons of the Air—North, South, East, and West, whom he found quarreling among themselves.

"My friends," asked the youth, "why do you fight?"

"Because each of us wants the inheritance which our father, Old Air, has left," answered the boys all at once.

"What kind of heritage did your father leave?" asked the youth.

"A pair of boots that will go faster than the wind can travel," answered North.

"A hat that makes the wearer invisible," replied South.

"A stick, one side of which will kill and the other bring to life that which is dead," responded East and West.

"I can settle your dispute for you," said the youth. "Leave the heritage here with me and you four boys go to the top of that ridge and stand in a row. When I wave my hand, run toward me. The one who arrives first will win all the inheritance."

"All right," agreed the boys.

As soon as their backs were turned, the youth grabbed up the boots and pulled them on his feet. Then snatching up the hat, he placed it on his head. He seized the stick and cried, "Boots, take me to the stump where my youngest sister entered!"

Away he sped. North, South, East, and West ran after him, but they could neither see him nor catch him.

Soon the youth reached the cleft in the stump. A large black woman (Moor) responded to his knock.

"Tell your mistress to admit me to this palace," said the youth.

"No one is allowed to enter here," replied the woman, barring his passage. With one stroke of the stick, the youth struck her dead and entered. Then when he was safely inside, he turned, struck her with the other side of the stick to bring her to life again, and went to find his sister.

He found, as he had suspected, that she was the mistress of the house.

"My husband is a fish," exclaimed the frightened sister. "If he finds you here he will kill you."

"Do not fear," the youth assured her, as he put on the magic hat. "He will not see me until I wish it."

When the fish returned home, he found his wife crying.

"What are you weeping about?" asked the fish. "You have never cried before."

"I was thinking of what you might do if you had some relative of mine in your power!" replied the princess.

"You need not cry about that. It would give me great pleasure to entertain a relative of yours."

With that assurance, the princess brought forward her brother and introduced him.

"Why have I the honor of this visit?" asked the fish. Thereupon the youth told him how his mother had wept for years over the loss of her beautiful daughter and how he had promised to find the daughter and bring her home again.

"I know how much your sister is missed," said the fish, "for I, too, have a sister, who was stolen by a giant. If you return to me my sister, then you may take your own sister home to see her mother. Here are some of my scales. Whenever you are in danger or need me, say to them, 'These scales came from my brother the fish.' "

On the following morning the youth put on his magic boots and said, "Take me to where my second sister can be found!"

The boots took him to another great palace, where once again he was met at the door by a negress, whom he had to slay with his stick and bring to life again.

After he had found his sister, the princess, and explained to her why he had come, she exclaimed, "Oh, my husband is a bull! He allows no strangers here. He will gore you to death if he sees you!"

"Do not fear. When I wear my hat he cannot see me." And the brother put on his hat and became invisible.

As had happened at the house of the fish, when the bull came home he found his wife in tears and assured her that he would not harm any of her kindred. When the youth was brought forward and introduced, he explained his mission and was told the same thing about the stolen sister.

"If you will bring back our sister to us," said the bull, "you may take your sister to see her mother. Here are some of my hairs," he continued, pulling out a group of hairs from his side. "If you need my help, hold them and say, 'These hairs came from my brother the bull!' "

A third time, the youth put on his boots and told them to take him to the place where he could find his oldest sister, and in a twinkling he came to a third large palace.

This time the frightened sister said, "My husband is an eagle. He allows no strangers to enter here. He will pluck out your eyes if he finds you."

The youth hid himself under his hat. Then when the sister had won her husband's approval and the youth was presented to tell his mission, the eagle also told him how his sister had been stolen by the giant, and made the same proposal for her return to him. He gave the youth a feather, which he was to address if he should need aid.

Finally the youth set out in search of the giant. Donning his boots at the palace of the eagle, he said, "Boots, take me to the Princess of Harmonaca, who knows everything." And the boots took him. From this princess he learned that the soul of the giant who had stolen the sister of the fish, the bull, and the eagle reposed in the bottom of the sea. The giant spent much of his time in the sea to be with his soul. "But even I do not know what will kill this giant, nor where is his vulnerable spot," concluded the Princess of Harmonaca.

Next the boots took the youth to the home of the giant, which was near the sea. When he arrived, the giant was in the sea communing with his soul. A fourth time his trusty stick killed the guards at the door and gave him entrance. Finding the mistress, who was the princess he sought, he told her who he was and why he had come. When he saw that she was beautiful, he fell in love with her at once and determined to marry her.

"Oh," wailed the princess, wringing her hands, "my husband eats human flesh! He will devour you if he finds you here!"

The youth put on his magic hat to assure her that the giant would not find him, and then said to her, "You must find out for me in what form the giant's soul lies in the chest at the bottom of the sea, what will open the chest, and in what spot the giant can be slain. Then I will slay him and take you away to be my wife."

"I will do my best," replied the princess.

"I smell human flesh!" roared the giant as he entered. "If you do not give it to me, I'll eat you!"

"That is impossible," replied the princess. "With all of the guards at the door, who could enter here excepting you and me? Something is wrong with your nose."

The giant sniffed and searched and searched and sniffed, but, finding no one, at last he lay down to rest. The princess lay down beside him and began to caress him.

"Many years we have lived together," she said, "and still you have not told me where you keep your soul, nor what it is like."

"Go on, crafty one!" replied the giant in jest. "Who knows what you are trying to do to me? Yet we have lived together for a long time and I will tell you. My soul is in an oaken chest at the bottom of the sea. It is in the form of a dove. No harm could ever come to me if it were not that in that dove is an egg. Whenever that egg is broken upon my forehead, I shall die."[1]

Next day when the giant had returned to his soul chest, the princess told the youth what he had said. The youth went outside to watch. When the giant came home, the youth drew from his bag the scales of the fish and repeated, "These scales came from my brother the fish." Immediately the fish appeared before him.

"What is it?" he asked.

"In the sea is a chest," explained the youth. "Go and bring it out to me."

The fish swam away and soon returned with the oaken chest, which he set before the youth. There was neither lock nor key; so the youth took out from his bag the hairs of the bull. Calling to him the bull, he asked him to break open the chest with his horns. This the bull did, and out flew the dove.

Summoning the eagle quickly, he told him to catch the dove. With the fatal side of his stick, he cut her open and removed the egg. Putting on his magic hat, the youth took the egg and entered the house, where he found the giant already weakening.

"Something has happened to my soul!" he was crying.

With careful aim, the youth broke the egg against the giant's forehead, and the giant fell dead.

At once the youth married the princess, and they and his three sisters went back to their parents' house.

It was not long after Regina had told me this old Spanish story with its delightful Indian touch of personifying the four cardinal points that I visited the Taos pueblo, found my friend Avelino at home, and heard from him the Indian version of the same folk-tale.

We sat together in the main room of his adobe house, with the door tightly closed. "All time you ask me 'bout I tell you

---

[1]Compare with the fatal dove's egg in "The Son of Tata Juan Pescador," by Riley Aiken, this volume.—*Editor.*

one story. I tell you now one story. When other peoples ask
you 'bout dis story I not tell it to you, 'cause Indians dey
don' like it I tell you stories. Dey think maybe so I tell you
Indian secrets like Indian Bible." He looked quizzically at me,
and I nodded my understanding and promise.

The room was long and narrow with a hard-packed, cleanly
swept mud floor. At one end hung the pole-for-soft-things,
draped with gay blankets, hand-woven sashes and *mantas,*
elaborately bordered with yarn embroidery. Beneath it tightly
rolled mattresses, covered with cotton materials, made a long,
low seat. At the opposite end was an adobe seat built in with
the wall. Back of the door a low wall stretched as a wing to
shield and complete a corner fireplace. Skins of small birds and
bunches of herbs hung from the rafters. The only note of in-
harmony was a wooden kitchen table against a side wall, covered
with figured mustard-colored oil cloth and flanked by two
straight chairs. In one of these sat Avelino, with his blanket
drawn tightly about him from waist to knees and his moccasined
feet placed close together upon the mud floor.

"Dis story it Messican story," continued Avelino. "It 'bout
dat big—how you call dat lily [little] animal live on ground
like snake, but it have legs?"

"Lizard?" I asked.

"Yes," he agreed with a nod, "it 'bout dat big lizard. Long
time ago, one Messican man he live wid his wife and wid his
tree daughter and his lily baby boy. Dey very poor, dose
peoples. Dat man he have to haul wood on one burro and sell
him to dose peoples in Santa Fé.

"One day dat Messican man when he go in dose woods to
cut down one tree for firewoods, he hit dat tree wid one axe
four time. When he hit it dat four time, one giant lizard
he jump out.

" 'Who hit my house?' he say to dat man. But dat lizard he
scare dat Messican man so he didn't say nothing. Den dat lizard
he look around and he see dat axe. He point to dat axe and he
say to dat man, 'It is you! You hit my house. You got to pay
me for hitting my house.'

THE METAMORPHOSIS OF A FOLK TALE

"Den de man he tell to dat lizard: "I cannot pay you nothing. I got no moneys to pay you. I got nothing but my wife and my childrens and my burro."

" 'You bring me one of dose girls to pay me,' dat lizard he tell to dat man.

"Next day when dat man he go out to get more woods, he take dat oldest girl wid him. When he hit dat stump, dat giant lizard he jump out and dat girl he jump, too, and he make loud noise 'cause he scared by dat lizard, he jump out so quick.

"Dat lizard he look at dat girl, but he don't like him. He say to dat man, 'Dis girl he too ugly. I no like him. You bring me other girl.'

"Dat man he take girl home. Next day he bring other girl; he bring dat second girl wid him. Dis time it all same like dat other day. When dat man he hit dat stump, dat lizard he jump out and dat second girl he make a loud noise—how you call it? Yes, he scream—and dat lizard he don' like it dat dat girl scream; so he tell to dat man, 'Dis girl he too ugly. Tomorrow you bring me dat other girl. Maybe so I like him.'

"Next day dat Messican be bring dat tree daughter. When dat lizard jump out, dat girl he don' scream. He jus' jump back but he don' scream. So dat lizard he look at him and he say, 'Dis girl he one pretty girl. I take him.' And he take dat girl into dat stump and dat man he don' see dat girl no more.

"Dat Messican man he very sad. He don' like for it dat dat lizard take away his girl. Dat baby boy he grow up. He one big boy now and dat man he tell dat boy 'bout how dat lizard he done take away his sister. So dat boy he tell to dat man how he going to find dat lizard and take dat girl back to his mother. Then he tell it to his mother, 'You fix me some lunch by my bed. I go away early tomorrow morning to find my sister.'

"Dat mother he don' like it for dat boy to go away, but he fix dat lunch just like dat boy he say, and next morning dat boy go away a long way. Pretty soon, when de sun it get 'way up in de sky, dat boy he see one mountain lion, one eagle, one hawk and one ant, all dose animals fighting. He go closer. He

131

see one dead deer. All dose animals dey fighting for dat dead deer.[2]

" 'Why do you fight, my friend?' ask dat boy to dose animals. 'Dat deer he have plenty of meat for everybody. You wait. I divide dat deer for you.'

So dat boy he take out his knife and he cut up dat deer. Dat mountain lion he biggest dan dose other animals; so dat boy he give to dat lion the biggest piece of meat. To dat eagle he give dat next biggest piece. Den he give to dat hawk de tree biggest piece and to dat lily ant he give to him a lily piece.

"Den dat boy he go 'way, but dat lion he say to him, 'Come back. You take for you dis hair from my breast. Some time maybe so you need me. If so you need me, you put dis hair on your chest and you be one lion, too.'

"One odder time dat boy he start off; he walk lily way. Den dat eagle he call tell to dat boy to come back. Four time dat boy he come back. Dat eagle he give to him one eagle feather. Dat hawk he give to him one hawk feather, but dat ant he wait long time. He don't know what to give to dat boy, you see. He tell to himself if he give to dat boy the end of his body behind, he have to give, too, his legs and maybe so den he cannot walk. He tell to himself if he give to dat boy one leg, he have to walk all time sideway. 'I give him one of my feelers,' say dat ant. He tell dat to himself. Den he give one feeler to dat boy and dat boy he go 'way to find sister.

"Pretty soon now he see one girl taking care dose sheeps. Dose sheeps dey want to go one way. Dat girl he want dose sheeps dey go odder way. He have hard times wid dose sheeps. Dat boy he run to where dat girl he have hard times and he drive dose sheeps for dat girl. Dat girl he says thanks to dat boy and he say to dat boy, 'You come to my house. My father he give to you some foods.'

"Dat boy he very hungry. He like it to get foods. He go 'way wid dat girl. When dat girl tell to his father how dat boy he help him wid dose sheeps, dat father he give to dat boy new

---

[2]Compare with the division made by Juanito in "The Son of Tata Pescador," by Riley Aiken, this volume.—*Editor*.

moccasins, 'cause dat long walks it wear out dose old moccasins, and he give lunches to dat boy.

"Dat boy he like it to have dat girl to take him home for one wife. Dat father he tell to dat boy if he stay four days at dat house and he help dat girl to take care dose sheeps, den he take dat girl home to be his wife.

"Next day dose sheeps dey so hungry for grass dey run away from dat boy and dat girl. Dey run away to dat spring. Dat buffalo he come out to eat up dose sheeps. Den quick like lightning it hit one tree; dat boy he take out dat lion hair, and he put dat hair on his chest. Pretty soon, quick, he turn into one lion and he jump on dat buffalo. All day dat boy and dat buffalo dey fights. At sundown dey stop fight and go home.

"Next day it happen just like I tell you. All day dose two fights, but neither one he kill dat odder one. Tree day all same fight; nobody he is kill.

"On fourse day dey fights again. Den dat buffalo he call loud to dat girl to give him one drink from dat spring. Dat girl he run get water, but he not give water to dat buffalo. He give it to dat boy. Dat water it magic water. It make dat boy strong so he kill dat buffalo. He tear open dat buffalo to take out his heart. He goin' to burn dat heart, 'cause dat buffalo he bad giant buffalo. When he take out dat heart, it break and one box it fall out of dat buffalo his heart. Dat box it fall on ground and it break open. One dove it fly out of dat box.

"Dat girl he tell to dat boy to catch dat dove. Pretty soon, quick, dat boy take out dat hawk feather. He turn to one hawk. He fly up and catch dat dove. He tear dat dove in breast to get his heart and one egg it fall out of dat heart.

"Dat girl he tell to dat boy 'bout one giant lizard. He very bad giant. He live not so far and he eat up peoples. In his house he one giant man. When he go outside, he put on big lizard skin. Nobody, nothing it can't kill dat giant but dat egg when it hit him on forehead.

"When dat girl he tell 'bout dat lizard skin, den dat boy he know dat giant he is the one take his sister. He tell to dat girl wait for him. He take out dat eagle feather. He turn into one eagle, and he go to find house of dat giant lizard.

"Pretty soon when he come to dat giant house, dat giant he look up. He see dat eagle, and he catch him in his hand. He put one lily stick on his roof and he tie dat eagle leg to dat stick. Den dat giant he go 'way. Den dat boy he take out lily feeler and he make hisself into one lily ant. He take dat dove egg and he crawl down wall. Den dat lily ant he slip under door. He find his sister, he sleepin'. Dat lily ant he make hisself one boy. He wake up his sister and he tell to him he is his brother. He say to him, 'I change into one lily ant when dat giant lizard he come home. You must not step on me when I lily ant.'

"Pretty soon dat giant he come home. He take off dat lizard skin. He hang it dat skin on the wall an' he lay down and go to sleep. Quick dat boy throw dat egg. He hit dat giant on fore-head. Dat giant he make a loud yell an' he fall back dead.

"He turn into one big stone like mountain. You can see dat mountain if you go north from Taos. It big mountain all same like big man. He lie down on his back.

"Den dat boy he break lily piece from dat big stone and he take it in his pocket. He go 'way with his sister. He go find dat odder girl and dey all dose tree go home to see dat mudder.

"Every night when dey want go to sleep, dat boy he take dat stone from his pocket. He mark with it on de ground like one house, and pretty soon one house it come where he mark. Dey go sleep in all dose house, 'til pretty soon dey go home to dey mudder. Dat is all 'bout dat giant lizard. Some day maybe so I tell you nudder story."

And Avelino accepted the whole package of cigarettes which I had offered to share with him.

How the
TEHUANA WOMEN
Became Handsome

By Hugh McGehee Taylor

WHILE the Mexican Southern Railway was in 1911 extending the line from Oaxaca to Tlascolula, I went in an official capacity to an engineer's camp to make estimates on construction. I found everybody planning to go to Oaxaca for the Sunday bull fight and other festivities, and when on Saturday night the engineer and fireman for the locomotive assigned to the camp reported that they had to take it in to the shop for repairs, I announced that the whole kit and caboodle might go. In this camp, as in others, the construction gang was made up of men—many of them with their families—from almost everywhere between the Río Grande valley on the north to the Suchiate on the southern boundary. By daylight next morning the whole camp—men, women, children, and even the Chinese cook—were piled on the flat cars behind the engine, Oaxaca-bound.

With nobody left to interrupt me, I had by noon completed the calculations I was working on. Then I ate the lunch left cooked by the Chinese and started out for a walk. Coming to the little mountain stream that skirted the camp, I saw a good hole to take a swim in. I needed a bath. I went back for towel, soap, and clean *ropa interior,* and was soon plunging in the cold water. Somehow, when I undressed, I sensed that somebody was looking at me; yet I could see no one. After I had dried off and put my boots on, I saw an old woman seated about two hundred feet away. She had probably taken in the entire performance.

When she saw that I noticed her, she came forward and, smiling, observed, "You Americans are like us; *les gustan bañar* —you like to bathe."

"Are you sure that Mexicans like to bathe?" I asked, teasing.

"But I, I am not a Mexican," she answered with pride. "I am a Tehuana, and we bathe every day. These *arribeños*—people from the high-country—I believe they never bathe."

Her slur at the *arribeños* told well enough that she came from the hot country. There is always a feeling between the folk of the high country and those of the low country—the *tierra caliente,* regardless of race. One cannot insult a Totonaca, a Zapoteca, or a Maya more easily than by calling him a Mexican. To these Indians "Mexican" means nothing but Nahuatl, and no matter how the world may classify them, they never classify themselves as Mexicans. The old woman's dress, her independent air, and her accent all proclaimed her to be what she had stoutly professed—a Tehuana. She was old enough to be my mother, was still good-looking, and fairly intelligent. I felt that I might get some sort of story out of her if I could get her to talking.

Accordingly, I invited her to have some coffee with me; she readily accepted the invitation. After she had drunk a cup, with milk and sugar, and had eaten a few teacakes of Chinese production and then had a second cup poured out in front of her, she smiled at me genially and rubbed her stomach.

"Doña Juana," I said—for she had told me her name, "they tell me that the Tehuanas and Zapotecas are kinsmen. Are you related to the Zapotecas?"

"We are not Zapotecas," she began her story. "They came from the north; we came from *sol sale*. We have lived with or near the Zapotecas for *siglos*. We are kin now from intermixture, but we were not always kin."

"You came centuries ago from where the sun comes up?" I repeated, as I poured out more coffee and offered a cigarette.

After she had put the *cigarro* to a match I held and had

drawn a few breaths of smoke, she answered, "Yes, *señor*, we came from *sol sale*. Our mothers told us when I was young that many *siglos* past we did not live in this country, but in another country far away where the sun comes from."

"Do you mean Yucatán?"

"No, *señor*. We lived in Yucatán before the Mayas were there."

"Perhaps from Palenque or Chichen-Itzá?"

"No, *señor*. Those were Mayan towns."

"I should like to know the *cuento*," I said.

"This is not a story," she answered. "It is the truth. I never learned the name of that country we came from, but it was a land where the sun shone all the time and it never rained. Yet a great river flowed through the land. At times this river rose to great heights and overflowed all the land. Then the people planted and raised food to live upon. They raised a great deal, for the soil was *bendita* (blessed). But there were many people, and the food became scarce because there were so many to eat it. Some years the river did not bring enough water to irrigate the soil, and then thousands died. The people had boats, for in the time of the waters there was no other way to move about; then they had to take their grain and cattle back to high lands. Everyone knew how to handle boats, both to sail and to row. The years when water did not come down were terrible, with much misery and many deaths.

"After one such drouth, the cacique of our people, who had had nearly all the food taken from him by the government, called all his people together.[1] The men talked and the women talked. Then they loaded all they had on the boats and went down the river until they came to the salt water.

"They were decided on going somewhere where there was land without too many people. The wind came from *sol sale*; so the boats went toward *sol pone* (sunset). The Tehuanas stopped at every favorable place to see if there were good lands and

---

[1] This was probably not Joseph. He knew that the seven lean years were coming and prepared for them. "The government" was probably some N.R.A. of a later date. The Tehuanas were farmers and were not unionized, probably did not have a vote. So "the government" took all they had.

not too many people, but wherever the lands were not poor the people were many. They found plenty of fish in the salt water; so they fished and ate, and rowed on, or sailed when the wind was fair. There was land on both sides of the salt water, but always where the soil was good there were too many people to fight.

"So they rowed and rowed, and the men rowing so much became very thin. The women had nothing to do, and they became fat and strong. We are still so. Our women are fat and much stronger than the men, and thus we are unlike other people.[2]

"After some time the land stopped on both sides the salt water. Some of the men wished to return, but the women said, 'No. We will go on. If we go back, we shall starve. Going forward, we can do no worse than die. There must be land on the other side of the water. Maybe it is just what we want. We will go on.'

"They came to some islands and found people there who did not wish to let them have even water.[3] They fought our men, but our men did not wish to fight back. The women pushed them out of the boats and made them fight until the boats were supplied with all the water needed.

"By now a woman, a princess, was directing the Tehuanas.

"They came on west. It rained and they saved all the water they could and they kept on west. Then a great storm overtook them. Many boats were wrecked and many people drowned.

---

[2]I have never been in Egypt, but from what I have read that land fits the description of the country left by the Tehuanas. I have never believed that the Tehuanas had common origin with the Zapotecas, among whom women occupy the miserable position of slaves to the men, not only rearing children but laboring outside the house; they are not clean and they carry themselves as subjected ones. Among the Tehuanas, the handsomest people I have seen in North or South America, the women are upstanding, clean, washing their clothes and bathing every day; they run the stores, the butcher shops, and banks and do what farming is done. Their "lord" is a wizened small man who does nothing but fish a little, hunt a little, and "play husband" when the woman wishes—for there are children. In Egypt, if historians are correct, women occupied as high a position as the men. Among the Totonacas the women are also quite independent, strong, clean, their dresses always white, but in color, features, and other characteristics the Tehuanas differ as much from them as they do from the Zapotecas.

[3]Perhaps the Canary Islands, the aborigines of which were warlike.

TEHUANA WOMEN

The wind blew for many days and always towards sunset. When the storm quieted, there were but forty boats left together; the others were lost and probably all the people in them drowned. The survivors waited for a day hoping to find some of the lost ones, but none appeared. Then the women told the men to row on, that it was useless to wait any longer.

"They rowed on and on and put up the sails to help them whenever the wind was right. They came to more islands, some large, some small. On a long island there were many people. The women thought to remain there, but there was too little to eat. The people on this island ate *crocodilos*. They could not stay with crocodile-eaters.[4]

"So they got back into their boats and went on, toward the southwest this time, for the people of the islands told them there was land without people in that direction.

"It was as the islanders said. A week later they came to a land broad and flat. And there were no people there and there was no fresh water. It did not rain, and before our people came to where the cocos grow and found a stream of fresh water, they were drinking salt water. Near this stream they found a beach where thousands of turtles were laying their eggs.[5] Our people were very tired of fish, and they ate all the turtles and turtle eggs they could hold. For a time they feasted; then the turtles went away, and the people had to find something else to eat. They had brought seed with them. They prepared ground and when the rains fell they planted, but the seed did not come up.

"Along the stream were many coco palms, but our people did not know the coconuts were good to eat. One day one of the women saw some monkeys throwing down coconuts from the trees and eating those that broke open. She called other women and they ran the monkeys away and took all the nuts and ate all they could hold. After that everyone had a belly-ache, an awful belly-ache."

---

[4]The long island might be Cuba. Crocodiles were sacred beasts in Egypt. The Tehuanas would naturally be shocked to see alligators, which look so much like crocodiles and which Doña Juana called *crocodilos*, eaten.

[5]Forty miles west of Progreso is a beach where turtles in great numbers still come to lay eggs.

Here Doña Juana rubbed her stomach and, in sympathy with pains that were suffered centuries and centuries gone, went through a most vivid pantomime of a lady with the belly-ache.

"For a long time the people would not eat the coconuts. Then they found that by eating moderately no harm came. Not long after this they found a place farther west where plenty of *plátanos* (bananas) grew. From the people on the islands they had passed they had learned to eat these. They found deer, rabbits and birds. There was plenty of food. Their teeth stopped falling out and the women began to have healthier children. But our women were no longer the playthings of the men, and since those times the Tehuanas have never had many children. As a result our people have never become numerous. Our mothers said that if they had too many children there would not be enough land and soon the whole population would be starving.[6]

"Then the Mayas came, from I know not where. But they were many, too many to fight.

"Our princess called the women together and said to them: 'We cannot stay here with the Mayas. Their men treat their women as we were formerly treated. If we stay here, not only will we have to fight them but, with the example of the Mayan men before them, our men will become so domineering that we will either have to fight them or else go back and become their playthings. Let us go on west where there are no men.'

"The women all agreed with the princess and now they waited for a chance to go. While they were yet waiting, the Mayas all went for a week of feasting and worshiping of their gods to a city they were building. Then the princess called all the women and ordered them to tell their men to load the boats and prepare to move farther west. The men, led by a young man who favored the princess and with whom the princess was really in love, refused to help load the boats or to go. There was a bitter fight and many men and some women were killed. The men were subdued. Then the Tehuanas moved to the country

---

[6]The Tehuanas still practice birth control.

where they have lived ever since. It is our country today.[7] They had got maize from the Mayas. They planted it and it grew well, and not since that time have our people ever wanted for food.

"Some time after this final move a party of Zapotecas, hunting, came to where our people lived. They were headed by a handsome young cacique, very gallant. When he saw our princess, he wished to have her for his wife and asked her to go north with him to his country and become queen over his people.

"She said to him: 'You are very kind. You are the head of your people and of your house; I am the head of my people and of my house. You may come and live with me as my *marido* for a while; then you will return to your people and I will stay with mine. If the child is born a boy, I will care for him until he is weaned and then you may take him and bring him up a Zapoteca. If the child is born a girl, I will keep her and you may come again and we will see if there will not be a son.'

"The young cacique agreed. When the child came, it was a boy. The princess cared for him until he was weaned and turned him over to the Zapoteca. She sent for him and he came again and brought with him a number of his young men who became *maridos* to the unwed Tehuana girls, but they had to agree to leave half the boys and take half the girls, for there was a shortage of men among our people.

"The Zapoteca men were strong and so were our women; in consequence the children born to these couples were equally divided between boys and girls. This coupling made our children strong. It made the Zapotecas more beautiful, for as a rule they were not handsome. When you see a handsome Zapoteca today, you may be sure he has Tehuana blood in him. When you see a Tehuana not handsome, you may be sure she has Zapoteca blood in her. The arrangement was sad for our women. They had to give up half their children, and they were widows half the time.

"Later the Mayas found out where our people had gone and

---

[7]The Isthmus of Tehuantepec, noted among all travelers for having the best-looking women in Mexico.

came and tried to take them back. But our men and our women, too, fought them and kept them off until the Zapotecas, whom our princess had sent for, came. The Tehuanas and the Zapotecas together drove the Mayas back to Yucatán and they did not again bother us.

"The Mexicanos came. They were ugly, too. They ran over us and also over the Zapotecas to fight the Mayas. But the Mexicanos did not molest us and they left us alone in our *tierra*.

"Thus it was, *señor,* that the Zapotecas came to be related to the Tehuanas."

Doña Juana sighed. We heated the coffee again. She drank another cup, rubbed her stomach comfortably again, and bade me a pleasant *buenas tardes.* After this I saw her a few times, but never alone for confidential talk. At her request I sent her a corset and Butterick's fashions. Her husband, who had purchased her many years before I saw her, was an American frontiersman. He said his name was Castelloa, but that is all he ever told me about himself. The couple never had any children and Doña Juana bossed him around in true Tehuana style. Several months after I got the story of the Tehuana migration and the explanation of the ascendancy of the Tehuana women, Mr. Castelloa was killed, near Oaxaca. When I tried again to find Doña Juana, I was told that she had gone back to her *tierra.*

The FLAMING FLOWER[1]

By Catherine J. Stoker

"WEEP not, little one," said Cuca to Jesusita, the girl-widow, sitting in the shadows in Cuca's *jacal.*

"But, Cuca," sobbed the girl, "Miguel's brother has taken the field from me, and says I have no longer a place in my *jacalito.* He says the corn that Miguel and I planted together belongs to him as eldest brother, and if I wish to eat I must seek work. I cannot even return there tonight, for he himself thrust me out and closed the door in my face."

"Hush thee, *chica,*" Cuca soothed the girl. "There, yonder, is a corner for thee, and God has always sent to Cuca *tortillas* enough for her mouth and that of any other *cristiana* in need of a morsel to eat. Life teaches us much, little daughter, and tears gain us naught. Dry thy tears, and I will tell thee a story of our race. It is called by us old ones who know the history of our people, which we keep hidden from the laughing scorn of the foreigner, 'The Flaming Flower.' It is the story of how brother learned to hate brother. It is the story of the seed sown in man's heart in the beginning of our race, that now has yielded so abundantly in Juan's heart. It is out of the history of our race before the hated Spaniard came to our shores four hundred years ago. It tells how Xolotl, our first king, sought from Mictlanteceutli, god of lost souls, the Flaming Flower to exalt himself and rule the world, thus satisfying his greed and lust for power.

---

[1] While she has given the tale a somewhat different setting, the author, Mrs. Stoker, wishes it known that she has followed it as she heard it in the state of Zacatecas and that the proper names are reproduced as nearly as she could transcribe phonetics to paper.—*Editor.*

PURO MEXICANO

"Before the Spaniards came, we were a very old and highly-civilized race. Our land was a treasure box filled with opals and jade and turquoise and yellow gold. It held clear rivers teeming with fish, valleys golden with corn, mountains upon which fell the sun-god's fleeting colors of rose, gold, sapphire, and purple. The cities of Mexico were gay and beautiful; their markets were filled with luscious fruit, flowers, green vegetables, fish, and game. Gold, much gold, precious stones, fine cotton robes, soft pelts of the tiger and deer were all for barter.

The Chichimecs, Xolotl's subjects, followed and obeyed implicitly the priests of Texcatlipoca, and their god's blessings were upon them. When Texcatlipoca dwelt with our people, he taught them to till the land, to sow seed, to reckon the days and nights, which whirl into cycles. He taught them to make the fish sleep in the water with the herb he gave. No cruel spear to tear the fish, nor hook to tease them into boats was needed. Texcatlipoca taught the art of hewing stones for temples and homes. 'Twas he that unfolded the secret of how to bring the sweet waters from their mountain source into the fountains of the cities by a system we now call the viaduct. He gave the people the arts of welding copper and gold, of bending iron, of beating and cutting silver and gold into beautiful ornaments and setting them with gems, and of weaving the rabbit's hair into cloth. He gave them the skill of the bow and arrow, the fleetness of foot in the race. Goodness ruled the world, and brother loved brother, for Texcatlipoca lived with man."

"Cuca," interrupted the girl, "was Texcatlipoca like the Holy Virgin Mother?"

"More like the good Señor Jesu-cristo," answered Cuca. "I think perhaps 'twas he who lived with us at that time, only our language called him by the name of Texcatlipoca," and Cuca touched the rosary in her pocket and crossed herself.

"But one day," she continued, "there came to the Chichimecs a great sorrow. Mictlanteceutli, the god of darkness and lost souls and Texcatlipoca's enemy, had caused them to do evil. The enmity between the two gods was old. Whence it had come, who knows? Texcatlipoca must leave us, for evil now dwelt in the world. But before he went away he called together his priests who served him and instructed them. When he bade the people goodbye, he told them not to fear, for some day he would return and would never again leave. Somehow, after Texcatlipoca left, the song of the bird was less sweet, the sun-god's glory dimmed, the blue turned gray, the world seemed sad and indifferent.

"Xolotl, the king, seeing the hearts of his people saddened and discouraged, called together his council of wise men and priests. During the wakeful hours of his nights a plan to save his race had come to him, for they were saying Texcatlipoca would appear no more. The day for the council to meet came. A solemn hush prevailed as each member entered the king's presence and knelt before him with downcast eyes, for no one was permitted to look upon the king's person. When all were seated, seconds ran into minutes, minutes into hours, but the silence of their thoughts remained unbroken. At last the king arose and stood before them. Now, for a Chichimec king to stand in the presence of his subjects was always an indication that some grave or tragic thing was taking place.

" 'What thoughts have ye with which to stir the hearts of my people, my brothers?' he asked. All kept silence. 'Your silence speaks ill for plans,' he said. And still none answered.

" 'Then, I shall speak,' he cried. 'Many moons have passed since our god Texcatlipoca left us with his promise to return. We wait and watch, but we see no sign of his coming. The hands of our people hang down, the *milpas* give little harvest. Our weaker neighbors look more and more to us for protection, and Texcatlipoca comes no more.'

"As he said this, the wail of the priests filled the court. King Xolotl raised his hand for silence and continued, 'My brothers, many nights have I sat in thought; many days has my soul been sad within me as I have looked and seen the indifference of my people since Texcatlipoca went away. Once our land was the fairest; our young men were the fleetest of foot; our women were the most skilled in weaving and embroidery; our gold was enough to supply our needs and more. Now we see only indifference. The counsel of the priests of Texcatlipoca remains, but counsel of the wise men leaves our race untouched. Texcatlipoca comes no more. If we continue as we are, my heart is filled with fear, fear for the future of our race. So I have thought, my brothers, and last night as Oxomococ, the goddess of the moon, reigned in the sky over the sleeping earth, enlightenment came to my spirit. Daring and dangerous it is, and yet we face danger in this indifference that has come upon our race, and danger must sometimes be met with danger.'

" 'Speak to us, O excellent Xolotl,' said the head priest, 'for wise thou art. Texcatlipoca speaks no longer to us through oracles as in the past. Perhaps through thy lips he would speak to us now. Thy much meditation makes us know the counsel thou wouldst give is well worth weighing.'

"The king spoke: 'No thought of Mictlanteceutli troubled the heart of our race until the day when we listened to his counsel and consented to his persuasions. Then was Texcatlipoca grieved and departed from us. Before this Mictlanteceutli's power was limited to the realm of darkness. Now he has power everywhere. I have wondered in my distress if Mictlanteceutli will not give us his protection and counsel us how to lift the danger that is upon us.'

"The priests and wise men rose up speechless with horror. 'What!' at last cried the head priest. 'Wouldst thou seek to thrust us deeper into danger and make us false to Texcatlipoca?'

" 'Nay, nay, sit thee down. I seek but the best way and I am asking counsel of thee. But what is the end to be? Thou hast made sacrifices without number, O priest, and the words are not cold on thy lips in which thou hast said to me, "Texcatlipoca no longer speaks in signs and 'tis perhaps through thy lips he now would speak to us." '

" 'Thou sayest well, O noble Xolotl,' said the priest. 'Speak, for if he speaks and we listen, no danger lies there.'

"Long they counseled. At last the king persuaded the priests to seek Mictlanteceutli's aid and ask of him that he lift from them this indifference which had fallen on their people and make them again supreme over all races. But first Texcatlipoca received even more prayers and offerings of fruit and flowers than had been commanded, for the good god had not asked for the sacrifice of blood. Yet no sign came from him to abandon their contemplated journey.

"The day dawned for them to seek the god of darkness. All day they traveled. I know not the road they took. I only know that Mictlanteceutli's kingdom lies in the bowels of the earth. Finally, when the sun had gone from the sky and the curtains were drawn to hide the daylight, they came to the realms of Mictlanteceutli. At the gate of his kingdom sat an evil-faced keeper. 'Whom wouldst thou see, O king of the Chichimecs? Thou art surprised that I know thee? Mictlanteceutli is a god of knowledge as well as of power. He has waited for thy coming since the night of thy decision to seek him. Enter, thou and thy council.'

"The king and his wise men entered, and as they walked through the corridor they reasoned among themselves that Mictlanteceutli would perhaps aid them. When they entered the court and saw the god on his throne, which was covered with flashing gems and beaten gold, they fell on their knees and waited for him to speak.

" 'Welcome to my kingdom,' said the god. 'And what seekest thou of me?'

" 'We have come to seek thy aid to solve our problems, O great Mictlanteceutli,' answered the king.

" 'Thy problems shall be my problems, O Xolotl, if I can but aid thee. But why dost thou seek me? Never has my name been worshiped by thy people; no temple has been given to me where I may dwell among them. All thy worship has been to Texcatlipoca. Why did he leave thee after thou didst so long and faithfully serve him?'

" 'We know not, O Mictlanteceutli, why he departed, but he left us a promise to return. Many moons have passed, our people grow dull with indifference, and I fear that soon the Chichimecs will no longer be called a great nation. Texcatlipoca comes not. We must have a god who will protect us. We desire to make ours the greatest of all nations. We would ask thy aid to make our men the strongest, our young men the fleetest of foot in the race, our women the most beautiful and the most skillful of weavers. We would ask power to find the yellow gold. We would ask thee to teach us how to unite to us our weaker brother tribes that we may be supreme.'

"Turning to an attendant, Mictlanteceutli bade him bring the seed of the Flaming Flower, which only he possessed and which as yet had never been planted by man. The attendant returned with it in a golden bowl, and, kneeling, as Mictlanteceutli commanded him, Xolotl received the seed.

" 'This seed, King Xolotl, will give thee all the power thou hast asked of me if thou wilt sow it in thy *milpas*. The morning of the next day thou shalt reap the harvest of the things thou hast asked of me. But for this seed thou must pay me. Thou and thy race must swear loyalty and obedience to me. Thou shalt build me temples. Thy priests who now serve Texcatlipoca must be taught to serve me. Thou shalt teach thy children to serve me. This oath must be taken by thee and thy race. Then thou shalt become possessor of this seed and all its harvest shall be thine forever.'

"The king and his council took the seed, and gave their oath to Mictlanteceutli, for now they were sure that they held in their hands all the power they desired.

" 'Take the seed, my dear children,' said Mictlanteceutli. 'Sow it and reap my blessing.' And he laughed loud like thunder.

"They took the seed and departed. Xolotl with his own hand sowed the precious seed between rows of the golden corn. Such a magic seed! No rain from above, no tilling of soil, nor time nor sun did the seed require. The next morning Xolotl eagerly arose and went to his *milpas*. There between the rows of the golden *maíz* grew a strange plant bearing flaming red flowers, as though the bright *zarapes* woven by the skillful women of the Chichimecs had been laid over the *milpas*. As he marveled, the flower continued to spread and bloom before his eyes.

"Suddenly from a home near by came a wail of pain and woe as if death had come to the soul of the person crying. Xolotl stood still with fear. Then from west of the *milpas* came shouts of anger, the sounds of blows, and screams of the wounded and dying. War was born from the Flaming Flower. The sky grew black, and the thunder-god spoke. In his fury he sped an arrow from the sky, and the fire-god answered from Earth. Soon the tribal court was in flames. Xolotl heard the shouts of victory mingled with the wailing of women, as men took them by force from their husbands and families of brother tribes. He heard the sound of falling bodies, as the weaker brother strove to defend his possessions and himself, and went down in defeat. He saw athletes run, wrestle, and play the game of *pelota;* he saw them win, no longer by their skill and strength but by trickery and cunning.

"Where once peace and quiet had reigned, where men once had loved and understood each other, and little children had laughed and played under the turquoise skies, where minstrels had sung the songs of power and love, now there arose the wail of pain, the shout of war and hate. Xolotl sat down on a rock and looked at the harvest of the seed of Mictlanteceutli. This was not what he had expected. Rising up, he went to his court and sent for his council of priests and wise men. When they had entered and had knelt before him, they arose and stood awaiting his words.

"He said to them, 'What, O brothers, has come to pass? The seed Mictlanteceutli gave us has dyed our land red with blood. We have gained the tribes we asked for, the lands, beautiful maidens, but at what a price! Our sons lie dead together with those of the tribes over which we have won supremacy. The captive maidens wail in the bridal court and meet our kisses with hate in their eyes. The skill of our men who were fleet of foot and accurate with the bow has been marred by the greed of gain.' As the king finished the recital of the evils that had come to him and his people, tears such as women shed streamed down his cheeks.

" 'We shall return to Mictlanteceutli, O noble king,' said the head priest. 'We shall tell him that he has not understood ou: request. We shall tell him we wanted power, not hate; supremacy over the weaker ones, not death to our sons; strength to increase our lands, not cunning and trickery.'

"And because the priest was wise and holy, and served day and night Texcatlipoca, Xolotl and the council took his advice, and set the day when they should again journey to the kingdom of Mictlanteceutli. As they journeyed, their hearts were heavy with sorrow. At last they came to the kingdom of Mictlanteceutli. There he sat upon his throne. Black it was, for he was the king of lost souls, and no ray of the sun-god's glory penetrated his realm. The god greeted them with malicious pleasure and said, 'How goes the harvest from the seed of the Flaming Flower?'

" 'Ah,' said Xolotl, 'great Mictlanteceutli, surely thou didst mistake our request. When we swore allegiance to thee and planted the Flaming Flower seed, surely thou didst not know the disaster that was to come to our land. Cunning, trickery, greed, hate, passion, war, blood, and death are the harvest of the Flaming Flower.'

"Mictlanteceutli looked at the king, and suddenly the court rang with his laughter. At his laugh the blood of Xolotl and his council ran cold, for in it they heard again the war cry, the snarl of hate and greed, and the scream of captive women.

" 'Ah,' said Mictlanteceutli, 'didst thou not ask for power, new lands, beautiful women, supremacy over weaker tribes? Has not all this been given to thee since I granted to thy keeping the Flaming Flower?'

" 'Yea,' answered Xolotl, 'all these things are ours, but with the granting of our requests have come such sorrows that the gifts are not worth the pain. Take back the Flaming Flower and its harvest, we beseech thee.'

" 'I have kept my word to thee,' answered the god. 'Now thou shalt keep thy vows to me. For none who become my subjects afterward turn from me. Foolish indeed thou wert, Xolotl, and hast thou still so little wisdom as to think that one may return and undo that which he has done? Knowest thou not there is no such thing as going back? Not even I, Mictlanteceutli, the god of lost souls, can go back. An act that is done stands forever; and could I destroy the Flaming Flower from the earth, which I cannot do, its power has passed into the hearts of the race and thy people themselves will continue to reproduce it. Thou hast chosen, and thou must abide by thy choice.'

"And that is the reason that Juan shut the door in thy face, Jesusita, and took from thee thy *jacalito*, because Juan is reproducing in his heart the Flaming Flower."

JUAN GARCÍA
GOES TO HEAVEN

By FROST WOODHULL

THIS story General Jesús Jaime Quiñones, of the Army of the Republic of Mexico, told to Walter Tynan, District Attorney of Bexar County, Texas, and the District Attorney told it to the County Judge. General Jesús Jaime Quiñones is the reviver of the original *charro* culture. He has done more than any other man in Mexico to revive interest in those arts in which Mexicans originally excelled; and those arts were—or that culture was—horsemanship, roping, singing and dancing, story-telling, and making love. In these decadent days the word *charro* often means to Mexican ranch hands what "drug store cowboy" means in the United States. But originally the *charro* cult was composed of the aristocracy among those who knew and loved ranch life—the *hacendados*. General Jesús Jaime Quiñones has quickened national interest in the dashing clothes of which the original *charro* was so inordinately and properly proud. His own embroidered *sombreros* and jackets, his close-fitting *pantalones,* the legs made tight with silver buttons, his hand-made, high-heeled *charro* shoes and, above all, his saddles and his reatas are the wonder of all who have seen them; and this means spectators from the south of Mexico all the way to the 1933-34 World's Fair in Chicago.

But, as I began by saying, the General told the District Attorney the story of Juan García and his experiences in Heaven and the District Attorney told the story to me. It runs something like this:

My friend, as you must know, there has been no rain in

northern Mexico for nearly thirty years. The reason for this is that thirty years ago it rained so much for a few days that, in the opinion of those who make rain, the country should properly do without more for a long, long time. You may not believe it, but at that time it rained throughout all of northern Coahuila. It even rained on the hacienda La Mariposa. It rained on Las Rucias and the Encino Solo; on La Hacienda del Oso of which Señor Don Diego Boehme is the owner, and, although you may not believe it, it actually rained in El Valle de Zacate, where La Hacienda El Fortín is now situated. From there it rained over La Encantada and west almost to Chihuahua, where no rain has ever fallen. El Arroyo de la Babia was a raging torrent and those who lived on La Piedra Blanca and Santo Domingo, as well as those who lived at the Treviño headquarters and at San Gerónimo, very happily could not come to the towns and cities for many weeks.

But it happened, my friend, that, heavy as the rainfall was in northern Coahuila, it was much more heavy at Monclova and Lampazos, and was most heavy of all in the hills and mountains above and to the north of Monterrey. That was the time, my friend, when the mountain called El Diente, which is one thousand feet high, was in danger of being swept away.

Now, there lived in the city of Monterrey at this particular time, an *hombre* named Juan García. Juan García was just a "middle-class Mexican," but nevertheless he owned the most famous horse in the whole country. He was much larger than the ordinary run of Monterrey horses; he was a much better horse than anybody has in Monterrey at this time, and he possessed a virtue which few horses in northern Mexico had then or have now. This horse could swim. Very few horses in northern Mexico had learned to swim before this flood and I have never heard of a single one's learning to swim after it. The matter of teaching a horse to swim is much like teaching your son to swim. One cannot swim or learn to swim if there is no water; and that is why I say that the large grey horse of Juan García possessed a remarkable virtue. I do not remember telling you that the horse was a grey horse, nor do I know why the horse was grey, but that is a part of the story as it has been told to me many, many times.

My friend, can you picture the flood which swept down from La Babia through the Álamo Creek, and which swept down through the Valley of the Grass and the Alameda Canyon and on down through the Puerta Santana by the Nacimiento of the Sabinas River into El Río Salado, below which the mother dam called Don Martín now stands? All these gathered waters swept through Monterrey in a flood very deep, very strong.

All of which, my friend, brings us back to Juan García and his horse. You have been to Monterrey, as have thousands of other Americans. Now, it is possible that some of your countrymen may remember an arroyo which runs through Monterrey, although they may not remember, for our *aguardiente es muy, muy potente*. I have never seen water running through this arroyo in Monterrey. I was too young to remember when it rained in northern Mexico, and although I have been in Monterrey many times since the rain, nevertheless I have seen no water running through that arroyo. But at the time of the great flood, the water ran through the city of Monterrey with a depth of which no man has knowledge. It is enough to say that the worst rain, or perhaps I should say the heaviest rain (one may not say that any rain is a bad rain), produced the mightiest hero of northern Mexico.

Juan García's swimming horse must have been very wonderful and Juan García must have had courage. When the mighty flood was sweeping through Monterrey, sweeping with it chickens, pigs, children, women, and some men (most of the men had gone for help), Juan García proved himself to be a great hero.

You may remember, my friend, that many of the little houses in northern Mexico are built of adobe. Adobe, as you know, is made of mud, mixed perhaps with a little grass. Egyptians when they made their bricks always mixed grass with mud, but there must have been more grass in Egypt than there is in northern Mexico. When the rain fell and the wind blew and the flood descended on Monterrey, these little houses, being built in a country where rain should not fall, were melted down much as *piloncillo* melts when you mash it in hot coffee. The water washed the children and the pigs and the women and the chickens into the arroyo.

My friend, Juan García saddled his grey horse and dashed into the mighty flood.

Pigs, being fat, float on top of the water, and, being valuable, should properly be rescued. And Juan García, seeing a fat pig in danger, rescued it and took it safely to his little house high up on the side of the hill. After that, Juan García dashed into the flood and, with the aid of his mighty horse, saved from an unaccustomed death twelve women, three more pigs, and four men.

That was thirty years ago. It is the fact that when one is a hero on one occasion, thereafter his fame will grow, whether he be living or dead; wherefore the fame of Juan García spread mightily. He became the great hero of northern Mexico—the hero who rescued ten, fifteen, even twenty men and women from the mighty Monterrey flood. No matter where he traveled, he found that his fame had galloped ahead of him. No matter where he went in Nuevo León, Coahuila, or Chihuahua, his reputation had preceded him. The fame of Juan García spread over all of northern Mexico and he became, even during his life-time, the greatest hero of that country.

My friend, you may kill one man and he will develop into three men; you may ride one horse which no one on the ranch can ride and in time no other person in the world can ride that horse or be such a *jinete* as you are; thus the greatest lover in the world is developed also.

It was very bad luck, but Juan García had to die. And after Juan García had gone through many difficulties he finally arrived at the gates of Heaven. I cannot understand why he arrived without his grey horse. But, as a favor to me, picture Juan García at the gates of Heaven without his grey horse. *Muy importante* he was, and why shouldn't he be important? He knocked as befitted his rank. The assistant of Saint Peter opened the *mirilla* (the small gate in the big door) and asked the usual questions.

"I am Juan García of Monterrey, the hero of northern Mexico. I dragged twenty people out of the mighty Monterrey flood."

Saint Peter's assistant said, "Juan García, I have never heard of you."

"What?" Juan answered. "I am the hero of the mighty Monterrey flood, and who are you?"

And the gentleman at the gate said, 'I am Saint Peter's assistant."

And Juan answered, "Well, neither have I heard of you. Send for Saint Peter himself."

And so, impressed by the great confidence of Juan García in himself, the assistant sent for Saint Peter, who immediately came to the gate.

Thereupon the Angel Gabriel, as I truly believe Saint Peter's assistant to be, said to his master, "Don Pedrito, there is here a person who calls himself the greatest hero of northern Mexico and, according to his statement, he is named Juan García."

"Yes," said Juan García, who was listening, "I am the greatest hero of northern Mexico; I dragged twenty people out of the mighty Monterrey flood; and, as all know, I am entitled to come to Heaven and sit on one of the high places."

Then Saint Peter examined the records and said, "Juan García is really entitled to a seat in the Kingdom of Heaven. Let him enter."

And so Juan García went into the Kingdom of Heaven with Saint Peter on his right hand. Very soon they came to a man all silent with his hand in the breast of his coat, and he occupied a very high place in the hero section. Then Saint Peter said, "Napoleon, this is Juan García."

But Juan García interrupted, "Me! I will introduce myself! Napoleon, I am Juan García of Monterrey, Mexico. I am the great hero of the mighty Monterrey flood. I dashed into the flood and rescued twenty lives."

JUAN GOES TO HEAVEN

And Napoleon said, "Juan García, I am glad to welcome you to Heaven and I hope you will be very happy here."

And Juan García next went to Hannibal and introduced himself, saying, "I am Juan García of Monterrey, Mexico. I saved twenty-five men from the mighty Monterrey flood. I, too, am a hero."

And Hannibal said, "Juan García, you are a hero; I hope you will be happy here."

And after Hannibal came Cæsar, Julius Cæsar, I think it was; and after Juan had introduced himself as the hero of the Monterrey flood, Cæsar welcomed him into Heaven. And thereafter Juan García introduced himself and the story of the mighty Monterrey flood to Xerxes and Henry VIII and George Washington and many, many others, even to Pancho Villa. And, my friend, all of these heroes welcomed Juan García and expressed the hope that Juan might be happy on his high seat in Heaven. Thus Juan García came into Heaven as he had come into the praise of northern Mexico.

But, my friend, on one of the highest places Juan García came upon an old man who was all wrapped up in his sarape. Juan patted him on the back and said, "*Viejito*, I am Juan García of Monterrey, the great hero of the mighty Monterrey flood. I preserved thirty men from the mighty flood."

But *el señor del sarape* made no response.

Then Juan hit him harder on the back and said, "*Viejo*, listen! I am Juan García from Monterrey. I am the great hero of the mighty flood, and I have come to Heaven to sit on one of the highest places."

Then the old one raised his *sarape* from around his face and said, "Pfffffffffttt."

And Juan García was terribly shocked. To Saint Peter, who was not very far away, he said, "This *hombre* is making fun of me. Pancho Villa and Cæsar and Hannibal and the other heroes have welcomed me, but this *viejo* has said only 'Pfffffffttt.'"

And so, my friend, Juan García demanded of Saint Peter a complete explanation. And Saint Peter slapped the *viejo* on the back, and said, "Juan García of Monterrey wishes to introduce himself to you. He is the hero of the mighty Monterrey flood."

And the *viejo* again lifted his *sarape* from around his face and again said, "Pffffffffttt."[1]

And Saint Peter said to Juan García, "I am sorry, my friend, but this is Noah, and he don't give a damn about your Monterrey flood."

---

[1]Footnote! Don Pancho Dobie says that no article can be erudite unless it has a footnote. This footnote explains "Pffffffttt." Such a thing is a "Bronx Cheer" or a "Razzberry." To illustrate either, stick the tongue loosely between upper and lower lips, loosely held, then blow upon the tongue vigorously from underneath. This will cause the tongue to vibrate in such a manner that hot air will escape from off the top of the tongue.

The EAGLE LOVER

By BERTHA McKEE DOBIE

ON the dining-room wall of Señora Carmen P. de Morales' house in Mexico City, is an arresting picture done by herself in the finest needlepoint. It shows an eagle crouched on the breast of a prostrate maiden, who is unclad except for a blue headband and a bright feather. An arrow has pierced through the two bodies, and the eagle's feathers are disarranged and broken.

When asked why she had imagined for her needle-picture so strange and violent a subject, she said, "But I did not imagine. The picture tells an ancient legend of the Mexican people. It relates to the two orders among the Aztecs, the Knights of the Eagle and the Knights of the Tiger, symbolic of day and night."

This is the legend:

What matters the kingdom or where it was or how it was called? Always, as the story is told, it was a part of Anáhuac, and within its narrow confines was born the loveliest princess of far-off times. She was born for the rejoicing of her parents, the sovereigns, and for fulfilling the prophecy of the priests, who had predicted the coming of a star without equal for brilliance—a princess who, kindled with love, would make of the Mexican lands a paradise.

The delicious little princess, of unexampled beauty, fulfilled the presage. Her life was all love. She loved the clear skies of her country, which smiled to see her, and the burnished mirror surface of the lakes. She loved the flowers and the songs of birds. Thus, loving always and always loved, the most beautiful maiden of the Mexican lands saw her existence glide on.

But the sovereigns of that short kingdom were disquieted

and impatient. Disquieted they were by the uncommon nature of the beautiful princess, impatient that she accept some one of the advantageous alliances that were proposed. But the maiden rested no thoughts on the elegance and gallantry of kings and princes who laid siege to her. Lost in the gardens of her father's palace, among birds and flowers, sky and lakes, she lived in a dream of love.

In the most hidden recess of the garden she lay at ease on the turf. Her eyes wandered caressing the distance until they stopped upon a point that oscillated in space. It was a little point, insignificant, but it moved with a marvelous grace, describing wide circles in its measured flight. This point, so small, so insignificant at the beginning, drawn by the maiden's glances, descended from the heights with exquisite elegance and, growing larger and larger, at last took position beside her. It was an imperial eagle.

A rejected suitor, last of an interminable list, felt a surge of hate and jealousy which, breaking out from the breast, rose to the head,—the head crowned with the device of a Tiger Knight. Finally he dragged himself dispirited to the recess where every day the lord of the heart and of the heights visited the sweetest princess. And the eyes of the disdained lover saw how her breast rose and fell with impatience; how her eyes, shadowed by long lashes, scanned the blue sky; how the pure body, free of tunics and robes, lay with a voluptuous delight on the carpet of grass and rose petals. And his eyes saw also the point, small, insignificant, that in the turquoise depth of space traced the complicated filigree of a poem; saw the titan of the heights descend in great and majestic spirals. The Tiger Knight will swear by the most sacred that the gigantic bird approached at slackened speed and placed itself over the nude body of the princess. He will swear that he saw her in the extremity of happiness and love open her arms and encircle the eagle's neck. He will swear that he saw the powerful and richly plumaged wings open and caress the smooth curves of the divine body.

And when the bent beak was lowered to seek the miniature

coral of the princess' mouth, the Tiger Knight with convulsive hands seized the bow, stretched the cord, and, sharpening the arrow with all his hate, jealousy, and despair, let it fly, to pierce through that idyll of regal feathers and sweet flesh.

LEGENDS *from* DURANGO

By Everardo Gámiz

(Translation by Bertha McKee Dobie)

Sacrifice Mountain

THE tribe of the Michis dwelt in a picturesque valley
formed by abutments of a gigantic mountain range which,
with breaks of more or less importance, extends throughout the
southeastern part of the state of Durango. From certain
particulars of their vestiges it appears that the Michis were
of Mayan origin. If so, their tribal name signifies *fish;* and,
since among the Mayas zodiacal cults existed, the fish must
have been for the Michis the supreme divinity.

Tradition declares that they were a powerful tribe, essen-
tially warriors, and that they extended their dominions over
a vast territory. They were a populous tribe, as is clearly demon-
strated by the innumerable remains to be found on the prairies,
in canyons, flats, and creek beds, and even on mountain tops.
Their capital, Michilía, which they themselves destroyed, was
a great city, to judge from traces yet visible.

Michilía had for cacique about the year 1555 a very strong,
valiant, and worthy man named Tobe, who had carried his
triumphal arms to the southern range of the Mezquital. All his
subjects feared, loved, and respected him, because to energy
he united goodness and to generosity valor. His people, in an
ambience of liberty, peace, and work, advanced rapidly, and
to this progress Indians who had emigrated from the south,
fleeing the conquerors, contributed the arts of their especial
civilizations.

One day there arrived before the monarch an Indian who
told him that a large army commanded by Spaniards found

162

itself, in warlike array, a few leagues from the city. Tobe, knowing the imminent danger that threatened his people, ordered the inhabitants of the city and of places roundabout to come together immediately that they might consider what attitude to assume before the Spanish invader. Although some thought they should abandon their country and take refuge in the mountain crags, others maintained that they should defend their territory inch by inch; and in the end this determination prevailed. They raised a considerable army, which marched out forthwith under orders of the cacique himself to meet the conquering army, captained by Don Francisco de Ibarra.

The place where the first encounter took place is not known, but it is said that the conflict was bloody and the issue undecided. On the following day, the conquerors having cut off retreat to the capital, the Michis lost heart and retired to the cordillera that limits the Valley of Súchil on the east.

Ibarra intended to leave the adventure and continue his march toward the north but, upon being pursued by the natives, saw himself obliged to fight. Fighting bloodily, the Michis again fell back toward the cordillera and began to ascend the mountain known today as Sacrifice Mountain. All the while they were climbing, they hurled down a rain of stones that caused considerable injury to their foes. The Spaniards again attempted to retire but again were obliged to prosecute the struggle.

According to tradition, this stage of the fight lasted two days. By the third day the Indians had attained the crest of the mountain, where they saw themselves completely cut off and unable, through lack of supplies, to continue fighting.

From that high place the capital of the tribe could be discerned far off toward the southeast. To the east the mountain overlooks a profound abyss. Imagine with what feelings the monarch, looking into the distance, gazed for the last time upon Michilía. Imagine the emotion that racked his frame as he considered that those homes were soon to be occupied and stained by the conquerors.

Standing there on the mountain top and gazing out in silence, Tobe, cacique of the Michis, took a resolution so desperate that to think of it staggers the mind. He broke his bows, destroyed his shield, and, having given with a glance his last farewell to the city of his forefathers, hurled himself from the precipice. All the indigenes, without a single one staying behind, followed him to death.

The Spaniards, seeing that the shower of arrows and stones had ceased, even though they suspected a ruse, ascended to the crest, and there they found bows, *macanas,* and shields broken into bits. The Michis lay in a formless heap at the bottom of the abyss. It is said that Ibarra, standing on a high peak, contemplated the vast and beautiful panorama spread out before his eyes and, upon descrying far in the distance the city of Michilía, raised his eyes to heaven as if repentant of his work. The tears rained from his eyes and, greatly moved, he exclaimed, "How sublime a sacrifice for liberty!"

When the queen of the Michis received word of her husband's death and the annihilation of the best part of the army, she, acting upon instructions he had given her, called the tribe together and, haranguing them from an eminence now known as Queen's Hill, ordered them, rather than fall into the conquerors' hands, to destroy the capital and its outlying villages and emigrate to the intricate sierras of the Mezquital. Then, worthy spouse of a hero, she hurled herself down the precipice to death. To this day herdsmen tell of seeing a woman dressed in white on the hill-top and of hearing a multitude shout.

Traveler, whoever you may be, when your eyes contemplate Sacrifice Mountain, remember that on its summit was enacted one of the most brilliant deeds of antiquity, that while an heroic race was plunging dizzily down the abyss it was leaving on the summit, very high, a name of honor, an example of patriotism, and a glorious memory that makes proud the state of Durango.[1]

---

[1]Such accounts of Indian heroism are not uncommon. Cubas tells of a similar sacrifice among the Ópatas:

"Persecuted by General Gandara with very superior forces, in consequence of an insurrection, they refused to surrender themselves, even after each one at his post had shot his last arrow. Their captain, with some few who had survived the contest, took refuge on the summit of an almost inaccessible mountain and there awaited the

LEGENDS FROM DURANGO

The Virgin of the Valley[2]

After the disaster suffered by the Michis on Sacrifice Mountain, Don Francisco de Ibarra learned that the tribesmen were gathering in the capital. Fearing that to abandon the region in pursuit of his journey would be taken as an indication of weakness, he ordered Captain Don Juan Vicente Zaldivar to remain and subdue the inhabitants.

The wife of Captain Zaldivar was Doña María de Oñate, sister of the conqueror Don Cristóbal de Oñate. According to tradition, she was a woman very virtuous, very much beloved, and very devout. She succored the poor when they were sick or in want and exerted herself for their spiritual advantage as well.

One day about the year 1560, as she was leaving the *pueblo* of Súchil, where she had gone on some errand of mercy, Doña María saw in the top of a mesquite tree a doll and ordered it to be brought to her. She put the doll in a covered hamper and rode on to her *hacienda*.

When, having arrived, she opened the hamper, she was amazed to find that the doll had disappeared. Immediately she sent two servants out on horseback to search. They found the doll in the top of the same mesquite from which Doña María had taken it, placed it in a little box, and returned to the *hacienda*. But when the box was opened, it contained no trace of the restless doll.

Her interest thoroughly aroused, Doña María ordered horses put to the carriage, and herself returned to Súchil. The doll

approach of General Candara's emissaries, who had intimated their submission. Believing themselves humiliated at the demand for the delivery of their arms, they declared to the envoys of the general their resolution to deliver themselves up to their conquerors without abandoning their arms. Upon General Gandara's insisting in his demands and they in their resolution, their conduct decided him to take them prisoners by force, which they avoided by an act worthy of the ancient Spartans, in throwing themselves over the precipice at the moment the general's troops were ascending the heights."—*Editor.*

[2]This and the two following church legends have been selected from several included in Señor Gámiz's collection of *Leyendas Durangueñas* because of their delicious naïveté.—B. M. D.

was in the tree top. It was again confined and with innumerable precautions brought to the *hacienda*. But the lady found herself again deceived. She returned immediately to the tree. This time the doll disappeared as she was taking it down.

From these persistent refusals to be taken away, Doña María deduced that the doll was a saint who desired a chapel to be erected to her at that place and no other. Being possessed of the greatest religious zeal, she determined to fulfill the desire of the saint, who became known as Purísima Concepción del Valle del Súchil. She summoned some people who dwelt near to lay the first stone of the temple at once. It is told that when the first stone was laid, there immediately burst forth a spring of clearest water.

The temple constructed is the one that exists today, and in the atrium still grows the ancient mesquite in the tip of which the Virgin appeared one 8th of December—a date annually commemorated in the *pueblo* with great *fiesta*. And there are those so ingenuous as to say that the spring comes out from under the high altar.

El Señor de Los Guerreros

Back in the times of Spanish rule there went out from the *pueblo* San José del Tisonazo of the Indé township on a first Friday in March some natives to hunt. It was scarcely dawn when on the edge of the *pueblo* one of them discovered under a corpulent mesquite an object that attracted his curiosity. The object proving to be a wooden crucifix, he called to his companions. They returned with that saint to the center of the village, and with the help of the people who at once gathered improvised an altar under a brush-roofed porch.

During the whole day the villagers danced before the altar of him who had appeared, and when they left him alone the night was well advanced.

On the following day the saint was in the same place in which he had first appeared. Again he was taken to the *enramada* and the *fiesta* of the day before was repeated. During the night the saint returned to the trunk of the ancient mesquite.

"Indeed," said the Indians, "this man does not wish to be where we wish him. We shall be compelled to fashion his house even here."

They topped the tree some two meters above the ground, and placed the saint on the tall stump. Then they began to construct a little chapel and an altar that had as nucleus the mesquite trunk.

In that place, then, lives and dwells El Señor de los Guerreros —The Lord of the Warriors—since that was the name they put to the saint. Little by little he created for himself such fame as a worker of miracles that he drew visitors from neighboring *pueblos* and even from distant places. They tell that on a certain afternoon there arrived in a carriage, with the sole object of testing the power of the Señor, some people who did not credit his apparition or his sainthood or his faculty for performing miracles. They brought three long and thick wax candles, which had dynamite bombs inside. If the saint were miraculous, he would escape the ruin that the bombs would make in exploding.

After examining the saint and his sanctuary in a detailed manner, the visitors delivered the candles over to the sacristan and told him to light them after they were gone. They left at once.

It followed that, on going to light the candles, the sacristan heard a voice proceeding from an uncertain place which said to him, "Don't light those candles!" The sacristan looked around without seeing a living soul. Hesitatingly he again made a light and was again bringing it to the wick of one of the candles when the voice said with more energy, "Don't light those candles."

Then the man searched boldly inside and outside the chapel, but never a person did he see. He went back in, heavy with confusion but resolved to light the candles, since such was the will of those who had brought them, perhaps in fulfillment of some command. When he had drawn near the candles and was about to light them, the mysterious voice repeated the command with still more authority, "Don't light those candles." The sacristan then told the priest what was passing, and the priest ordered the candles brought to him. Inside them he found the sticks of dynamite.

But that was not all. It followed that the individuals who subjected the saint to such proof, having gone out from the *pueblo* very late in the day, continued traveling through the night, with the idea of putting themselves beyond any trouble that might start when the bombs exploded. In the darkness they did not notice that an arroyo was in freshet. They plunged in, their carriage was overturned, and they all were drowned. Such, according to the legend, was the punishment the Lord of the Warriors imposed upon those ill-intentioned ones.

Each first Friday of March a great *fiesta* is made in San José del Tisonazo in honor of the Señor of the Warriors. This *fiesta* is attended by tens of thousands of persons proceeding from many leagues roundabout and even by persons from other states of the Republic, who feel themselves drawn by the miraculous saint. The place is, moreover, constantly frequented by those who come to fulfill promises made to the saint in payment of some grace. In the month of March, 1928, the Señor of the Warriors had in his sanctuary 1,346 objects representing as many miracles, and from the month of April in that year to January, 1929, 217 objects were brought to him.

El Señor del Rebozo[3]

When the Spanish missionaries came to America, they found established in the minds of the aborigines the superstitions of idolatry; and, in order to convert the Indians to Christianity, they had to use proceedings that would impress the conscience through the senses. No doubt this necessity accounts for the apparitions of virgins and saints abounding in those times. Such apparitions had to be planned with a degree of intelligence, so that no distrust of their pretended reality might be awakened. Under these conditions appeared the Lord of the Rebozo.

---

[3]A *rebozo* is a long cotton scarf worn by humble Mexican women.

LEGENDS FROM DURANGO

They tell that on a certain night about the middle of the seventeenth century some drivers arrived at one of the principal houses on the Hacienda de Concepción de Poanas, where they were given lodging. It was not known who they were, where they came from, nor where they were going; nor was even the direction they took ever known. Among other things they brought a box loaded on a mule. This box, tightly nailed, they left forgotten—so they made it appear—in the house when they went away very early the next morning.

One day the *rebozo* belonging to the mistress of the house was missing. She searched everywhere. She moved clothes baskets, boxes, wardrobes, and trunks, and went at last to look behind the box left by the *arrieros*. As she drew near, she was delighted by a fragrance as of flowers and began to wonder what the box contained. More in sprightly jest than anything else, she exclaimed as she went to the box, "If you help me find my *rebozo*, I shall unnail you to see what is inside you."

Great was the lady's surprise to see her *rebozo* thrown into the middle of the room. Surmising that in the box was hidden some talisman or other miraculous object, she told the *cura* what had occurred. The box was unnailed and found to contain an image of Jesus—*un Nazareno*. Pinned to the saint's breast was a paper with this inscription, "The Lord of the Rebozo."

This saint is the patron of the Hacienda de Concepción, where it has a place in the chapel, with the especial duty of looking after *rebozos*. In thinking of this, I ask myself why they have not invented a Lord of the Sombrero and, if by chance there is such an one, what he thinks of these people who wander through the streets in the height of fashion. Also it would be a good thing to invent a Lord of the Coat-tails, because in this respect we go very badly.

El Llorón

Throughout the month of October, 1905, I found myself on vacation at the Rancho de Alemán. The ranch is situated in a picturesque valley formed by abutments of the Sierra de Michis, one of the powerful spurs that the western Sierra Madre makes in the state of Durango. Through the valley flows the river also named Michis.

Some six kilometers at most from Alemán is a low place called The Little Ovens—*Los Hornitos*. Here there exist traces of a great many furnaces in which metals were reduced during the time of Spanish domination, and these furnaces, together with the slag piled near them, are evidence that long ago rich mines of silver and gold with a percentage of lead and some tin mines as well were worked in the valley of the Michis. In the Little Ovens flat are also remnants of small villages and of fortress towers constructed by the Spaniards for defense against the Indians.

Well, then, one night toward eight o'clock I found myself here in a hut, given over to problems of writing that I do not now recall, while some woodcutters seated on a huge trunk that served as a kind of sofa in the *patio* were gabbling with one another.

Of a sudden they thrust themselves precipitately into my room and, with very visible signs of fright, fastened the door.

"What happens?" I asked in surprise.

"Praised be the most Holy . . . cross yourself, little master. Ave María Purísima!"

All crossed themselves and a woman began to pray the Magnificat.

"What passes?" I insisted.

"Hear, hear you. It is El Llorón."

"What Crying Man is that? What are you talking about? Be assured that what you hear is like nothing else than the howling of a dog."

"No, *señor*," said one of the countrymen, a man already up in years, toward whom for his calm nature and judicious conduct the others showed esteem. "It is the Crying Man. Listen, listen yourself. This comes about inevitably on this very day each year."

"In most parts of Mexico there prevails the fixed superstition of a Crying Woman. Where is the Crying Man?" I said with air of denial and in a somewhat ironic tone to him who had spoken.

LEGENDS FROM DURANGO

"This is nothing at all but a superstition that causes in you folk a terror entirely unfounded. I wish to convince you that what we hear is the howls of some dog. Let us go to the place from which they proceed."

Conquering their terror, they accepted my invitation and we left the hut. The cries appeared to come from the glen on the farther side of the river. Thither we directed our steps, not without the nervousness that an experience of this sort causes. Our investigation had no result and served merely to fix belief in my companions' minds.

When we got back to the house they told me the legend of that Crying Man who on every 15th of October lets his pitiful groans be heard.

During the year 1812 or thereabouts, when the war of independence was agitating our country, there lived at The Little Ovens a Spanish miner who had on hand a considerable quantity of coined money and silver bars. As the confused condition of the country made him fear for both his capital and his life, he resolved to abandon the region, but in full confidence that peace would shortly follow, when he could return to care for his business. Since he did not consider it practicable to transport his wealth, he decided to hide it.

This Spaniard had a wife and a baby a few months old. Having made arrangements for his journey, he busied himself during several nights in digging a pit to hold his riches. He proposed to bury the money and bullion the night before his setting out and to have a workman in whom he had always placed trust to help him. By coincidence this workman also had a wife and baby.

The evening before undertaking the journey, the Spaniard called the workman to him and communicated his thought. The workman went then to his house and indiscreetly told his wife the business that would take him from home during the night. He went back to his master's house, and the two men at once directed themselves to the selected place, conducting on mules the treasure they were to hide.

The laborer's wife, who had heard it said that potentates

were accustomed to bury with their riches those who aided them in the task, began to fear for her husband's safety. Remembering the good heart she had observed in the rich miner's wife, she resolved to beg her aid against the so imminent danger.

The good lady first suggested that the woman follow the Spaniard's steps and beg him for the life of her husband. But then she herself saw that this action would but increase the danger, since the Spaniard would see the security of his treasure still more seriously threatened. Then she formed a plan to make her husband put himself mentally in the place of his presumptive victim—a plan that resulted in a horror to set the hair on end.

She put on the Indian woman's clothes in order to present herself to her husband in this disguise. Then, her little daughter in her arms, she turned resolutely toward the place where she knew her husband to be.

She arrived at the precise moments when the rich miner was cutting off the poor workman's head and rolling the body into the pit. She was so filled with horror and fright that she could not speak a single word and was on the point of dropping her baby. The Spaniard was greatly astonished at the appearance of her whom in the darkness he believed the dead man's wife. Without saying a word or demanding any explanation, he aimed a blow at the head of the woman, who fell lifeless on the verge of the pit, into which her body was then kicked. The baby girl, who had fallen on the heap of removed earth, was crying at the top of her lungs.

"And this child," the rich man considered, "why should she live and what could I do with her? Would not her very existence cause what has occurred to be suspected? Let her follow the same fate."

Picking her up with his foot, he hurled her after the mother and then gave himself to the task of filling up the pit, where he was burying his material riches and, without suspecting it, what he had most loved in his life, as if Destiny, implacably cruel, were punishing forthwith his hideous crime.

When he finished his task, the birds were saluting the dawn, and the mountains, wearing their night-caps of fog, were already becoming clear in outline, and a scud of rosy cloud was announcing that day of blood. He seated himself over the filled-in pit, and there he experienced such rare presentiments and so intense a fright that he arose and fled like a madman to his house. There the wife of the unfortunate workman was awaiting the lady's return.

"What does this mean?" asked the miner.

"It means that I am awaiting your wife, who went to beg for my husband's life."

"Heavens! what have I done?"

The desperation of that criminal is easily imagined. He passed that day in a veritable delirium. With darkness, he went back to the place of the crime, where he groaned all night. And when dawn was spilling its light over the land and little birds were greeting the day with joyous trills, that assassin put an end to his life by hanging himself from an oak limb.

Since then annually on the night in which that frightful event took place, the spirit of the miner renews its laments, being in the opinion of the vulgar a soul in pain which sees afar off the day of its liberation.[4]

El Naranjal

It is told that in a tangled part of the Sierra Madre, under the jurisdiction of Santiago Papasquiaro, there existed in a remote epoch an extraordinary placer mine of gold which many people worked. For the reason that the gold in its native state occurred in balls of different sizes, resembling oranges, the mine was called El Naranjal—The Orange Grove.

The mine was situated in a valley in the bottom of which was an ever-running arroyo. This arroyo flowed out through the only place that gave access to the little valley, since elsewhere

[4]Very similar is a story in *Historia de San Ángel*, by Fernández del Castillo. A long ago resident of San Ángel, suburb of Mexico City, killed his brother to get sole possession of the property they owned jointly. He commanded his head man, a black, to kill and wall up his brother's widow and child, whom he expected to come to the house. Then he left. During his absence the black walled up a woman and child—the wife and daughter of his master, come unexpectedly from Spain.—B. M. D.

the folds of the surrounding mountains were too escarped to admit a way of entrance. Legend assures us that the valley was a wild place, with varied and luxuriant vegetation and a rich flora. The mountains were compactly covered with enormous pines and oaks, and in the depths of the valley the tortured, poetic canyons sang with the lullaby of playful waters. Little houses showed here and there amid the dense growth, and the shouts of the miners harmonized with the murmurs of waters, the chant of birds, the rustling of leaves, and the perfume of resin and flowers.

From that place, which, from the description of it that has come down, must have been an invitation to dream, innumerable Spaniards fled the savage incursions of the Indians in the colonial epoch. According to report, in order to elude all danger, they obstructed the only possible entrance to the valley, which has never been rediscovered.

They tell that now and then the river carries golden sands in the form of little balls and that these proceed from the legendary and fantastic placer mine of El Naranjal. Ingenuous persons believe that in that place there yet exists an enchanted city, and they assert that they have heard the ringing of powerful bells at twelve of the day, at three in the afternoon, and at the hour of prayer, and at intervals during the night the watchman's whistle. And people have speculated that the enchanted city is under the earth, in a gigantic subterranean cavern, the entrance to which it is possible to find.

The report goes that the products of the fabulously rich placer of El Naranjal were conducted to Santiago Papasquiaro's town and stored in a great vault of the master's house, called the Red House, and that these treasures have, through diverse circumstances, remained hidden. Many have sought but none has found.

The Legend of
HOLY GHOST CANYON

By Maude McFie Bloom

THIS is a Christmas story of the time of the *conquistadores*. It was the twilight hour of the sixth of January in the year of our Lord 1599, Twelfth-night. The sleety winter wind, sweeping ceaselessly down from the white peaks above, buffeted, blinded, staggered the three lone white men who, with their laden donkey, were desperately seeking shelter and defense, a place to hide in before their last powers went and night came. For behind them moved, as silent and sinister as shadows, a war party of painted nomad Indians. To the three everything looked unfamiliar—the canyons all deep and shadowed, the mountains darkly timbered throwing their gloom on the snow, and not a single familiar landmark in all the vastness. They had penetrated this wild land for bear meat and tallow, especially needed for the many sick in the new colony called San Gabriel, and they had found what they sought. But now, as the darkness of night came on and they sensed the nearness of their savage pursuers, their spirits were heavy with the doubt that they would ever again experience the warm hearths and warm hearts at San Gabriel in the deep valley by the wide river.

Equally the men were Spaniards, but in birth they were not equal. Being Spaniards, they knew that human society must needs have strata, and each in complete serenity knew himself of worth in his own place. The *caballero* could not flourish without the muleteer, nor the muleteer without the *caballero*.

Nor could any of them get along without the patient, plain little *burra*. Fidel, the muleteer, told her so time and again. Between the two existed complete understanding. Whenever, in some ticklish place where it was a matter of life or death that her four feet be safely put, the *burra* would slant backward one of her great furry ears toward her master, Fidel took it that she asked advice and gave unstintingly. Praise he gave also.

"Well done, my beauty," he would say. "Greater carefulness could not be. When we arrive in San Gabriel by the river, Fidel will bring many more cedar boughs for thy stable. Yes, yes, thy present need is water, but have patience, poor little one, have patience."

Just ahead he could hear Captain Ramón muttering curses at his frost-bitten fingers. The leader, Don Juan, had veered off toward a cliff wall on which faintly showed a trail. Perhaps, Fidel was thinking, it led to a cliff house, such as the friendly *Pueblo* Indians now living in the valleys had once occupied. A new anxiety beset him. Would the *vereda*, if such it were, be wide enough for his *burra* and her enormous load?

Then, "A trail!" he heard Don Juan shout. "We can defend ourselves from above. *Adelante!*"

The ground was dry, free from ice, but steep and unevenly eroded. The donkey was nervous and inclined to balk. Fidel went ahead, feeling out every step of ground for his *burrita*.

"Come on, my beauty," he encouraged. "What is to happen to us if you make up your mind to stop? It is you the *Indios* wish. That is certain. *Arre, burra!*"

Fidel knew that he should be calling upon some saint for protection. But upon which one should he call? There was a strangeness in not being able to decide this grave matter. For months, safe in San Gabriel, he had mulled over the legion array on the church calendar. But now, simply it would not decide. Fidel knew that should Don Juan or Captain Ramón be saying prayers, they were saying them to the mighty Santiago, patron of soldiers. But it was not for him, a humble muleteer, to pray to Santiago. For him what saint would have most power? He could not think.

He could neither see nor hear the *caballeros*. On a perilous curve a blast flung at the muleteer and his *burra* so savagely that only the man's quick skill kept her from being hurled into space. For a moment both man and beast were unnerved.

"*Dios!*" gasped Fidel. "I have to decide. I must implore some saint or other to stop the wind. What is it the *padre* says when the mass is ended? *Ay! El Espíritu Santo,* that is it." The Holy Ghost. Over and over he said the potent name.

And El Espíritu Santo heard his prayer. From immediately overhead sounded his master's shout, "Fidel, my man, are you there?" It was the voice of the valiant, iron-willed explorer and colonizer, the nobleman Don Juan de Oñate, captain-general and governor of New Spain's northernmost province, Nuevo Méjico.

First the *burra* was hauled up by a rope tied about her middle. Then, with difficulty, for his legs were stiff, Fidel scrambled up by means of shallow toe-holds in the rock wall.

On top was a cave, empty but blackened with smoke. To deflect the aim of any arrows that might be sent their way, Fidel hung across the front of the cave Governor Oñate's long silk and wool blanket, hand-woven back in Zacatecas, his *tierra.* He tied the *burra* in the back and hobbled her feet. She had thirst, was crazed for water. Fidel knew by the way she lipped his hand and shuddered.

The wind was knife-edged. Fidel said, "In time the moon will set. Then will I climb down to find dry wood for a fire that your Excellency and the *Señor Capitán* may have warmth."

"I would not have thee expose thyself to such peril, good Fidel. One well-aimed arrow and you would drop to the canyon floor, leaving thy poor wife and children on the colony," answered Don Juan.

"*Pues, Señor,* at the same errand of gathering wood, I could bring up a skin of water for your excellencies and the beast."

"But no!"

Fidel went back to his *burra.* In what a way she looked at him and sighed! "*Paciencia,*" whispered the *peón* into his donkey's ear. If ever those two sleep, my angel, Fidel will have the kindness to fetch you a drink."

A glow of reflected camp fires showed on the opposite wall of the narrow canyon. Presently above the roar of the wind rose the yells of Indians. Dimly their shadows in postures of the scalp dance played upon the cliff wall within view of the three Spaniards.

But Oñate spoke quietly. "My friends, have you remembered what day it is?"

"Yes, my *Comandante*," responded the captain. "The Feast Day of the Kings, when we give gifts to our children. Am not I a man of family?" His tone was sad, for he doubted he would see his children again or they know how he died.

"And thou, Fidelcito?" Don Juan just raised his voice above the *burra's* uneasy noise.

"Yes, Excellency. But the little mother *burra* has much thirst."

"Close thy mouth about the animal! Is a beast to be considered above a man?"

Then, as if repenting his sharp words, Oñate continued, "My friends, our Spanish Day of the Kings, the children's gift day, is not observed in all nations as it is with us. Among heretic nations the Kings are called the Wise Men; and not the day on which they brought gifts to the little Jesucristo but the day of his birth is celebrated. On it they shower not only the children but the poor and one another with gifts."

"A pleasant custom—for the heretics," admitted Don Ramón. "But I like much better our own Day of the Kings—*El Día de los Reyes*."

"Speaking of kings," the governor mused, "Ramón, look at us here in this unexplored new world. We, the Spaniards, the conquerors, are kings. Dios! we shall extend the kingdom of New Spain northward to the Strait of Arian (Santa María, grant we find it soon!), eastward to Quivira and the Ocean Sea which our fathers crossed to conquer this infidel land, westward to the Island of California. All, all by force of arms for our royal master Felipe Segundo, whom may God preserve!"

"Whom may God preserve," echoed the captain and the muleteer.

"This, my friends, is what being a king means to Oñate."

"To me," mildly but earnestly began Don Ramón, "being a

king has a different meaning. I see this province—for if one be exact, your Excellency, this is a desert region with sierras more as oases than aught else—as a kingdom for men like me. I see on it sheep—the most beautiful wealth of all. They can get along with water once a week. In six months a lamb weighs as much as its mother if the feed has been good, and very often a ewe drops twins. Then there is her coat of fine wool, which we cut off in mercy to her. And when she is old and past profit, we give her for food to our dependents. Sheep need attention only twice a year, at lambing and shearing. Finally, a man can lose three-fourths of his flock and still not be down to the soles of his boots. Ewes, wethers, and bucks, these are what will make wealth in this land. And wealth is power."

The great Oñate nodded a thoughtful head. Then he turned to Fidel. "And thou, Fidelcito, what may be thy idea of kings?"

"Of kings," said the *peón*, "I, being a humble and ignorant man, know nothing. But it is said of the kings that they are kind."

The two *caballeros* were moved unexpectedly by the revelation of how small was their servant's world.

Fidel waited with the patience of the humble until his masters slept. Then he girt a rope about his body, slung the leathern bottle over his shoulder, and tied his long, straight hair close to his head. Committing his all to the new protector, he stepped softly to the left front of the cavern, lay down and slid his short, strong legs over the brink.

But he had not counted on the force of the wind. On the instant it seized half his body as if it were a broken branch, flinging it in a semicircle clear of the cliff, and then swinging it pendulum-wise from side to side. He felt as powerless as a leaf in the vortex of the winds. Yet like bands of steel his fingers held and the new saint gave him power to make his bulk heavy. Almost as suddenly as the wind had snatched him up it let him drop against the cliff. With careful, painful pulls Fidel drew his body back into the cave.

Rubbing his bruised limbs, Fidel became aware that his feet

had touched no shelf in the rock face. Yet he had been sure one was there. It must be in the center front, he decided. So when his breathing came slow again he stole carefully around Don Juan's recumbent body to the exact middle point, where a slight groove was formed in the rock.

This time Fidel studied the wall until he was sure that a faintly darker line was the remembered shelf. He waited for a lull in the wind. Then he let himself down, found the toe-holds one after another, and presently stood again in the path up which he had driven his *burra*.

He was confident from the size and steadiness of the reflected fire that the Indians had found a cave shelter. Perhaps a spring of water was in the cave, but how could he pass the Indians to fill his bag? So Fidel pondered. On he went, feeling his way, careful not to let the Indians know of his presence. The sound of the wind was strong enough to cover his stealthy movements. He was not much afraid that an Indian would come upon him unaware, for his sense of smell was keen for the blended odor of grease paint and tanned hide.

Once down on the valley floor, Fidel found himself close enough to the Indians to count them about the camp fire, which was placed well to the front of a broad but shallow cave. There were about thirty of the unholy devils, some singing in voices wilder than a coyote's howl, some circling about the fire, gyrating, gesticulating, their shadows printed on the wall across the canyon.

Soon the adventurer noticed that one or another of them would step out into the valley darkness and after a few minutes return visibly refreshed. "Water!" the *peón* said to himself. "If they can get it, I can." With greater caution than he had yet used, he followed the next Indian who left the cave, and found a well hacked through the ice to flowing water. He filled his leathern bottle and turned to his further business of gathering firewood.

Fidel had not been long out of the cave before the uneasy

caballeros awoke. They were confident that their disobedient servant had gone to his death.

"Miserable son of a burro!" grated the captain.

"The ignorant, stubborn fool!" exclaimed the governor. "But he was a faithful one." And then in a moment he added, *"Dios!* 'twas a rash act, but noble."

The thought took hold. What a grip of duty on the simple man, what quiet courage! Nor was this a sudden impulse, an isolated act, but rather did it spring from the root of him. On this King's Day night prophetic vision came to Juan de Oñate. Not to him and his kind, but to all the Fidels—to the undemanding, inarticulate, toiling, enduring peasants—belonged this new country and they to it. His own class would gain no firm footing. Ramón's would cling more tenaciously, combatively for a few generations. But in the end the Fidels, kindly, happy-hearted, fearing nothing, would possess the land.

The governor strode up and down the confines of the cavern. Once he paused beside the *burra,* laid his hand on her ugly gray back. *"Dios!"* he muttered. "I have regarded that brave fellow as little better than this beast."

Yet something was due to discipline. Don Juan considered what course to pursue if, after all, the disobedient one should return to the cave.

"Hear you not something, my governor?" exclaimed the captain.

"Distinctly, Ramón. Hark to that whistling manner of hard breathing. 'Tis Fidel! By all the saints, the man has made it."

"The wretched one has lost his courage and is scrambling back," said Ramón. "Nor can I fire when he reaches the top lest the Indians be upon us."

But the great Oñate had made up his mind about discipline. "Peace, Ramón," he said. "For a brave man there is no punishment. Lie down and keep silence."

Not quite so noiselessly as he had slipped out to perform his urgent duty of kindness Fidel clambered in again, muttering "El Espíritu Santo" in thanks not only that he was safe but also that he had not awakened his masters. He unfastened the firewood from his back, and then felt his way to where the *burra* was tied. The *caballeros* heard him fumble about for a depression they had remarked in the rock floor, heard the gurgle of the water poured from the leathern bottle, heard him mumble to the snuffling animal.

Governor Oñate lay very still. The high moments of prevision were past. The muleteer was safely back—a drudging *peón*, no more. His mind turned to his own life and to his life's failure if when morning came the Indians should complete their scalp dance. He had done his utmost. He had battled jealous rivals for years, had experienced every form of delay at the hands of two viceroys. He had used all his private fortune and most of his family's to man and equip the colonists. San Gabriel was an established outpost with home fires kindled and house of worship builded. And all to go out ignominiously in a cave! Given longer time, he could have shaped more safely for the Fidels and the Ramóns and the friendly Indians. He could have told his plans and his dreams to little Cristóbal, already mannishly brave, sober and gay by equal turns. The soul of Oñate was sick with sorrow. It was his blackest, bitterest hour.

Suddenly a curious excitement stirred him—a quickening of sensation, a loosening of physical bonds, an inflooding of some new force. It was as if his inward being were drawn to the surface. The very air seemed to move. Something mysterious was beating in upon his consciousness. He was strong again, stronger than ever before.

"*Excelencia,* are you awake? *Mi Comandante,* Don Juan!" Ramón's voice was full of awe, mounting to panic.

Oñate sprang up, crossing himself. Ramón was jabbering familiar curses, as if to ward away the startling strangeness that surrounded them.

The cavern was filled with light, a dazzling blue light. There was a whirring on the air as if huge wings were nearing. The blue radiance intensified. It overpowered in each of the men the last sense of self. They knew it now for what it was—a Visitation. In its presence they bowed, swayed, fell face down on the rocky floor. Yet distinctly, indelibly was imprinted on them the sight of the humble muleteer squatted beside his *burra,* his countenance as awestruck as their own.

A voice sounded in their ears, mighty as the tide's roar. "The wise are become as fools; the fool is become as wise. Truly a king is one who is kind. Thus saith the Holy Ghost, El Espíritu Santo."

Night again enfolded the Spaniards. And utter silence shut in the canyon. At dawn they descended and easily found the way home to San Gabriel, saved beyond all doubt by the Holy Ghost, as are all the faithful who to this day have need of help in the quiet Cañon del Espíritu Santo.

This legend, still living, has three versions, told from the slant of each of the three men who experienced the Visitation. To Don Ramón the Visitation was white man's magic, tremendous, which so terrified the Indians that they slunk away.

Don Juan de Oñate's reaction was personal. The Presence was for him. The events of that night of the Kings so blent in him that his attitude toward the common people among his colonists was ever after altered. He understood them and was kind. Ten years later when San Gabriel was to be moved to a new location (Santa Fé), when rival aspirants and political intrigue had caused Don Juan to resign, the colonists with amazing self-assertion refused to accept the viceroy's choice, Captain Juan Martínez de Montoya, and chose for themselves their first leader's nineteen-year-old son, Don Cristóbal.

And lastly there is Fidel's plain account of what sport it was to play bear and fool the Indians on that night of the Feast of Kings, in 1599; and how it was that he brought down the Power.

Old-Time_

NEW MEXICAN USAGES

By Alice M. Crook

THE domestic usages here set down, as I have found them in New Mexico, are of course dwindling. Some of them, like the ceremonies pertaining to marriage, go back to a time in Spain anterior to the discovery of America; others, like the manufacture of *cáscara*, illustrate how the *conquistadores* and their followers—or were *all* people of Spanish blood who came to the Americas conquerors?—adapted themselves to the primitive and also adapted the primitive to themselves.

Cáscara, which means literally *bark, peeling, husk, eggshell*, etc., is the name of an ancient cosmetic used until recent years by the feminine population of the settlement of Pojuaque; probably it is still used on some out-of-the-way ranches. To make it, the women gathered the bones of cattle, burned them blue-white over a slow fire of cow chips, and then ground them to powder upon a stone *metate*. Into this powder they worked pure homemade soap (in later years Castile soap), a white root, pounded up, called *inmortal* (immortal), and a number of other ingredients unknown to me. The mixture was moistened, rolled to about an inch of thickness upon a cloth, and left to dry. Later the *cáscara* was cut into small squares, snow-white, slightly gritty, and similar to chalk. A woman would rub one of these cakes over face and arms until her skin was very white. Besides being much valued as a whitener by those with dark skins, *cáscara* was used as a preventive of sunburn. Now that powder may be cheaply bought, women, even of the poorest class, no longer go through the tedious process of making the cosmetic.[1]

The ceremonies attending marriage are obsolescent but not obsolete, although few daughters are now contracted while yet little girls by their fathers, as in the old days. However, the making of a formal engagement is still practiced in the following manner. First the prospective groom's father sends a letter by head male relatives, sometimes as many as twenty men participating, to the father of the prospective bride. Upon receiving it, he reads it aloud to his daughter. After a lapse of at least three days, she may send her answer in a letter to be delivered by a number of her male relatives. If the answer is affirmative, the groom's parents announce an engagement reception about a week later. The bride-to-be and groom-to-be are introduced at this function and become acquainted with the future in-laws. The wedding probably is set for a week from that date. In the old days the wedding could be set for any future time, but during the interim the engaged girl must at a *baile* never dance with any but her affianced. Just before the wedding, the groom-to-be presents to his future wife a trunk of clothes. It may contain wearing apparel sufficient for years to come—and, of course, her wedding dress. In the trunk, also, is her badge of marriage—her black *tápalo*. Never again must she wear a hat. The groom paid a pretty penny for the *tápalo*, and it should last a life-time.

As the wedding day approaches, relatives gather for miles around at the home of the bride. For days the groom's relatives bake and prepare for the wedding feast. The bride is dressed in her lovely garments by her godmother, and the ceremony at the

---

[1]In *The White Chief*, a novel of remarkable fidelity to New Mexican life, Mayne Reid in describing the folk gathering for a *fiesta* says: "The prettier faces peep forth; and you may see, from the softness of the complexion, that they have just been washed free of the *allegria* that for the last two weeks has rendered them hideous." Then he subscribes this note:

"The *allegria* is used by the Mexican belles to preserve the complexion and get it up towards some special occasion. . . . When it is washed off, the skin comes out clear and free from 'tan.' The *allegria* is the well-known 'poke-weed' (*Phytolacca decondra*)."

In some parts of Spanish-America deer-horn, burned and powdered, formed a chief ingredient of a cosmetic.—*Editor*.

church takes place. When it is over and the wedding group emerge, they are met by two men, one playing a violin and the other a guitar. The wedding party returns to the bride's house, following the musicians. That night a *baile* is given and relatives and friends crowd to the house. Hired singers begin the long song *Entregar*. It is about the giving away of the bride; the name actually means in English to "hand over." After the song, the dancing, feasting, and merry-making begin, to continue most of the night.

A pretty custom, no doubt dating back to ancient days, is the one of "blessing." If the daughter and her husband are about to leave for their home some distance away from that of the parents, the daughter pleads, "Papa, bless us." Then they kneel before her father, who makes a cross sign and touches his daughter's lips and those of her husband, while he murmurs, *"Dios te haga un santo."* (God bless you.)

While each year the *tápalo* is being more and more discarded, the younger women will borrow one from an older relative or friend to cover their heads while attending a funeral. It seems to designate sorrow. Some people call the black shawl the *rebozo*,[2] but actually in New Mexico the *rebozo* is a scarf that is tied over the head for warmth and covered with the *tápalo*, or black shawl.

Mattresses were made from earliest times of wool, carefully washed, dried and spread evenly into a thick pad, which was tied and sewed together. These wool mattresses are still much in use. They are warmer than cotton, much softer, and cleaner, for they must be taken apart at least every two years, washed and remade. The wool wads up in that length of time.

In many isolated settlements, factory-made brooms are entirely unknown. The hard dirt floors and yards are clean-swept with the *escoba chiquita*, a short, tied bundle of swamp grass, gathered from marshy places.

Yeso is a white gypsum, burned and ground upon the *metate*

---

[2] In Mexico City the *rebozo* is a long blue or brown cotton scarf, or shawl, worn by women of the lowest social class over the head or shoulders and used as a carry-all for bundles and babies. Women who wear the *tápalo* are a grade up in the social scale. —*Editor*.

to powder. A small amount of it is mixed with water and brushed on the hard adobe inside walls of many New Mexico homes. It makes a smooth, hard, very white finish that does not rub off. Sometimes the *yeso* is left white, sometimes tinted to a pink or a green and used on the inside of porches. It has more than one use. The artists who painted the old, old *santos* used it as a first covering.

A white earth is also obtained in many localities, some being near Cerrillos, and, mixed thinly with water, brushed on the adobe plaster. But this is not as satisfactory a finish as *yeso*.

Some of the names of home remedies are not pure Spanish and therefore not found in any Spanish dictionary. I have written them down as they are pronounced in the Spanish way of spelling. One of these is *incerrado,* a poultice made of pitch from the pine tree, *punche* (native tobacco), *ojía* (a root obtained from the mountains), and other ingredients, mixed with grease and applied to parts affected. It is a sure cure for imbedded splinters, boils, and abscesses. *Ojía* root is also made into a tea and drunk to break up colds. *Inmortal,* used in making *cáscara,* is steeped into a tea and drunk for various ailments. *Yerba de la víbora,* obtained near Santa Fé, seems to be a fine panacea for rheumatism. *Tecomaca* is a preparation containing *inmortal, alusema,* and a great number of other herbs and roots, ground and boiled into a sticky substance called *alquitrán* (tar). Then this pitchy mess is rolled into bits the shape of a finger and kept in a closed can. If anyone develops a headache, eyeache, or earache caused by *aire,* a tiny piece is warmed over a stove and stuck to the temple, close to the eye, or behind the ear, as the need may be. Rose petals dried and rubbed to a powder between the hands are used in various medicinal concoctions.

The native children pull up the greyish *pinque* weed and invert it until milky balls form on the root. They pull these off and chew them like gum. It tastes, they tell me, a great deal like rubber.

Drying is one of the best native methods of preserving food. Meat is cut into strips, salted, and hung on the clothesline.

PURO MEXICANO

When cured, it is pounded into shreds, cooked, and served with a hot *chile* sauce. Corn is cut from the cob and dried. It makes a tempting dish in the winter time. Squash is sliced and spread out on cloths in the sun to dry and then stored away in white sacks. After soaking all night, the squash is cooked with salt and onions until tender and served in *chile carriva,* flavored with *orégano* (wild marjoram). Strips of pork loin are dipped in this *chile carriva* mixed with other flavors, and fried in hot fat, or else hung up and dried after being dipped. In either form it is very palatable.

To make *chile carriva,* the spines and seeds are removed from a number of the red *chiles,* and the pods are placed in a pan and dried for a few minutes in the oven. Then they are put into cold water and worked with the fingers. The peelings are finally separated, skimmed off with the fingers and thrown away. The red water that is left is *chile carriva.* This sauce may be heated, but even the natives never *boil* it. The infernal regions could have nothing as hot as boiled *chile carriva.*

Chile grows hotter in some parts of the country than in other parts. The natives usually prefer the *chile* grown from Pojuaque to Chimayo, which they say is milder. I do not see the difference.

Panocha is a delicious dessert composed of wheat sprouts. It is made in the following manner: The wheat is washed and spread on a cloth in a dark place for about ten days, at the end of which time it has sprouted. Then it is dried in the sun and ground on a *metate* or in a mill. The powder is mixed with hot water and baked for about twelve hours in the *horno* (the round bake oven seen outside many native homes). Nothing else is added; yet the cake is very sweet.

Small white Spanish cheeses made in the settlements that dot the valley through which the Río Grande runs, are peddled from door to door in Santa Fé. They are made from either cow or goat milk and have no special name, being called only *queso* (cheese).

For the rennet in this *queso,* the cheese maker uses the *cuajo* that she carefully removes from the vicinity of the liver of a butchered beef. She salts the oblong mess and hangs it on the clothesline to cure. When she is ready for her cheese making, she soaks the dried *cuajo* in a jar of water overnight. The next morning she adds some of this water to a little milk, which she lets stand until it clabbers. Then she squeezes out the whey and pours it back into the jar containing the *cuajo*. She does this because the water in which the *cuajo* is soaked is not strong enough to clabber a large amount; so she clabbers a small vessel of milk first and uses this as a "starter" for a larger quantity. If she makes cheese regularly, she can keep the rennet going without a new piece of *cuajo* by pouring a little whey back in the jar each time.

SONS *of the* DEVIL

By JOE STORM

"LOOK at them wild devils go," Jim Jackson whistled, as he sat back on his reins and gestured towards a band of about forty horses "high-tailing it" along the crest of a ridge. Soon they disappeared on the other side.

Jackson was a cowman of the old school. He knew cattle, horses, Apache Indians, and the wild animals that are commonly shot. For many years he had ranged in the country where we were riding, the Mescalero Apache reservation, in the heart of the White Mountains of southeastern New Mexico.

"You say those horses are wild, regular mustangs?" I asked, for I had the idea that wild horses were legendary rather than real.

"Yes, wild, unbranded and untouched by rope."

"Why doesn't someone corral them and sell them?"

"Better men than you have tried to catch these horses, boy. If you can even get a rifle shot at them, you are better than most people. Why, they smelt us out a long time ago and have been keeping out of sight for a good time now. They are up there now where a mountain goat could not keep up with them. They've been running and breeding that way for generations."

"Where'd they come from?"

Jackson stuffed his pipe and took his time about lighting it. Then we jogged on.

"There's a story the Apaches tell about that," he began. "Back in the days of Geronimo and long before when there was bitter warfare between the Mexicans and the Apaches, the Mescaleros made it their business to steal horses from the *rancheros* both in this state and in Old Mexico. In this way some of the best mares and studs of the Spanish breed came into

190

their hands. When they finally settled down on their reservation, they brought a few of the prize specimens with them.

"Now, among the noted horse thieves of the tribe, as they tell the story, was a warrior named Cow Bird, and he'd got hold of a big black stallion they called Diablo. Lots of the Indians thought he was a medicine horse. If what they say is true, he must have been part human and part maniac. Why, he and Cow Bird carried on regular conversations with each other. The Indian was about as queer a specimen as his horse. He hadn't an equal for riding pitching horses, and they say Diablo wasn't the only animal he held conversations with.

"But the most peculiar thing about Diablo wasn't his power to talk. It was his dislike for the smell of chile. The faintest whiff of that stuff simply made him insane. And whenever his nostrils got irritated that way he would be possessed by a desire for the taste of blood—the blood of the carrier of the chile, anybody's blood, even the blood of his own master.

"Well, one time Cow Bird's band was getting low on arrowheads; so he decided he would go by himself back into a mountain where flint was plentiful, make up a supply of ammunition, and associate with himself and the spirit world a while. He rode Diablo.

"While he was up there some Mexicans got wind of him. He was the ringleader against them, and now that he was unprotected by numbers they thought their chance had come to get rid of him.

"So one night a Mexican snaked up through the tall grass and bushes to Cow Bird's tepee, intending to stab him in sleep. He was as noiseless as a shadow, and, even if the Indian had been awake and alert, the Mexican could have matched knives with him, but there was one thing he did not take into account. He had eat a special bait of chile for supper. That horse was staked right out close to the camp.

"Diablo smells the chile about the time the spy begins to get close enough to be nervous about his business. He sniffs kind of easy at first, and then be blows his nose. He knows it's going to start to take a-hold of him; so he breathes just a little at a time. 'Damn that stuff,' he thinks. And he gets all out of breath and heaves a big sigh. It's too much for him. With one jump he breaks his rope and shakes himself in the moonlight. His little red eyes is bulging out a foot, and his long, yellow teeth is bared for the kill.

"Cow Bird is awakened by a muffled scream—and then a sound like a pig squealing with his head in the trough. By the time he can reach the scene of the racket, Diablo is devouring chile-saturated flesh.

" 'Now, this is good and bad news all at once,' the Apache says to himself. 'For it is good I'm not laying up in bed with a knife in my chest. And still it is bad—awfully bad.' Cow Bird tries to be reasonable. 'Come now, Diablo,' he implores—'enough for tonight.'

"But the big stud is crazy mad. He knows what he is doing but he just can't help himself. He curls back his lip and starts a rush that is full of meaning. But an Indian is never behind when it comes to thinking. With the speed of a painter he side-steps the charge; and before the black can turn for a second attack, Cow Bird is on his back and holding on for dear life. Right here, son, is where a great ride takes place."

At this crucial point in the story, Jackson knocked the ashes out of his pipe, and began explaining. "If you have ever ridden an outlaw," he directed at me, "you will know that it's either stay on or fall off some place where you can get to shelter soon after you land. Usually you are so scared of the consequences if you fall, you will make a ride you never thought was in you.

"Well, Cow Bird was about the best rider the horseback Indians ever knew of. He had an instinct for knowing just what a horse was going to do next, no matter how fast he did it. He had a special instinct for Diablo.

"The black does a sunfish to the moon, comes down on his back, rolls over and goes into some awful contortions. At times he flies sidewise through the air, very much like a killdee; and at other times he turns over and over in the tall grass. But that Indian seems to be on like a wart. He's off on his feet at the fall and back on again before the horse can get to him. Diablo goes into a white-hot rage; and at times he gives the Indian some mean knocks. This keeps up most of the night, until Cow Bird feels that he can last out no longer. 'Soon,' he thinks, 'will I hunt with my departed brothers in the Land of the Sun.' But Diablo is tiring steadily as morning draws near. Then he stumbles and falls hard and knows he's whipped. But the Indian is whipped, too, if the horse only knew it. Neither can regain his feet. The Indian lies to one side and his blood-stained face must have looked old in the grey morning light. The black, his once glossy coat a mat of dirt and blood, finally manages to stand.

" 'Master,' the outlaw spoke, 'if I could, I would kill you. This I know—and that I love you. I will travel to the high places, where the air is pure and I shall be free. There will I regain my strength and mind. Come not for me, master, lest I kill you. And remember, in days to come, that I have told you the liberty of the horse will outlast that of the red man.'

" 'Devil-horse,' the Indian answered back, 'go where you will; you have borne me well. My people will not disturb your freedom.'

"As the sun was setting four days later, Cow Bird heard a shrill, high nicker come over a breeze from the west. 'Diablo is lonesome,' he says to himself. 'He will be back begging for forgiveness before the sun sets on another day.' But Cow Bird was only half right, it seems. For when Cow Bird rose the next morning and went to catch his best sorrel mare, all he found was a pair of chewed-up hobbles. From that day to this, wild horses have roamed over the slopes of Old Baldy. 'Sons of the Devil,' some call them."

CATORCE

By J. Frank Dobie

IN December, 1932, I and my friend Tom Newberry of Chihuahua City were camped for a few days, hunting, in the Sierra Madre about fifty miles northwest of that city. We had as *mozos* a *mestizo* named Justo and a pure-bred Yaqui Indian named Cruz, living far removed from his tribesmen in the *quebradas* of Sonora. Justo could not tell a story as long as the beard on a flea, but Cruz was as fecund and tireless a story-teller as one could find in either the Orient or the Occident. He had stories about bears and burros and giants and fairies and princes and princesses and witches and magical words and devils and everything else under the sun. When, after supper while we sat around the camp fire, he got well launched into a story, his black face would twist up and his voice would sound as if he were crying. He had a way of running one fairy tale into another and then into another so that really there was no reason why he should ever end. Once or twice I fell asleep while he was talking, for, to tell the truth, some of his stories did not interest me. Others did, this one among them. It is known in Puerto Rico, and perhaps elsewhere, as the story of Juan Catorce.

One time there was a man named Catorce (Fourteen). He was named that because he lived by fourteens. He had to have at one meal fourteen hectolitres of *frijoles*, fourteen dozen *tortillas* and fourteen gallons of coffee. True, he ate but once every fourteen days, but then he ate so much that he could not possibly earn enough to buy his own food. So he would go from place to place offering to work for his board, but as soon as people learned how much he ate he would lose his job. Finally

CATORCE

he went far away from home and offered himself to a very rich *hacendado.*

"All right," said the *rico,* "I'll furnish all you can eat and you work as hard as you can. We milk a great many cows on this hacienda, and in the morning about three o'clock you are to get up and begin milking."

"I will milk, do anything," answered Catorce, "but remember I eat plenty, enormously, and tomorrow is the day on which I am going to be hungry."

The *rico* laughed and told the head cook to prepare breakfast for an especially hungry man. When milking time came, Catorce learned that more than thirty barrels of milk must be extracted from the cows. He was ravenous and as soon as he milked a barrel of milk he would taste it and then, unable to restrain his hunger, swill it down. Thus he milked and swallowed ten barrels of milk, by which time the army of other hands had milked all the other cows.

Then they all went to breakfast. The cooks had boiled an extra pot of beans and cooked several dozen extra *tortillas,* but Catorce—and the cooks also—soon found that there was not nearly enough food to satisfy him. All *rancheros* know that milk is baby's food. The barrels that Catorce had drunk were like so much water. Only a sense of decency kept him from gobbling up all the food on the breakfast table; he had a regard for the other men, but he went away hungry.

After breakfast the *patrón* came out and told Catorce to go with a little peon driving two yoke of oxen to a big high-wheeled wooden *carreta* to haul in wood.

"With both hands—willingly—I go," answered Catorce. "But remember that when I get back I want some breakfast."

He and the peon drove the gigantic cart out into the foot-hills and halted in the woods. They got out to chop wood. Now the peon was suddenly dumbfounded to see Catorce grab his *machete* and cut the throat of an ox, then of a second ox, then of the other two, all before they were unyoked. He started to run away, but Catorce called him back.

"What is the matter, *hombrecito* (little man)?" he called.

195

"I am dying of hunger and have to eat something. Here, help me pile up some wood to make a fire."

Without saying a word and trembling in all his joints, the peon went to piling up wood. Meantime Catorce gutted the oxen. "More wood," he yelled, and went to piling up a mountain of it himself. Then he struck fire to it and threw on the four ox carcasses. He had not bothered to skin them. About the time the hair was well scorched, he began gobbling them down.

"It is not a full meal," Catorce said, "but I can make out until we get back, and now I feel enough strength in myself to load the cart with wood."

Catorce flew about hacking logs, dragging them up, and pitching them on the *carreta*. The peon was amazed, paralyzed. Catorce paid no attention to him until the *carreta* was loaded with such a load of wood as no human being ever saw before. The *carreta* was strong, massive. The wood was stacked so high that the peon had to shade his eyes to see the top of it.

[I remember how at this point Cruz squinted his eyes and, following them with his upstretched hands, seemed to be reaching for the stars.]

"All right, let's go," bellowed Catorce.

"But we have no oxen," squeaked the peon.

"Pish, we don't need any oxen. Climb up and get ready to drive."

Now, the peon knew he had a madman to deal with. But Catorce did not give him time to hesitate. He caught the *hombrecito* and pushed and poked him up to the top of the load, where he settled among the timbers like a mouse among corn stalks. Then Catorce grabbed the tongue of the wagon in his left hand and, waving his *machete* in his right hand, made a direct line for the hacienda. The trees that were in his way he cut down with one lick each. At the gulches and canyons he simply lifted the *carreta* across.

People at the hacienda saw the load of wood approaching. It was a miracle for height. Figure to yourself their amazement at not seeing any oxen hitched to the wagon. Catorce was a playful fellow, and as he neared the hacienda he stopped for a minute among some trees, where he could not be seen, tied the tongue of the *carreta* up, and then got behind it and pushed. The great load of wood kept him invisible from the watching people, and the *carreta* seemed to be moving by its own will. The *patrón* and his wife and all the other people were gazing with' their mouths open when the *carreta* came up.

"Where must I unload the wood?" asked Catorce, stepping around in front of the master.

"Why, right over there—but where are the oxen?"

"Oh, I ate them, I was so hungry, and I am still unbreakfasted."

"All right," said the *patrón*. "Now you will fill up. The cauldrons have been boiling *frijoles* all day and the granary has been disgorging corn for enough *tortillas* to feed the biggest regiment that Don Porfirio Diaz ever sent out. Unload and then eat."

Catorce lifted up his little finger and helped the peon down, unloaded the wood, and went in to eat. He seemed to have enough this time.

That night the *hacendado* had a long consultation with his wife. "This fellow," he said, "works for nothing but his board, but it seems to me that his board will make the hacienda barren. In the morning I am going to discharge him."

"No, do not do that," said his wife. "He is an extraordinary hand. You know how long you have been wanting to get those *sitios* of brush by the Santa Clara cleared. You know how little progress the men make on it. Put Catorce to work there and watch how the brush and timber fly. Feed him on old bulls. The hacienda has many hundreds of them."

The *hacendado* thought this a good suggestion. In the morning he told Catorce his plan.

"I am very, very *contento* with my master," Catorce said. "I need some real exercise. Also you are to remember that although I eat considerably when I do eat, I require food only every fourteen days. All I want now is a good axe and I'll start to clearing the land. Do you have a blacksmith?"

"Yes, I have a blacksmith," the *hacendado* answered,

"Then order him to make an axe as I direct."

The *hacendado* gave the order.

"I want an axe," Catorce told the blacksmith, "fourteen *quintales* in weight with the handle fourteen hectometers long."

A *quintal* is a hundred-weight. The blacksmith went to work. He had to have fourteen men help him forge the axe metal and lift it on to the anvil. It took him twelve days to do the job.

Then the *hacendado* directed Catorce to the vast swamps and forests and thickets of the Santa Clara.

"Where is the *administrador?*" Catorce asked when he arrived at the camp of the men who were clearing the land.

"Yonder he is," answered a peon.

"Well, *señor administrador,* show me the boundary line."

"It follows this *sendero*—a straight breach through growth," answered the *administrador.* "We have been cutting on it a whole year, but the brush grows up behind us almost as fast as we cut it down ahead."

"I can see a thread through the jungle," said Catorce, "but I do not call that a real *sendero.* It is too narrow and it is not very long."

"It is five leagues long," said the *administrador,* "but the line goes on and on far beyond the point of the *sendero.* Maybe you can see that flag away beyond where the *sendero* ends. Away and away beyond it is another flag, and then another. The line goes on and on *hasta la cola del mundo*—clear to the tail-end of the world."

Swinging his axe, Catorce set off, hewing right and left, clearing a *sendero* eighty feet wide. He worked so fast that before long he disappeared from the *administrador's* sight. He cut down the trees and the brush ahead of him at such a pace that he had to trot in order to keep up with his own licks. It was late afternoon when he got back to camp. On his return trip he cleared a stretch of ground eighty feet wide alongside the first *sendero.* The *peones* had to scuttle to get out of his way, for they were camped right in his path.

The next morning they saw a herd of bulls coming, driven by

vaqueros. They were old bulls but fierce, bellowing, running, fighting.

"Good!" Catorce called out. "I am ready to eat. Kill fourteen while I pile up some wood and brush to make a fire."

Two vaqueros roped a dun bull and with great difficulty and much yelling dragged it up and were throwing it down to cut its throat.

"What a bother!" Catorce said. "What a fuss over an ant!"

He grabbed his *machete*, leaped among the bulls, and right and left either cut their throats or hacked their skulls in two. He ate and was contented.

Then the *hacendado* came out, viewed the expanse that Catorce had so quickly cleared, and was also contented. By the time another meat day came Catorce had the vast *sitios* of the Santa Clara all cleared.

His fame spread. Now the king of the country came out requesting his aid in killing a gigantic serpent with seven heads that was destroying cattle and people, a creature so mighty that none of the king's subjects could kill it. As a reward for destroying this beast the king had long offered the hand of his daughter.

"I do not want to marry," Catorce said to him. "All I want is my food, but I will destroy the serpent."

Catorce went out into the sierras, found the serpent, cut each of its seven heads off, took out all the fangs, which he pocketed, and skinned it. He brought the hide to his camping place and stretched it over some trees to make a shelter.

Then the *administrador* of the Santa Clara courteously offered to guide Catorce to the king's palace. When they reached the city, they saw a great *fiesta* in progress.

"What is the occasion for all this?" Catorce asked.

"Why," a citizen replied, "a heroic man has killed the great serpent, has brought in the seven heads and presented them before the king, and now as a reward he is about to marry the princess."

Catorce was only mildly interested, but he went to the palace.

199

He asked of the king, "Does each one of the seven heads have fangs?"

The king was surprised at such a question, but it was reasonable. He demanded the heads for examination. Of course the fangs were gone.

"Here they are," said Catorce, pulling them from his pocket. "When I killed the serpent I cut the fangs out."

Thus the man trying to steal the credit due Catorce was exposed. The king asked to see the skin of the serpent also. Catorce went back and brought it in. When he flipped it over the palace, it covered the building and grounds as a handkerchief covers a fallen acorn.

"Very well, the princess is your bride," said the king.

"But I don't want a wife," Catorce answered. "All I want is my rations. Why, the idea of a wife that comes up merely to my knee, even if she is pretty!"

"But my decree is that whoever killed the serpent must marry the princess," answered the king. "It is proven that you killed the serpent."

So Catorce married. He killed other serpents and had to marry other princesses, and he had his rations every fourteen days as long as he lived.

"I came in by Laredo
And went out by Silao.
Listeners polite,
It's your turn now."

Thus Cruz the Yaqui story-teller ended his tale.

The
LITTLE WHITE DOG

By Hugh McGehee Taylor

IT was a winter night down in the brush country of the Texas border. The mesquite coals of the camp fire added to the brightness of the flames. The Engineer and twelve Texas-Mexicans, after putting in the day surveying, had eaten supper, some of the men had helped the cook wash the dishes and cooking utensils, and now with one end of the Engineer's cot pulled up to the fire so as to afford him a comfortable seat, all were grouped about what is—intensely so in cold weather—the center of a camp, the fire.

On the preceding night the Engineer had entertained the men, in Spanish, with stories of Mexico, where he had lived and worked for many years. By agreement they were to do the story-telling tonight, and Apolinar—his name shortened to "Polinar" and even "Poly"—had been selected to tell the story. His day's work finished and his *ollas* of beans for breakfast simmering on the coals, Apolinar sat down opposite the Engineer.

"Now we are ready; you can commence," said the latter. Apolinar Vásquez then, with few pauses, related the following story very much as it is here written. His mention of the Cuban revolution was as casual as was the remark of another Mexican in the region concerning a flower that the Engineer asked about. "This flower," he said, "is with us called *coreopsi,* but that is not the name *botánico.*"

This ranch is one of two old *porciones*, El Perdido and Las Vargas, that together are called El Coyote. The owner before the Confederate War was Don Luis Cantu. Don Luis had no male children, but he had a lovely daughter about nineteen years old. Her name was Liza. At this time her mother was dead.

The owner of the ranch west of us was Don Miguel. He was a wild *ranchero* and he also carried on smuggling between Monterrey and Corpus Christi, through Guerrero. The streets of stone houses in Guerrero then were not empty of souls. Many people lived there then, and the men stole cattle and horses on both sides of the Rio Grande, and what they took on one side they sold on the other.

This Miguel was twenty-seven or twenty-eight, stocky, thick-necked, bullet-headed, one who admired himself and considered himself to be a great success with the *señoritas*. He was quick with both the knife and the pistol, and the people said he was afraid of nothing. He drank a good deal and gambled. Now he was paying court to Liza.

Her other lover was Don Carlos Guajardo, a man very gallant and *un caballero de a tiro*—entirely a gentleman. As the oldest son, his father being dead, he was the head of the Guajardo family. There was no doubt that Liza favored him. He asked Don Luis for her hand and she was given. Then he went to Monterrey to purchase her wedding clothes and to bring the bishop from Laredo to marry them.

These arrangements were made while Don Miguel was away on one of his smuggling trips. When he returned to find the wedding promised, he rode in a fury to El Coyote, there to front Don Luis. He demanded that Liza marry him and not Don Carlos.

"But she has already been asked for and given," responded Don Luis.

No matter. He demanded to see Liza herself. Don Luis refused. Then in his fury the mad Miguel knocked the old man down and ran over his body into the house, calling loudly for Liza. She had seen and heard what had passed. She came at him like a tigress and drove a dagger into his arm before he could get out of the way.

She was making another stab when old Esteban, foreman for

many years under Don Luis, caught her arm, saying, "No, child, no! Leave him to me!"

But Miguel was too quick. He ran out of the house, sprang into the saddle, struck spurs, and was beyond the sweep of the knife in Esteban's hands. His *mozo* dashed after him. All this was in the time it takes a whirlwind to sweep across the *patio*. When Liza bent down to her father she found him unconscious. Alone she raised him up, but she had to have help to carry him to his bed. He was old, Don Luis was. The blow, the shock made him very weak. For a long time he lay ill. When he was better, the candles burned at his head and feet.

Before they were lighted, however, Don Carlos arrived with the bride's clothes and the bishop. The bishop was in time to give Don Luis the supreme unction and to hold the funeral in Matamoras. But the wedding had to be put off. A sister to Liza's mother took her in charge until the period of mourning should pass. She remained, living with this aunt, in Matamoras.

After his attack on Don Luis, Miguel disappeared. Carlos and others hunted him on both sides of the Río Grande, but not for a long time did they hear anything of him. Meantime Carlos took charge of Liza's property. Twice a month he rode to Matamoras to see her and give an accounting. He went to Mexico City and collected from President Díaz the money that Don Luis had loaned him for his revolution. At first he made these trips well attended, but in time he took only his *mozo*. Each carried a sword and rifle.

One night they were set upon by six men. The *mozo* was hit on the top of the head by a bullet that knocked him to the ground but did not greatly injure him. Carlos received a sword thrust in his body, at which he threw himself from his horse and hid in the brush, sword in hand. His horse ran off but came back looking for him, and then the attackers fired. Here they made a mistake, for the *mozo* had recovered his rifle and now he aimed by the flashes of the enemies' guns and killed one. He moved to one side so that the flash of his own gun would not make him a target; when the enemy fired he made another shot that killed a man. A third man of the attackers ran to hide himself and came within reach of the sword of Carlos. As his entrails were ripped out, he gave a death cry. Then the other attackers left. No one of the three dead men was known to Carlos or his *mozo*. Nor could the judge, who was notified, identify them. A comfortable amount of money, both Mexican and American, was found on the bodies. A part of it was used to bury them; the remainder was kept by the judge. *Rurales* took up the trail of the escaped attackers, but it led into a main-traveled road and was lost.

After this Carlos rode well guarded. Under his management Liza's affairs and his both prospered. Cattle were a good price. Just before his death Don Luis had delivered four hundred head of steers to some men in Corpus Christi, who paid for them in gold and shipped them to Cuba, where a revolution had used up all the cattle. To these buyers Carlos sold other cattle from his and Liza's ranches in Texas. He also sold cattle to a contractor who was grading the railroad bed from Matamoras to San Miguel.

With so much business to attend to, the year of mourning passed quickly for Carlos. Now, a second time, the date for the wedding was set. Carlos brought the bishop from Victoria, as the one in Laredo was getting too old to make long trips. Friends from Monterrey, from Corpus Christi, from the border ranches in Texas and Tamaulipas and other places came. Carlos chartered all the hotels in both Matamoras and Brownsville and chartered also the ferry so that anybody could pass in either direction without paying a centavo. The civil wedding was held soon after dark; the church wedding was to be held at daylight. Don Francisco, uncle to Liza, gave a rich banquet and there at his house the wedding party was dancing, waiting for the morning to come.

Soon after midnight the door guard came to Carlos and said: "There is a stranger outside on a fine horse, both of them all covered with mud. He says that he can not come in, but he asks for you to come out to receive his *felicitaciones*."

Carlos was in high good humor. He went to the door and called out, "Who is my friend?"

THE LITTLE WHITE DOG

The only answer he received was a pistol shot through the heart. The unknown rider clapped spurs to his horse and went tearing over the cobblestones into the brush. Darkness and the chaparral swallowed him up before men could mount and catch him.

Liza had followed Carlos to the door. She saw him fall. She gathered him in her arms and his blood ran all over her hands and dress. He was dead.

For a long time Liza lay ill. She would take no food. The bishop remained for several days giving what comfort he could. Then a nun from Monterrey came and took charge of her. This sister was young and gentle and loving, and she persuaded Liza to eat. They both went to the ranch. Legally Liza was the wife of Carlos, but the church had not added its blessing and for this reason she did not consider herself married. She signed over all of Carlos' property to a kinsman of his.

Months after the fatal wedding night Liza received a letter from Miguel, sent from San Luis Potosí. He had, he said, just been informed of the death of "your sweetheart and my friend." He said that he was going to wind up his business at once and come to Texas. "It is my duty," he wrote, "to come and be tried by the courts for the death of Don Luis. If they do not hang me, I will hunt down the man who killed Carlos, and avenge you. For a time I hated Carlos. I loved you too, and could not otherwise than hate him. Yet he was my friend from boyhood. Long ago all hate went away."

This Miguel was astute. He knew women and he knew Liza. His letter touched her and she had the courts remove the charges against him. No doubt he had counted on this, for he waited until the charges were dismissed before he came. Then when he presented himself to the sheriff and was told that there was nothing against him, he pretended surprise. After he had remained at his ranch a few days, he sent Liza a note asking that she allow him to call and pay his respects. He thanked her for having had the charges against him removed. "I have already begun working to find out who the murderer of Carlos is," he added.

Liza replied in a note that Miguel might come to see her. "Nevertheless," she said, "you need not hunt for the murderer. Nuestro Señor (Our Saviour) will take care of the punishment. The guilty one will not go free."

Miguel came. He showed great respect and solicitation. He found a few things to do for Liza. Soon he called again. Then he increased his visits until there were few days when he was not at her home. He took care to work himself into the graces of the servants. With most of them he succeeded, but not with old Esteban. Liza finally reproved the old man. After that he said nothing, appeared outwardly polite when he met Miguel, but watched him closely.

Then one day a horse without a saddle but with the bridle still on came limping into the ranch. It was evident that he had been shot. Esteban recognized the horse as one that had been ridden by a vaquero working with a herd of cattle to the south. He rode in that direction, was gone two days and one night, and returned with his head down. He had found three murdered vaqueros and tracked the herd to the Río Grande, across which thieves had driven it.

Liza sent for Miguel. He would, he said, recover the stock at once. He rode off furiously. A week later he returned to report that he had followed the herd into Mexico until the tracks were blotted out by those of other cattle. Not long after this more vaqueros were killed, more cattle stolen. Again Miguel promised to bring the guilty to justice; again he reported failure.

Don Francisco, Liza's uncle, now compelled her to take refuge with him in Matamoras. "They will kill you next," he said. In Matamoras she soon learned that all of her cattle in Texas had been driven off and that old Esteban had been wounded. And now Miguel came to her with offers of money to pay her taxes and help keep up her ranch. He had the idea that she was without resources. She thanked him but declined aid. She, in fact, had plenty of money from the sales of cattle that Carlos had made for her and from the debt paid by Don Porfirio Diaz.

Then one night one of her herds on the Mexican side of the Río Grande was attacked. But the vaqueros were not caught asleep. They reported that while they were fighting, a stranger came to their aid and killed two of the bandits; they killed another. But nobody could identify a single one of the dead men. Liza sent for Miguel, saying that, as he wanted to track her enemies down, now was another chance. The messenger came back with word that Miguel had been absent from his ranch for two weeks.

On the very day that the messenger returned, Miguel himself appeared to Liza at her uncle's house. He said to her: "I came upon the men just as they were attacking your vaqueros. Two of them I killed; your vaqueros killed another and then ran away. Had they not been cowards, we should have killed all the attackers. These, no doubt, are the *bandidos* who killed your vaqueros in Texas and stole your cattle there and who also are responsible for the murder of Carlos."

Liza, and her uncle and aunt also, were very grateful to Miguel. He came often to see her now. He ate little, drank not at all, and grew pale and thin. Finally he confided to Liza that he had rather die than live without her. She consented to marry him.

He went to Monterrey to buy the wedding garments for the bride and arrange with a padre there who had long been his friend and confessor to perform the ceremony. On his way back to Matamoras something very strange happened. While the stage was crossing the Arroyo Colorado, Miguel was eating an orange, as the other passengers observed. He had peeled it, had eaten a lobe, and was carrying another to his mouth, when two long, slender hands caught his arm. The passengers saw the fingers of the two hands grip into the flesh of Miguel's arm while he struggled. They yelled to the driver to stop. When he did, a small white dog that no one had before this observed leaped out of the coach and ran off howling. Miguel had fainted.

He was revived and the stage went on. He arrived at the hotel in Matamoras very ill. Doctors examined him and found that his pulses were too full, his heart beating too fast. They prescribed a cordial, but he refused it, saying, "I have promised

Liza never to drink again." Finally he dropped off to sleep.

The next morning when he awoke he called for coffee. A *criada* brought it with a glass of hot milk. As he lifted the coffee to his lips, the servant girl saw the two hands reach from the air and catch Miguel's wrists. She ran from the room screaming. When people who had been alarmed ran in, they saw Miguel struggling with the hands. Then they saw a little white dog run out of the room. Miguel was in a stupor. Foam was on his lips. The coffee was spilled all over the bed.

A doctor brought Miguel back to consciousness. Soon he insisted on having breakfast. He ate it without molestation.

Meantime Liza had gone to her ranch expecting to be accompanied back to Matamoras by Miguel. When she returned on the third day of his illness, she went at once to the hotel to see him. Sitting in his room dressed, he heard her voice and got to his feet to greet her. The hands came and caught him by the throat and forced him back into his chair. People in the hotel heard him choking and gurgling. They saw the door to his room close suddenly. When they tried to go into his relief, they found the door locked. When they forced an entrance, a little white dog ran out between their feet.

They found Miguel in a fit, frothing at the mouth, red streaks that were turning black on his throat and wrists. He finally came to, screaming, "You cannot keep me from it, Carlos! I will marry her!"

Now Don Francisco came. As he entered the room, Miguel shrieked out the same cry, "You cannot keep me from it, Carlos! I will marry her!"

He stood and looked at the wild man without saying a word. Then he went to Liza. "You must not marry that man until we find out what it is that troubles him," he said. "He is either crazy or he is . . ." He did not finish the sentence.

This was on the third day of Miguel's stay in the hotel. The stage from Monterrey brought the padre who was to perform the wedding ceremony the next morning. He called at once to see the man who was to be bridegroom. He found him sleeping under an opiate that the doctor had given. When Miguel aroused, he told the padre of the three appearances of the hands. The padre had confessed Miguel several times, knew about his smuggling and other sins.

Now he said, "Miguel, you have never told me all. I must insist upon a full confession. You are keeping back something that is at the bottom of all your trouble."

This speech made Miguel wild. "What have I done now that I must confess?" he cried. "I have drunk no wine, played no cards, seen no woman since I returned from San Luis Potosí and visited Liza."

"This may all be true," answered the priest. "But there is something you are holding back. I do not know what it is, but I will know. You must confess."

Again Miguel denied.

"Listen!" said the priest. "I am only a man, but I represent the good God, and God knows you have done some awful deed. You cannot hide from God. The hands that you imagine you see and feel are His punishment."

"Look at these marks on my wrists and throat," cried Miguel. "They are plainly of long, strong fingers. Do you think they really came out of the imagination?"

The padre crossed himself. "Confess," he said. "You have not yet told me the truth. Confess. No confession, no ceremony."

A long, low howl of a dog answered this speech. It seemed to come from somewhere in the room. The padre got up and looked, but he could find nothing.

To end the talk, Miguel now suggested that the padre accompany him to the home of Don Francisco to see Liza, whom he himself had not seen since his return from Monterrey.

In order to receive guests fittingly, Don Francisco had put on the white shirt and black suit he had bought for the wedding between Carlos and Liza. He had just seen a caller to the door and was standing behind it thinking when he heard the sound of approaching carriage wheels and then the knocker.

Many had noted a strong likeness between his features and those of the dead Carlos. And now as he opened the door and presented himself, the man in front of him was utterly maddened. It was Miguel.

"I killed you once, Carlos," he screamed. "I will kill you again!"

"Yes, you killed me," answered Don Francisco, pretending to be Carlos. "You stole Liza's cattle to make her poor. You killed her vaqueros. You schemed to get Liza and get her property, too. But I, Carlos Guajardo, know where the stolen cattle are."

"You lie!" screamed back Miguel. "I hid those cattle so that no one knows where they are. The men who helped me drive them off I killed so that they could not tell."

Miguel was entirely out of his head. Neither the padre nor Don Francisco now said anything. Other people had gathered, drawn by the wild cries.

Even though he was mad, some instinct in Miguel made him mark a horse tied to a post across the street from Don Francisco's house. He bolted towards the horse. When he was nearly to it, a little white dog suddenly appeared at his feet. He kicked at it and missed. At the same time the dog's teeth grabbed the calf of the leg that remained on the ground. Miguel fell with a lunge that brought his head against a sharp rock of the curbstone. The blow killed him instantly.

Some weeks after this second fatal ending of a wedding for her, Liza went to Monterrey and took the veil. A prairie fire later burned up the house on her ranch and that on Miguel's ranch also. Thus all things pass.

Ranchero
SAYINGS *of the* BORDER

By HOWARD D. WESLEY

THE hour was late, and myriads of stars were twinkling in the sky. Everyone in the truck load of football supporters returning from Laredo to Hebbronville had been looking up, trying to locate the *Oso Grande* (Great Dipper) when the little Mexican girl asked this startling question, *"Qué tantas estrellas hay en el cielo?"* (How many stars are there in the sky?) I began to explain seriously, with somewhat of a pedagogical air, that no one knows exactly how many stars there are in space.

Again Estela spoke up with enthusiasm, "I know how many there are; *son cincuenta.*"

I said, "Oh, there are many more than that. What makes you think there are only fifty?"

Her quick reply was, *"No puede contarlas; por eso son sin cuenta"* (they can't be counted; so they are countless). *Cincuenta* (fifty) is pronounced the same as *sin cuenta* (countless).

Time-honored puns such as this are common in the speech of dwellers along the Texas-Mexican border, as they are among all Mexicans. The life of the Tejano (the Texas-Mexican) is bound up in *cuentos* (folk-tales), *corridos, canciones* (ballads), and *dichos* (folk-sayings). As this folk-lore is transmitted, it naturally receives additions and undergoes variations. If a man cannot sing the plaintive tunes, typical of a people whose moods are heirlooms of a Spanish-Indian ancestry, his friends will comment, *"No es Mejicano."* Every happening of any importance, whether unusual or commonplace, from the shooting of a bootlegger by a ranger to a big cattle drive, is developed into a new song or saying. Quite often the puns and *dichos* have

211

no meaning to the hearer unless he knows the incidents that gave rise to them.

One night I was listening to an old Mexican *ranchero* tell stories of early border days. "Did you ever hear the *dicho* about *la romana de Tacho?*" he asked, and then proceeded to explain the meaning. In the early days along the border there were only a few stores. The keeper of one of these stores, a man called Tacho, was very careful not to give his customers overweight. He would often throw an article on the balance and remove it immediately, giving perhaps thirteen or fourteen ounces instead of sixteen. From this practice of his, *"como la romana de Tacho"* (like Tacho's scales) became a common phrase among the ranch folk in allusion to someone's being cheated or beaten in a deal.

An incident said to have given rise to another common expression concerns a man who sold *tacos*. He made his *tacos*[1] from jack-rabbit meat. As the story goes, even though it seems impossible to one who knows how many rabbits there are in South Texas, the restaurant man found that cats were more cheaply and easily caught than *liebres,* and in time his horrified customers discovered that they were dining upon the flesh of stray cats. At any rate, I have been told that this is the story from which originated the proverb, *"Ten cuidado que no te den gato por liebre"* (beware that they don't give you cat meat instead of rabbit).[2]

On the border ranches many Spanish expressions are used in much the same fashion as our common phrase "from the sticks." When a speaker wishes to ridicule some one for stupidity, he may say, *"Trae el rancho encima"* (the ranch sticks out all over him). A boy who shows by his action or his unfamiliarity with town life that he is ranch-bred is characterized by the *dicho, "No puedes negar el rancho"* (you can't deny that you are from the country). Another *dicho,* Spanish in origin, that

---

[1]The *taco* is a kind of native sandwich made of fried corn paste folded with meat, cabbage, and other vegetables inside.

[2]This proverb is found in picaresque literature of Spain and probably was brought over to the New World by the *conquistadores* and has since been adapted to local circumstances.

expresses the same thought is *"No puedes negar la cruz de tu parroquia"* (you can't deny the cross of your parish; that is, your origin is apparent by your conduct).

One ranch saying comparable to "Birds of a feather flock together" is *"Siempre la res busca al monte"* (cattle always seek the cover of the brush). Another is *"El que es buey hasta la correa lame"*, or, as I have also heard it, *"El que por su gusto es buey hasta la coyunda lame"* (he who by his own liking is an ox even licks the yoke-strap). In other words, he who is content with what he is will never progress. I have also been told that the saying can be used with this significance: If you are determined to be an ox, take the consequences. The saying goes back to Spain, where the difference between the plodding ox and the fighting bull of the arena is marked.

Another strictly *ranchero* expression is *"Está cerrado de un tiro."* This is used when a stranger, knowing no Spanish, is unable to express himself to the ranch hands. It means "His head is as thick as a post." When some one is trying to tell or do something of which it becomes evident that he knows little, or when some one attempts to butt into a conversation, we often hear said, *"Pues, que sabe el buey del freno?"* (what does the ox know about the bridle?) Let the horse wear the bridle and the ox tend to his own business.

When a person sneezes, another may ejaculate, *"Jesús!"* At first one might think this an instance of onomatopœia, since the word *Jesús* sounds like a sneeze, as does our mocking exclamation, "Who is she?" The ejaculation is made, however, as a prayer that the sneezer's health will be guarded so that the evil one may not enter while he has his mouth open.

Some other expressions, for most of which there are English analogues, are *"Comiste gallo?"* (Did you eat a fighting cock?) and *"como agua para chocolate"* (like water for chocolate, which is hot). The first is a clever way of asking, "Are you angry?" and corresponds loosely to our saying, "He must have got up on the wrong side of the bed." The other expression is applied to one who is angry. A saying something like "He left him cold" is *"Le dejaron como él que silbó en la loma"* (they left him like the one who whistled on the hill). This *dicho* of the border arose from a particular incident. A herdsman plotted with some thieves to steal his employer's cattle, cross the river with them, and go into business for themselves. They had a *señal*, so that confederates would know when it was safe to steal. The cattleman noticed the disappearance of his stock and at last caught the men. They told him that his vaquero was an accomplice, but he would not believe them. To prove the point they explained their signals and told him to go to a certain hill at night and listen. Surely enough, the herdsman came upon the *loma* and whistled. We say, "They caught him red-handed," meaning that he was caught in the act. Mexican dwellers in the prickly pear country say, *"Lo pescó en las tunas"* (he was caught in the *tunas,* the fruit of *nopal*). In certain parts of Mexico, it is said, the Indians harvest the wild *tunas* as their principal crop. Each one has a certain portion of the *monte* which he claims as his and guards against poachers. The hands of a *tuna*-picker become stained red with the juice of the fruit. A man who is caught in another man's patch is thus caught red-handed in the act.

A very common saying among the Mexican people is *"No creas que la luna es queso porque la ves redonda"* (don't think that the moon is cheese because it looks round). This saying derives from a fable told about the coon *(tejón)* and the coyote.[3] Some of the Mexican fables are much like those of Uncle Remus, except that the coyote and the coon are the characters instead of the rabbit and the fox. Señor Coyote is always regarded as everyone's enemy, and people like to see him outwitted. Well, Señor Tejón was fishing in a pool by the edge of an open well one night, and before he knew it Señor Coyote had come up on him. As it was useless to attempt flight, Señor Tejón had to use his wits. The reflection of the full moon was plainly seen in the clear water. "Señor Coyote," said Señor Tejón, "if you will not harm me, I will give you half of that cheese." Then Señor Tejón showed Señor Coyote the golden

---

[3]Compare this fable with "Br'er Coyote," by Sarah S. McKellar, and "Sister Fox and Brother Coyote," by Riley Aiken, both in this volume.—*Editor.*

image of the moon in the water, and Señor Coyote plunged in to get it. While he was drowning, Señor Tejón ran merrily away.

Another coyote story, illustrating that "the leopard cannot change his spots," involves a dog. Bruno, a ranch dog, loved to hunt and, contrary to custom and the unwritten laws of animals of the brush, became a close friend of Señor Coyote. Whenever either made a kill, he would share with the other. So Bruno, to be neighborly, asked his friend to visit his master's ranch. Señor Coyote at first declined, since he knew that the other dogs at the ranch were his blood enemies. But Bruno insisted. The *patrón's* daughter was to be married; there would be much *cabrito* and other delicacies; the dogs always got the scraps. The coyote could pose as a dog and join the party; no one would know the difference. Accordingly, Señor Coyote was under the table at the ranch the night of the feast. The table was large and was placed out-of-doors. The guests dined and then the celebration became hilarious. The bottles of *mescal* and *tequila* were passed freely and all present nipped heartily. A few became sufficiently intoxicated that some bottles were dropped and a little of the contents spilled. The dogs ate bones and scraps that were tossed upon the ground and they lapped at the spilled *tequila*. Señor Coyote did likewise. The liquor was even better than he had expected. He felt overjoyed. He wanted to sing. Bruno warned him that if he should sing he would be discovered. The *tequila* had more influence than Bruno, and he sang *burc—burc—burc—il*. The other dogs recognized him at once by his song and, rushing after him as he attempted to escape, killed him. Had he been wise, he would have followed the maxim *"En boca cerrada no entran moscas"* (flies do not enter a mouth that is closed). However, *"Perro que come huevos sigue aunque le quema el pico"* (a dog that sucks eggs will continue to do so even if he gets his mouth burned).

Doubtless the *mañana* philosophy of the Mexicans has been over-emphasized, but, nevertheless, there is a prevailing trend among border folk never to do a thing today if it can be put off until tomorrow. Many Anglo-Saxon Americans have fallen into the same attitude, especially in ranching communities, whether from association with the Mexican vaqueros or because the climate and environment are conducive to such philosophy. Maybe there is some truth in the rather crude *dicho*, "*Panza llena, corazón contento*" (belly full, heart easy).

Several proverbs counsel to moderation in endeavor. An old Spanish proverb current among Mexicans is "*El que mucha abarca, poco aprieta*" (he who embraces much can tighten up on little). He who attempts many things gets little done. A similar expression, meaning "He has bitten off more than he can chew," is "*No puede beber el caldo y quiere tragar la carne*" (he can't drink the soup; yet he wants to swallow the meat). Much more typical as a ranch proverb is the saying "*A todo el tira y nada le da*" (he shoots at everything and hits nothing). Somewhat along the same line of thought is the proverb "*Nadar, nadar, y a la orilla ahogar*" (swim, swim, and at the very bank drown). Others express the not far removed idea that one should let well enough alone. A common saying is "*No descubres el pastel*" (don't uncover the pie, or, as we have it, don't spill the soup). Another is "*No menear el arroz aunque se pegue*" (don't stir the rice even though it sticks). Much more practical as advice is the saying, "*Más vale mal ajuste que buen pleito*" (a poor settlement is better than a good law-suit). But, on the other hand, there are "*gustos que merecen palos*" (some pleasures are worth the price).

Expressing the fatalistic doctrine of the Mexican, are many proverbs. What's the use of worry? "*Si Dios quiere*" (if God wills), it will happen anyway. So the best thing to do is to take life easy. "*Si quieres dichoso verte conformate con su suerte*" (if you wish to be happy, adapt yourself to your fate). Moreover, "*Si tu mal tiene remedio, para que te apuras, y si no tiene para que te apuras?*" (if your evil has a remedy, why fret yourself; if it has not, why fret?) Oftentimes the person who toils receives little credit or recompense for what he does. Some one else may indirectly become wealthy from his efforts. "*Nadie sabe para quién trabaja*" (one never knows for whom he works). Another *dicho* which points definitely to a belief in the lack of free will in life is *"El que nace para tamal del cielo le caen las hojas"* (he who is to be a *tamal* will be, even though the shucks have to come from heaven). The *tamal* is made from a paste of boiled corn stuffed with seasoned meat and rolled in corn shucks. *Tamal* is also used to designate one who is a loafer, or no-account; hence there is a double meaning. If a person is destined to occupy a certain position in life, he will occupy it despite contrary conditions. *"El que nace para guaje nunca llega a ser jícara"* (he who is born to be a gourd will never be a jícara, a finished vessel). Here, too, is a double meaning, since *guaje* figuratively means one who is foolish. *"Unos corren a la liebre y otros sin correr la alcanzan"* (some chase the jack-rabbit while others catch it without running). A few people are born lucky, and while others toil they get rich without trying.

They say that fate has its way with men. Never bet on *mañana*. According to a border tale, a young vaquero had a very beautiful horse. No horse could cut cattle like his *melado*, which, he vowed, should never have another master. One day when he returned home, he related that Don Andrés had offered him a hundred head of sheep for his mount.

"That's where two fools met," remarked one of his friends. "The one was a fool for offering such a price and the other for not selling."

"But, *caramba, hombre!* I can't part with my horse. No other man has ever ridden him and I hope will not."

Nevertheless, it was only next morning that his friend's words were proved true. When he went out to saddle his beloved pet, he found that he had died during the night of snake-bite. It seemed that fate had decreed he should not own such an animal. He realized bitterly, *"Un pájaro en la mano vale ciento volando"* (a bird in the hand is worth a hundred flying).

There is an old story of European origin which is retold often in America. A man lectured his son for being so lazy. He urged him to get up early and go to work: *"El que se levanta tarde ni oye misa ni compra carne"* (the late riser neither hears mass nor buys meat). The youth left the house, but instead of going to work lay down to sleep in the *patio*. It so happened that some thieves fleeing from justice, about to be overtaken, decided to throw the evidence over the wall. The stolen bag of gold fell upon the sleeping boy, awakening him. He took it into the house and said to his father, *"Al que Dios le ha de dar por la trasera ha de entrar"* (to him to whom God intends to give, it will come even though in a round-about way).

Not all of the Mexican people think like this. So it might be well to give a few *dichos* showing a prudent philosophy. *"Grano a grano llena la gallina el buche"* (grain by grain the hen fills her craw). This is somewhat similar to the English proverb, "Little by little, dripping water will wear a rock away." Another counsel to perseverance is, *"Vale más una gota que dura que un chorro que se para"* (a drip that lasts is more effective than a torrent that soon stops). Vigilance is taught in *"Al pescado que se duerme se lo lleva la corriente"* (the fish that sleeps is carried away by the current). Yet another is *"De pequeña centella grande hoguera"* (from a little spark a great fire). One signifying "Be prepared" is *"Como quiera nace el maíz estando la tierra en punto"* (the corn will always sprout if the land is prepared). Again, *"Regarás la tierra con el sudor de tu frente"* (you will water the land with the sweat of your brow). This is much the same as the Biblical injunction, "By the sweat of thy brow thou shalt eat bread."

Many *dichos* are concerned with love. Of a heartless one it may be said, *"El es como el carrizo, no tiene corazón"* (he is like the reed grass, he has no heart). Sometimes when some one carries stories to a youth about his sweetheart, perhaps that she has been out with another, the youth will say with an air of unconcern and resignation, *"Ojos que no ven, corazón que no siente"* (what eyes do not see, heart does not feel). Another very popular way to embarrass the young lover is to say, *"Eres el gacho,"* which literally means "You're the hunch-back," and really implies that he has been made out a "chump." His "time is being beaten" by another *joven*, who has made him a *gacho*. A girl who tries to "two-time," or hold two beaus at once, may be called a *mancornadora*. The verb *mancornar* means to tie the horns of a wild steer or ox to a gentle one in order to control or break him. Then the word *mancornadora* means one who ties two lovers together. She breaks the heart of one. A popular love song is called "La Mancornadora." There are many names used to designate a sweetheart. The word *chata*, which literally means "bulldog," is applied to both boys and girls who have a bulldog face. Some of the other common names for "girl friend" are *chulita, chora, chinita, prieta, nenita, huerca, morenita, trigueñita,* and *chamaca*.[4]

One of the most commonly used expressions denoting a poor culmination of a courtship or love affair is *"Me dió las calabazas"* (I was given pumpkin). The girl who wishes to discourage or jilt her wooer plucks a squash or pumpkin blossom and wears it on the left side of her breast to inform him politely that his attentions are no longer wanted. The people of Spanish descent are always very particular about proprieties. For instance, it is customary for an *amante* to have four numbers and only four in the serenades played at the window of his beloved. It is sometimes considered an outright insult to play more. It is also a custom for a lover, unless he be of the common vaquero type, to ask for the hand of his *amante* and then wait fifteen days to see if he is acceptable. The true origin of the *calabaza dicho* is hard to determine. It is not original in Mexico, since it occurs in Spanish literature. The color of the fruit and flower of the pumpkin signifies *desprecio*, or degradation. I have also been told that when a girl gave her sweetheart "the air" she wrote her message on a slip of yellow paper, and that since the *calabaza* is yellow the word was applied to the rejection. Due more credence is the assertion that the *dicho* comes from the etymology of the word.

---

[4]*Nenita* means little baby, and *morenita* means little dark one. The word *trigueñita* has almost the same meaning as *morena*. From the fact that wheat is of a dark brown color one who has a nut brown complexion is called *trigueño*. The word for wheat is *trigo*. *Chulita* means pretty little one. *Chora* is derived from the corrupted pronunciation of the English word *shorty*. *Chinita prieta* means dark little Chinese girl. *Chinita* has come to mean in familiar discourse any little country girl. *Huerca* and *chamaca* are just slang words for *girl* or *kid*. They are also used in masculine form.

PURO MEXICANO

Calabazar means to make foolish or to trick. A word used along the border, *calabacear*, means to make one foolish or to come out badly in a test. The lowly pumpkin was given the name and one who is tricked is made a *calabaza* or given the cold shoulder or double-cross.

Lastly I give a rustic *dicho* that is a good excuse for a boy who is accused by his fellows of showing the white feather. He will probably reply to such a charge, *"Vale más que digan que aquí corrió una gallina, que no aquí murió un gallo"* (it is better that they say a hen ran here than that a rooster died here). In other words, accepting Falstaff's argument on Honor, "a live coward is often better than a dead hero." And then why worry anyway about gossip either of love or war in a land whose natives with a shrug of the shoulders and a casual puff on the *cigarro de hoja* (shuck cigarette) effortlessly put off until tomorrow what they might do today? For in this Texas-Mexican border country *"La suerte y mortaja del cielo bajan"* (fate and a winding-sheet come down from heaven), all things happen *"como Dios quiere,"* and a sufficient answer to most questions is *"Quién sabe?"*

Songs of the
MEXICAN MIGRATION

By Paul S. Taylor

IMMIGRANTS to the United States have long composed songs out of their experiences in severing ties with home and country and in making adjustments to the new environment. The emotions of the Irish emigrant, bound for the States a century ago, leaving broken-hearted Irish girls behind him, are immortalized in the verses of "I'm off to Philadelphia in the mornin'." And Paddy, who, like the Mexican Juan Diego decades later, began work on the track, sang of his occupations:

> To work upon the railway, the railway,
> I'm weary of the railway . . .
>
> In eighteen hundred and forty-four,
> I landed on Columbia's shore . . .
>
> In eighteen hundred and forty-six,
> I changed my trade to carrying bricks.[1]

Like the early Irish and other immigrants from the Old World, the Mexicans have composed and sung ballads in which they, too, express their emotions of farewell, of loves, and of work. These have value not only for the student and lover of folk-lore, but for the social scientist as well, for in them the attitudes of Mexican migrants are mirrored simply but vividly. Although no adequate record of the songs has been made,

---

[1] Irish ballad, quoted in W. F. Adams' *Ireland and Irish Emigration to the New World* (New Haven, 1932), pp. 208-9.

contemporary study makes possible analysis and documentation of this aspect of the Mexican migration.[2]

The songs which have the migration as their theme are mostly *corridos;* i.e., doggerel verses in the form of a ballad. *Corridos* are common among the laboring folk of Mexico. They are sung by troubadours on street corners or in market places; often they are printed on sheets to be sold for a *centavo* or two in Mexico, or for a nickel in the United States.

The Emigrant's Farewell

The emigrant's leave-taking calls forth the accentuated sentimentalism in which Mexican popular songs abound. Here it clusters about the very real and potent ties of religion, love of country, love of native state, as the speeding train bursts familiar bonds. At Aguascalientes the emigrant has insufficient funds to obtain an immigration visa from the American consul, but nevertheless proceeds to the border.

DESPEDIDA DE UN NORTEÑO

¡Adiós! mi Patria querida;
yo ya me voy á ausentar,
me voy para Estados Unidos,
donde pienso trabajar.

¡Adiós! mi madre querida,
la Virgen Guadalupana,
adiós! mi patria amorosa,
República Mexicana.

Pues, en fin, yo ya me voy,
te llevo en mi corazón,
Madre mía de Guadalupe,
échame tu bendición.

AN EMIGRANT'S FAREWELL

Goodbye, my beloved country,
Now I am going away;
I go to the United States,
where I intend to work.

Goodbye, my beloved mother,
the Virgin of Guadalupe;
goodbye, my beloved land,
my Mexican Republic.

At last I'm going,
I bear you in my heart;
my Mother Guadalupe,
give me your benediction.

[2]Other *corridos* dealing with Mexican immigrants have been published in Manuel Gamio, *Mexican Immigration to the United States,* ch. 7, and by the present writer in *Mexican Labor in the United States,* II, viii, vi, and in *An American-Mexican Frontier,* pp. 144-46. The author gratefully acknowledges aid given at various times in the collection and preparation of these *corridos* for publication by the Social Science Research Council, the John Simon Guggenheim Memorial Foundation, the Board of Research of the University of California, and the United States Civil Works Service.

SONGS OF THE MEXICAN MIGRATION

Me voy triste y pesaroso á sufrir y á padecer, Madre mía de Guadalupe, tu me concedas volver.	I go sad and heavy-hearted to suffer and endure; my Mother Guadalupe, grant my safe return.
México es mi madre patria, donde nací mexicano; échame tu bendición con tu poderosa mano.	Mexico is my home-land, where I was born a Mexican; give me the benediction of your powerful hand.
Me voy á Estados Unidos á buscar mi manutención, ¡adiós, mi patria querida, te llevo en mi corazón!	I go to the United States to seek to earn a living. Goodbye, my beloved land; I bear you in my heart.
Pues yo no tengo la culpa que abandone así mi tierra, la culpa es de la pobreza que nos tiene en la miseria.	For I am not to blame that I leave my country thus; the fault is that of poverty, which keeps us all in want.
Pues ya voy en el camino y salí de Salvatierra, haz, Madre mía de La Luz, lo que yo vuelva á mi tierra.	So now I'm on my way, I've left Salvatierra; grant, Mother of Light, that I may return again.
Ya llegamos á Celaya con mucha resolución, ¡adiós, adiós, Madre mía, Purísima Concepción!	We've already reached Celaya, full of resolution; goodbye, goodbye, my Mother, Immaculate Conception.
Llegamos á Salamanca; adiós, Señor San Pascual, échame tu bendición Padre mío del Hospital!	We arrive at Salamanca; goodbye, San Pascual; give me your blessing, Father of the Hospital!
Vamos llegando á Irapuato de paso para Silado, Madre mía de Loretito, ¡haz que yo vuelva á tu lado!	We are arriving at Irapuato en route for Silado; my Mother Loretito, grant my return to your side!
Adiós, Guanajuato hermoso, mi Estado donde nací, me voy para Estados Unidos, lejos; muy lejos de tí.	Goodbye, fair Guanajuato, the state where I was born; I'm going to the United States far, far from you.

223

PURO MEXICANO

Ya vamos en el camino
llegando á ciudad de León,
y admirado me quedé
al ver su iluminación.

We are on our way again,
arriving at the city of León;
I was filled with admiration
to see its bright lights.

Al llegar á Aguascalientes
con mucho gusto y esmero,
no arreglé mi pasaporte
por la falta de dinero.

I reached Aguascalientes
with much pleasure and gaiety;
I didn't arrange my passport
for lack of any more money.

Luego pasé Zacatecas
con muchísima atención,
en el tren de pasajeros
se me partió el corazón.

Then I passed Zacatecas,
giving it much attention,
but in the passenger train
my heart was breaking.

Llegamos á la estación
que se llama de Fresnillo,
donde todo mexicano
visita á un milagroso Niño.

We arrive at the station
that is called Fresnillo,
where every Mexican
visits the miraculous "Niño."[3]

Pues muy cerca de Fresnillo
se ven los boscosos cerros
donde se encuentra también
ese Niño de Plateros.

And very near Fresnillo
the wooded hills are seen,
where there is also found
the Holy Child of the Miners.

Santo Niño del Fresnillo,
tú me has de favorecer,
Santo Niño de Plateros
tú me concedas volver.

Holy Child of Fresnillo,
you must grant my request;
Holy Child of the Miners,
allow me to return.

Ya va caminando el tren
hasta llegar á Torreón,
Santo Niño del Fresnillo,
échame tu bendición.

Now the train goes on
till it reaches Torreón;
Holy Child of Fresnillo,
give me your benediction.

Ya llegamos á Chihuahua,
pues ya de aquí me despido,
¡adiós, mi Patria querida!
¡adiós, todos mis amigos!

Now we reach Chihuahua,
so here I take my leave;
goodbye! beloved country,
goodbye! all my friends.

Ya con ésta me despido
de mi Patria Mexicana,
he llegado á Ciudad Juárez,
¡oh Virgen Guadalupana!

And so I take my leave
of my country, Mexico.
I have reached Ciudad Juárez.
Oh, Virgin of Guadalupe!

—Cecilio Chavez.

---

[3]Probably a man called "Niño Fidencio," who is reported to work miraculous cures.

224

SONGS OF THE MEXICAN MIGRATION

Deported

In the following *corrido*, it is separation from his physical mother which evokes the chief regrets of the departing laborer; there is tender reference in the last line to his "beautiful land," but the exaggerated sentimentalism of the previous song is lacking. The incidents of approach to the frontier are depicted. At Chihuahua the Mexican customs inspection is met. At Juárez (El Paso) the American immigrant inspectors examine rigidly, and the public health authorities impose measures of sanitation and personal cleanliness. The *gringo* officials lack "compassion" for Mexicans, and many are rounded up for expulsion from the United States. In protest, the migrant cries that his people are not bandits, but come only for hard labor.

DEPORTADOS	DEPORTED
Voy á contarles, señores,	I am going to sing to you, señores,
voy á contarles, señores,	I am going to tell you, señores,
todo lo que yo sufrí,	all about my sufferings
cuando dejé yo á mi Patria,	when I left my native land,
cuando dejé yo á mi Patria,	when I left my native land,
por venir á ese País.	in order to go to that country.
Serían las diez de la noche,	It must have been ten at night,
serían las diez de la noche	it must have been ten at night,
comenzó un tren á silvar;	when a train began to whistle;
oí que dijo mi madre	I heard my mother say,
hay viene ese tren ingrato	"Here comes that hateful train
que á mi hijo se va á llevar.	to take my son away."
Por fin sonó la campana,	Finally they rang the bell,
por fin sonó la campana;	finally they rang the bell.
vámonos de la estación,	"Let's go on out of the station;
no quiero ver á mi madre	I'd rather not see my mother
llorar por su hijo querido,	weeping for her dear son,
por su hijo del corazón.	the darling of her heart."
Cuando á Chihuahua llegamos,	When we reached Chihuahua,
cuando á Chihuahua llegamos,	when we reached Chihuahua,
se notó gran confusión,	there was great confusion:
los empleados de la aduana,	the customs house employees,
los empleados de la aduana	the customs house employees,
que pasaban revisión.	were having an inspection.

225

PURO MEXICANO

Llegamos por fin á Juárez,
llegamos por fin á Juárez
ahí fué mi apuración
que dónde va, que dónde viene
cuánto dinero tiene
para entrar á esta nación.

We finally arrived at Juárez,
we finally arrived at Juárez,
where I had my inspection:
"Where are you going, where are you
    from,
how much money have you
in order to enter this country?"

226

Señores, traigo dinero,	"Gentlemen, I have money,
señores, traigo dinero	gentlemen, I have money
para poder emigrar,	enough to be able to emigrate."
su dinero nada vale,	"Your money is worthless,[4]
su dinero nada vale,	your money is worthless;
te tenemos que bañar.	we'll have to give you a bath."
Los güeros son muy maloras,	The "blondes" are very unkind;
los gringos son muy maloras,	the *gringos* are very unkind.
se valen de la ocasión,	They take advantage of the chance
y á todos los mexicanos,	to treat all the Mexicans,
y á todos los mexicanos,	to treat all the Mexicans
nos tratan sin compasión.	without compassion.
Hoy traen la gran polvadera,	Today they are rounding them up,
hoy traen la gran polvadera	today they are rounding them up;
y sin consideración,	and without consideration
mujeres niños y ancianos	women, children, and old folks
los llevan á la frontera	are taken to the frontier
los echan de esa nación.	and expelled from that country.
Adiós, paisanos queridos,	So farewell, dear countrymen,
˙adiós, paisanos queridos,	so farewell, dear countrymen;
ya nos van á deportar	they are going to deport us now,
pero no somos bandidos	but we are not bandits,
pero no somos bandidos	but we are not bandits,
venimos á camellar.	we came to *camellar*.[5]
Los espero allá en mi tierra,	I'll wait for you there in my country,
los espero allá en mi tierra,	I'll wait for you there in my country
ya no hay más revolución;	now that there is no revolution;
vamonos cuates queridos	let us go, brothers dear,
seremos bien recibidos	we will be well received
en nuestra bella nación.	in our own beautiful land.

Corrido de Texas

The Texas *corrido* is a song of the laborer under contract, leaving his woman behind in Texas as he goes to the industrial North to avoid picking cotton. Similarities of theme and

---

[4]This may refer to insufficiency of money to meet immigration requirements, or to the fact that Mexican currency is not accepted officially.

[5]To work like a beast of burden, humped over like a camel.

PURO MEXICANO

phraseology between this and the Pennsylvania *corrido,* also a song of migration to northern industry, are marked.[6]

CORRIDO DE TEXAS

Mi chinita me decía
ya me voy para la agencia—
á pasearme por el norte
y para hacerle su asistencia.

De la parte donde estés
me escribes, no seas ingrato
y en contestación te mando
de recuerdos mi retrato.

Adiós estado de Texas
con toda tu plantación,
me retiro de tus tierras
por no pizcar algodón.

Esos trenes del Tipí
que cruzan por la Lusiana
se llevan los mejicanos
para el estado de Indiana.

El día 22 de abril
á las dos de la mañana
salimos en un renganche
para el estado de Lusiana.

Adiós estado de Texas
con toda tu plantación,
me despido de tus tierras
por no pizcar algodón.

Adiós Fort Worth y Dallas,
poblaciones sin un lago,
nos veremos cuando vuelva
de por Indiana y Chicago.

El enganchista nos dice
que no llevemos mujer
para no pasar trabajos
y poder pronto volver.

TEXAS CORRIDO

My woman used to tell me,
"I am going to the agency—
I'll roam around the north
and take care of you.

"Wherever you may be,
write to me, don't be forgetful;
and in reply I'll send you
my picture as a forget-me-not."

Goodbye, state of Texas,
with all your growing crops;
I am leaving your fields
so I won't have to pick cotton.

These trains of the T & P[7]
that cross Louisiana
carry the Mexicans
to the state of Indiana.

On the 22nd of April
at two o'clock in the morning
we left in a *renganche*[8]
for the state of Louisiana.

Goodbye, state of Texas,
with all your growing crops;
I bid farewell to your fields
so I won't have to pick cotton.

Goodbye, Fort Worth and Dallas,
cities without a lake;
we'll see each other when I return
from Indiana and Chicago.

The contractor tells us
not to take a woman along,
so as to avoid difficulties
and so as to return soon.[9]

[6]See *Mexican Labor in the United States,* II, viii.
[7]Texas and Pacific Railroad.
[8]A gang of laborers shipped under contract by an employment agency.
[9]The third and fourth stanzas are repeated at the end.

SONGS OF THE MEXICAN MIGRATION

Three Approaching Girls

In this *corrido* the migrant takes his woman with him. Gamio (*op. cit.* pp. 90-91) has published a *corrido* entitled *"La de la 'nagua azul"* (she of the blue skirt), which has numerous identical phrases, but also many minor differences and even entirely different stanzas. I obtained a third version, printed in Mexico City, from which I include here under the title *"Canción del Interior"* stanzas which are not found in *"De las tres que vienen ai."* It adds a portrayal, somewhat ambiguous in detail, of some of the sex entanglements which are aggravated not only by uprooting of local ties, but also by the heavy preponderance of males in many of the Mexican colonies of the United States.[10] The emigrant's mistress in the United States is enjoined to remember that half his earnings are due to his family in Mexico. She proves "ungrateful"; the emigrant, torn alternately by love for her and by disillusion—the meaning is decidedly ambiguous—now thinks fondly of his wife, who, so a sad letter from his parents informs him, has just died. Bitterly he leaves his mistress with a warning that she, too, will suffer from inconstancy.

DE LAS TRES QUE VIENEN AI

De las tres que vienen ai
cual te gusta, valedor?
esa del vestido rojo
me parece la mejor.

Vente, deja de moler,
ya no muelas nixtamal,
vamonos pa' Estados Unidos,
que allá iremos á gozar.

Chatita, ai viene el tren,
oyelo que silvos da,
no más un favor te pido,
que no llores por allá.

OF THREE APPROACHING GIRLS[11]

"Of the three that are coming,
which one do you like, partner?"
"That one in the red dress
seems to me the best."

"Come on, stop your corn-grinding;
don't grind corn any more.
Let us go to the United States,
for we shall enjoy ourselves there.

"Sweetheart, here comes the train;
hear it whistle there;
One favor of you I ask,
don't cry while we are away."

---

[10]See "Some Cultural Adjustments: Family," II, pp. 192-203.
[11]Words and music furnished by courtesy of Concha Michel and Frances Toor.

PURO MEXICANO

Querido, ya voy cansada,
y apenas aquí es Torreón,
para no sentir cansancio,
cántame una canción.

Qué canción tan rebonita,
que jamás la había oido yo,
cántame otra más bonita,
y después te canto yo.

Yo le dije al renganchista,
yo le dije que volvía,
pero que no venía solo,
que hora traiba compañía.

No me mandes para Tejas,
ni al Estado de Oklahoma,
son puntos muy desgraciados,
que aborrecen al que toma.

Todos vienen platicando,
que pasaron por San Luis,
y al llegar á San Antonio,
les robaron el valis.

Ya con esto me despido,
con apretón de manos,
estos versos son compuestos
por los nobles Mexicanos.

"Dear, I am already tired, and
here it is only Torreón;
so that I shall not feel fatigued,
sing me a song.

"Oh, what a pretty song, the
    prettiest
ever I have heard;
sing me another that is prettier still,
and then I shall sing to you."

"I told the contractor,
I told him that I would return,
but that I wouldn't return alone,
that now I'd have someone with me.

"Do not send me to Texas, nor
to the state of Oklahoma;
they are awful places
that make it hard for one who
    drinks.

"Everyone is talking of how they
passed through St. Louis,
and that on arriving at San Antonio,
their suitcase was stolen from them."

With this I take my leave
with a hearty handshake.
These verses are composed
by the proud Mexicans.

230

SONGS OF THE MEXICAN MIGRATION

Song of the Interior

Here the theme of the emigrant's relation to women is further pursued.

CANCIÓN DEL INTERIOR

SONG OF THE INTERIOR

Pero ya se va á llegar el pago
para que gaste mi querida,
la mitad es para ella,
y la mitad para mi familia.

But wages are going to start
so that my mistress may spend them;
half is for her
and half for my family.

Mira, no seas ventajosa,
tú gozas de lo mejor;
supiste que era casado
y que tenía obligación.

Here, don't take advantage,
for you enjoy the best there is;
you knew that I was married
and under obligation.

Ayer tarde recibí carta
que mis padres me mandaron
en que llorando me dicen
y suplican que me vaya.

Yesterday afternoon I got a letter
that my parents sent me
weeping; they asked and
begged me to come back.

Para irme para mi tierra
yo no hallo ni como hacer,
no más me pongo á pensar
que aquí dejo á esta mujer.

I don't know what to do
in order to go to my country;
I begin to think
that I'll leave this woman here.

Recuerdos de una ingrata
que en un tiempo yo la amaba,
pero mi orgullo ha sido
que no la he vuelto á querer.

I have memories of an ingrate
whom at one time I loved,
but in my pride
I have not loved her since.

Las aves ya no cantan,
los astros ya no alumbran,
las flores no perfuman
porque allí faltó tu amor.

The birds no longer sing
and the stars give no light;
the flowers have no scent
because your love has fled.

Chinita lo que te encargo
que cuando de mí te acuerdes,
¡ay! nunca, nunca olvides
que fuí tu adorador!

Chinita, I charge you
that when you think of me,
ah, never, never forget
that I was your adorer!

Pero fuí tan desgraciado
con querer á esa mujer,
que he jurado por el Eterno
no volverla ya á querer!

But I was so unfortunate
in loving that woman,
that I have sworn by the Eternal
never to love her again!

PURO MEXICANO

Tus ojos son dos estrellas	Your eyes are like two stars
que brillan por el panteón,	shining in the cemetery;
yo quisiera abrir tu tumba	I would like to open your tomb
para ver tu corazón.	in order to see your heart.
Ya con esta me despido;	And so I say farewell;
ya me voy á retirar,	I am going to go away,
pero al cabo que con otro	but finally with another
tú has de llegar á pagar!	you, too, will have to pay.

Effects of the Crisis

The great movement of repatriation began in 1930 because of economic depression in the United States. "Effects of the Crisis," together with the "Corrido of the Immigration Officers," both of which were obtained at Globe, Arizona, through the courtesy of N. D. Collaer, pictures vividly the effects of the depression: the cries of hungry children who have to eat prickly pear instead of meat, the cutting off of light and water, the end of gay dances, the sadness of the "flappers," the break-up of homes through divorce.

EFECTOS DE LA CRISIS   EFFECTS OF THE CRISIS

En este tiempo fatal	In these unhappy times
la crisis ya nos persigue;	depression still pursues us;
se come mucho nopal,	lots of prickly pear is eaten
lo demás no se consigue.	for lack of other food.
Como todos ya sabrán	Probably everybody knows
estos males tan prolijos;	about these many evils;
que hay hogares sin pan	that there are homes without food,
donde lloran nuestros hijos.	in which our children cry.
Las pianolas ya no tocan	The pianolas no longer play,
los bailes han disminuido,	the dances are fewer and fewer;
las flappers tristes invocan	the sad little flappers pray
que vuelva otra vez el ruido.	to have the gaiety return.
Se pierden casas algunas	Some lose their houses
porque los pisos no pagan;	because they can't pay rent;
han muerto varias fortunas	the fortunes have collapsed
de algunas que las poblaban.	of some who lived in them.

La crisis no nos afloja y el remedio no parece; nos ayuda la Cruz Roja que tanto se le agradece.	Depression does not turn us loose, and the remedy does not appear; the Red Cross gives us aid, for which we are very grateful.
No se ve luz en las casas ni llave de agua potable. La gente de malas trazas en estado lamentable.	No light is seen in the houses nor flows the water from the tap; the people are in tatters and in a deplorable state.
Antes se fumaba puro, era una alegría las calles; hoy de hambre se mira obscuro y se escuchan muchos ayes.	They used to smoke cigars, there was gaiety in the streets; now faces are clouded with hunger and many sighs are heard.
Los aboneros no aflojan siguiendo su profesión. y los deudores se enojan cuando van a su cantón.	The bill collectors do not relent in pursuit of their profession, and the debtors get angry when they come to the house.
Esta crisis decidida al mundo está desafiando. Si te falta la comida, no llores, sigue ayunando.	This sharp crisis is defying the world; if you have nothing to eat, don't cry, keep on fasting.
Ya nadie verás que engorde con las chuletas guisadas porque nunca es bueno el borde aquel de "Las Tres Hambreadas."	You'll see no one now who grows fat from eating broiled chops, because the fare never is good at "The Three Hungers."[12]
Divorcios han aumentado en estos últimos años; la crisis lo ha decretado con sus tristes desengaños.	Divorces have increased in these late years; depression has decreed it with its sad disillusion.
Ya con esta me despido, que sean ustedes felices. Aquí termina el corrido y sigue siempre la crisis.	And so I take my leave, may you all be happy. Here ends the song, but the depression goes on forever.

Corrido of the Immigration Officers

The theme of the next *corrido* is the arrival of United States immigration officers in the mining town of Miami, Arizona, to carry on their work of investigation and deportation. The

---

[12]This is a pun on the name of a restaurant and the poorness of meals.

devastating effects on the Mexican colony are pictured as the officers round up and jail deportees. Obedience to the laws—especially marriage and liquor laws—is counseled to avoid deportation, as the officers investigate after the manner of "the priest about to hear confession." Once the fate of deportation is ordered, then glad emotions upon returning to the homeland dominate; as an immigration officer has reported, the prostitutes, their own doom of deportation sealed, abandoned resistance to their fate with seeming relief, took up jokingly the slogan *"Nos vamos limpiar Miami"* (we're going to clean up Miami), and aided the officers to catch others of their own profession. The appeal to "protect our own industry" is a curious introduction of a slogan then prevalent in Mexico, roughly the equivalent of "Buy American."

CORRIDO DE LA EMIGRACIÓN

Miami es la población
que se haya muy atrasada;
pues llegó la Emigración
cuando menos se esperaba.

Se oyen no más las quejas
de todos sin distinción;
hombres, niños y viejas,
todos van a la prisión.

Si tú no estás bien casado
no te sirve el pasaporte;
te llevan los del condado,
á dormir allá en la corte.

Llevan las mujeres solas
y algunas que no lo son,
pobrecitas amapolas
que cortó la Emigración.

Con la mano en la cintura
se paran á investigar
como si fueran el cura,
cuando te va á confesar.

CORRIDO OF THE IMMIGRATION OFFICERS

Miami is the town
which has suffered many reverses;
for the "Emigration"[13] arrived
when it was least expected.

You hear only the complaints
of all without distinction;
men, children and old people
all have to go to prison.

If you are not legally married,
a passport is of no use to you;
the county authorities will take you
to sleep there in the jail.

They take away the single women,
and sometimes those who are not;
poor little poppies
cut down by "Emigration."

With hand on belt they pause
to make investigation
as though it were the priest
about to hear confession.

---

[13]Border Patrol of the U. S. Immigration Service.

SONGS OF THE MEXICAN MIGRATION

Yo voy á dar un consejo
á todo joven soltero,
que se mire en este espejo
aquí en suelo extranjero.

Que arregle su pasaporte,
no viva amancebado
porque va á dar á la corte
siendo al final deportado.

En el Globe, las mujeres
aclaman á Cristo Rey,
se olvidan de sus deberes
y algunas violan la ley.

Si tú quieres ser feliz,
cuando el Bravo hayas pasado
muestrale á este país
que sus leyes no has violado.

Si antes has hecho cerveza
y has vivido de alambique,
hoy te rascas la cabeza
no tienes ni que te explique.

Así, paisanos queridos,
en México los espero
y allá todos reunidos
en aquel suelo sincero.

Labraremos nuestro suelo
y olvidemos esta angustia;
bajo aquel bendito cielo,
protejamos nuestra industria.

Por fin llegó ya la era
de que me arrastrara el viento,
adiós México de afuera,
ya me voy para el de adentro.

Ya con esta me despido,
raza de mi estimación;
sin poder dar al olvido,
que me echó la Emigración.

I am going to give advice
to every young bachelor;
let him look in this mirror
here on this foreign soil.

Have your passport in order;
do not live with a mistress;
because you'll land in jail
and at last you'll be deported.

In Globe, although the women
acknowledge Christ the King,
they forget their religious duties
and some of them break the law.

If you want to be happy
when you have crossed the Bravo,[14]
show this country clearly
that you have not broken its laws.

If you used to make beer
and operate a still,
just scratch your head
and don't admit anything.

Thus, dear countrymen,
I await you in Mexico,
and there we'll be reunited
in that true country.

We will till our own soil
and forget our misery here;
under that blessed sky
let us protect our own industry.

At last the time has come
for the wind to carry me away;
goodbye, Mexicans in exile,
home to Old Mexico I go.

And so I take my leave,
race that I told in esteem,
without being able to forget
that "Emigration" deported me.

---

[14]The Río Grande.

PURO MEXICANO

The Deportees

The stay-at-homes have had their say, also, towards the returned emigrants. *Corridos* of this type were gathered in Jalisco, Mexico, during the years 1931 and 1932. Some were printed as broadsides; others were taken down from the singing or dictation of the troubadours. In the ballad that follows the deportees are mercilessly lampooned.

LOS DEPORTADOS	THE DEPORTEES
Les cantaré un corrido	I shall sing you a song
de todos los deportados,	of all who were deported,
que vienen hablando inglés	who come back speaking English
y vienen de desgraciados.	from those wretches.
Los tiran en donde quiera	They are shoved around anywhere
á puro mendigar,	and have to beg their way.
da lástima verlos	It's a pity to see them
que no traen ni para almorzar.	with nothing to eat.
Marchan para el norte	They set out for the north
con gran gusto y afán,	with high hopes and eagerness,
trabajan en el campo	but they work in the fields
como cualquier gañán.	like any field hand.
Se van al algodón	They go to pick cotton
y dan muy mala cala,	and get on very badly;
trabajan en el traque	they work on the track
ó en el pico ó la pala.	or with shovel or with pick.
Pues eso y más merecen	So they deserve that and more,
esos pobres paisanos,	those poor countrymen,
sabiendo que este suelo	for they knew that this land
es para los Mexicanos.	is for the Mexicans.
Se tumban el vigote,	They lop off their mustaches
y mascan su tabaco,	and chew their tobacco;
parecen la gran cosa y no	it seems the thing to do
cargan ni . . . tlaco.	and they don't have a cent.
Se pelan á la boston	They cut their hair close
como burros tuzados,	like a clipped donkey;
se van á las segundas	they go to second-hand stores
y compran trajes usados.	and buy worn-out clothes.

SONGS OF THE MEXICAN MIGRATION

Los corren los maltratan
los gringos desgraciados,
no tienen vergüenza
siempre allá están pegados.

Por eso yo me quedo
en mi patria querida,
México es mi país
y por el doy la vida.

They're insulted, mistreated,
by those *gringo* wretches;
they have no shame,
they are always beaten there.

That is why I remain
in my beloved country:
Mexico is my country
and for it I give my life.

237

PURO MEXICANO

Defense of the Immigrants

In answer to such as the foregoing attack, a repatriate makes "Defense of the Emigrants." Necessity forced them to leave Mexico, but in case of "intervention" their country will see that they have not become *"gringado* (Americanized). After all, although the *gringos* worked them hard, Mexicans received far better pay and treatment in the United States than the impoverished peons receive in their own country.

DEFENSA DE LOS NORTEÑOS	DEFENSE OF THE EMIGRANTS
Lo que dicen de nosotros casi todo es realidad; más salimos del terreno por pura necesidad.	What they say about us is nearly all the truth, but we left the country from sheer necessity.
Que muchos vienen facetos yo también se los dijera; por eso la prensa chica tuvo donde echar tijera.	I myself could have told you that many come back boasting; that is why the local press speaks harshly about them.
Pero la culpa la tienen esos ingratos patrones que no les dan á su gente ni aun cuando porte chaqueta.	But those who are to blame are those unkind employers, who don't give their people enough to buy a jacket.
No es porque hablo del país: pero claro se los digo que muchos trabajadores enseñan hasta el ombligo.	I'm not criticizing the country, but I certainly tell you that many of the laborers are naked to their navels.
El rico en buen automóvil, buen caballo, buena silla, y los pobrecitos peones pelona la rabanilla.	The rich go in automobiles, riding a good horse and a good saddle while the poor peones go about half naked.
Siempre el peón es agobiado, tratandolo con fiereza, donde le miran los pies quieren verle la cabeza.	The peon is always burdened, is treated with cruelty; the rich would like to see his head where they see his feet.

SONGS OF THE MEXICAN MIGRATION

Lo tratan como un esclavo
no como útil servidor
que derrama para el rico
hasta el último sudor.

Yo no digo que en el Norte
se va uno á estar muy sentado,
ni aun cuando porte chaqueta
lo hacen á uno diputado.

Allí se va á trabajar
macizo, á lo Americano,
pero alcanza uno á ganar
más que cualesquier paisano.

Aquí se trabaja un año
sin comprarse una camisa;
el pobre siempre sufriendo,
y los ricos risa y risa.

Los cuarenta y el tostón
no salen de su tarifa,
no alcanza para comer;
siempre anda vacía la tripa.

Que lo digan mis paisanos,
si yo les estoy mintiendo,
porque no hay que preguntar
lo que claro estamos viendo.

Mucha gente así lo ha dicho:
dizque no somos patriotas
porque les vamos á servir
á los infames patotas.

Pero que se abran trabajos
y que paguen buen dinero,
y no queda un Méxicano
que se vaya al extranjero.

Ansia tenemos de volver
á nuestra patria idolatrada,
pero qué le hemos de hacer
si está la patria arruinada.

They treat him like a slave,
not like a useful servant,
who pours out for the rich
his last drop of sweat.

I don't say that in the north
one is going to be well off;
nor because one wears a suit
is he elected to Congress.

One has to work there,
hard, in the American fashion,
but one succeeds in earning
more than any of our countrymen.

Here one works a year
without earning enough for a shirt;
the poor man suffers always
and the rich man laughs and laughs.

Paid forty or fifty cents,
never more than that,
he can't get enough to eat,
his stomach is always empty.

Let my countrymen say
if I am telling a lie,
for it's needless to ask about
what we can clearly see.

Many people have said
that we are not patriotic
because we go to serve
for the accursed *patotas*.[15]

But let them give us jobs
and pay us decent wages;
not one Mexican then
will go to foreign lands.

We're anxious to return again
to our adored country;
but what can we do about it
if the country is ruined?

---

[15]Literally "big feet," an uncomplimentary term applied to Americans.

PURO MEXICANO

Si han hablado de nosotros es por muchos fanfarrones que andan sonando los pesos cual si trajeran millones.	If they've talked about us, it is because of all the braggarts who go jingling their dollars as if they'd brought back millions.
Si no hubieran presumido ni quien nos dijera nada, porque todos comprendemos que nuestra patria es sagrada.	If they had not put on airs, there would have been no comment, because we all understand that our country is sacred.
Ya tenemos entendido que en caso de intervención vendremos de tierra extraña á servir en su ocasión.	We all know well that in case of intervention we'd come back from abroad to serve our country in her need.
Que no vengan de facetos les digo á mis compañeros; amigos, yo no presumo porque soy de los rancheros.	"Don't come back boasting,' I say to my companions; "Friends, I don't put on airs, because I am just a *ranchero.*"
Orden guarden y decoro esos que vienen del Norte. si no quieren que la prensa á toditos nos recorte.	Let them behave themselves, those who come back from the north if they don't want the papers to speak ill of us.
Porque todo están oliendo— no crean que son ellos sordos— y nos pudieran cazar como si fuéramos tordos.	Because they smell this all out— and don't believe they are deaf— they could shoot us down as though we were turtle doves.
Yo ya me voy para el Norte amigos, no se los niego; ahí les dejo á sus riquitos á que los torée Juan Diego.	Now I am leaving for the north; friends, I do not deny it; I leave you with your rich fellows— let who will be bothered with them.[16]
Muchachos, yo los convido á la Nación extranjera; no le hace que algunos digan que somos chucha cuerera.	Boys, I invite you to the foreign nation; don't be bothered if they say that we are mercenary.

---

[16]Alternative translation: let the common Mexican deal with them.

SONGS OF THE MEXICAN MIGRATION

The Two Rancheros

The final selection is a dialogue between two ranchers, one a returned emigrant, the other a man who had remained in Mexico. The repatriate boasts of his wealth and his exploits among women and in the prize-ring in the United States. He praises the mechanical efficiency, the order, and the high wages of that country, and remarks on the oppression of the poor in Mexico. But when he attacks Mexican religious beliefs as "deceptions" and implies that those who have not been freed from them by emigration are benighted, then his outraged fellow rancher, no longer able to contain himself, threatens him with his dagger. The repatriate recants, invoking protection of the very saints he so affected to despise.

PLÁTICA ENTRE DOS RANCHEROS

No critiques á tu patria,
no rebajes la nación,
procura siempre tener
de ideal, la emancipación.

Plática de dos rancheros
de calzón y sombrero ancho,
uno que había ido al norte
y otro no salía del rancho.

Norteño:

Si vieras como es bonito
esos Estados Unidos,
por eso los Mexicanos
por allá estamos engridos.

No te imaginas lo que es
vivir como un licenciado
buena camisa, buen traje,
buen abrigo y buen calzado.

CONVERSATION BETWEEN TWO RANCHERS

Don't criticize your country,
don't run down the nation;
try to have always
as an ideal, emancipation.

A talk between two *rancheros*
in "pyjamas"[17] and broad-brimmed hats,
one of whom had been in the north
and one who had not left the ranch.

The man who had journeyed north:

"If you could only see how nice
the United States is;
that is why the Mexicans
are crazy about it.

"You can't imagine how it is
to live like a lawyer,
with good shirt, good suit,
good overcoat and shoes.

---

[17]The characteristic loose-fitting white cotton pants.

PURO MEXICANO

Tu reloj con su leontina,
y tu fistol de corbata,
los bolsillos siempre van
bien retacados de plata.

No se conoce la crisis
por allá en el extranjero,
todos los trabajadores
ganan siempre buen dinero.

No me quedó que desear,
conocí el estado de Texas,
allí yo llegué a tener
una docena de viejas.

De esas mujeres bonitas
puras güeras de primera
esas que van por las calles
todas vestidas de seda.

Luego me pasé á S. Luis,
á Kansas á Santa Fé,
en Wuasintón que primor
de gozar me fastidié.

Los Angeles conocí
al derecho y alrevez,
tuteandome con los gringos
porque sé hablar el inglés.

Cuando conocí Arizona
ya era un gran boxeador;
no más mira que conejos
me porto, mi valedor.

Lo que es con esta canilla
pocos se paran el cuello,
no más con una guantada
los hago estampar el sello.

Todo esto que yo te digo
en nada te lo exajero;
ojalá me huvieras visto
por allá en el extranjero.

"Your watch on its chain
and your scarf-pin in your tie
and your pockets always filled
with plenty of silver.

"Depression is unknown
there in a foreign land;
all the workingmen
always earn good pay.

"I had nothing more to wish;
I knew the state of Texas,
and there I got as many
as a dozen women.

"Some of these pretty women,
classy blondes—the kind
who go through the streets
all dressed in silk.

"Then I went to St. Louis,
to Kansas and Santa Fé;
in Washington, how swell!
I got tired of so much pleasure

"I knew Los Angeles
forward and backward;
I got thick with the *gringos,*
as I know how to talk English.

"When I was in Arizona
I was a great prize-fighter;
just take a look at the biceps
that I carry around, partner.

"Few have my right to brag
about their muscles;
with a single blow of my fist,
I would put my mark on them.

"All this that I'm telling you
is no exaggeration at all;
I wish you'd seen me
there in a foreign country.

Pero tú nunca has salido
del rancho y de tu doctrina
creyendo en monos de palo
y isque en la virgen divina.

No hombre quítate esa venda,
no te dejes explotar
de hombres que dicen ser sabios
y que estudian para robar.

Vieras que bonito el norte,
hay mucha electricidad,
hay máquinas para todo
que es una barbaridad.

Con el aire comprimido
levantan en el espacio,
no solo rieles, durmientes
se levanta hasta un palacio.

La verdad que esos patones
se las jalan como astutos,
no son como esta nación
que está plagada de brutos.

Por allá hay protección
inteligencia y dinero,
por eso es que le suspiro
y le lloro al estranjero.

Aquí por un veinticinco
trabaja uno de sol á sol
no pasa uno de comer
puras gordas con frijol.

México será bonito
pero está muy arruinado,
se trabaja noche y día
y no sale uno de pelado.

Pero si cree uno en milagros
y en las ánimas benditas
y en irle á besar la mano
á los señores curitas.

"But you have never left
the ranch, or your parish school;
still believing in wooden images
and in the divine virgin.

"Come, man, unbandage your eyes;
don't let yourself be exploited
by men who claim to be wise
and who study only to rob.

"Look how splendid the north is—
lots of electricity;
machines for everything,
an enormous number of them.

"With compressed air
they raise up into space
not only rails and ties
but even whole palaces.

"The truth is those big feet
are considered very smart;
they are not like this country,
which is plagued with stupid people.

"Over there they have protection,
intelligence, and wealth;
that is why I sigh for it,
and yearn for a foreign land.

"Here for twenty-five cents
one works from sun to sun;
there is nothing else to eat
but *tortillas* and beans.

"I grant that Mexico is very pretty,
but it's down and out;
one works day and night
and never ceases to be a *pelado*.[18]

"And here one believes in miracles
and in blessed souls
and in going to the priest
in order to kiss his hand!

---

[18]A penniless Indian.

PURO MEXICANO

Y creelo que el capital
aquí nos tiene cegados
para podernos robar
porque son muy desgraciados.

No es que yo hablo de más
de los ricos cabezones
pero tú ya bien lo vez
que son puritos bribones.

Hay nos pintan el infierno
y también la ánima sola.
quisque á San Ramón Nonato
y también la ánima sola.

Nada de eso valedor
no te creas de esas boberas,
son puritas vaciladas
son puras conseguideras.

El que no había ido al norte:

Ya cáyate pues el osico
no hables de la religión,
se me hace que te despacho
á traer changos al Japón.

Voy que con este instrumento
yo te quito lo relajo
aunque seas gran boxeador
ahorita te saco el cuajo.

Y le enseñó un puñalón
al norteñito payaso,
que luego se le engrifaron
todos los del espinazo.

Y le agarró tal temblor
al ver tan filoso acero,
que se incó á pedir perdón,
el uno al otro ranchero.

"But believe me, the capitalists
have blinded us
in order to be able to rob us;
they are a lot of scoundrels.

"It isn't that I want to talk
about those rich men,
but you can see for yourself
that they are terrible thieves.

"They picture hell to us
and the devil with lots of tail,
as well as San Ramón Nonato
and also the immortal soul.

"Pay no attention to that, pardner;
don't believe those follies;
they are simply nonsense,
they are simply frauds."

The man who had not gone north:

"You had better shut your face
and quit talking about religion,
or I'll have to send you
to bring monkeys from Japan.[19]

"With this little tool
I'll change your tune;
even though you're a great boxer,
I'll cut out your rennet."

And he showed him such a knife—
to the clown from the north,
that it gave him the shivers
up and down his spine.

It gave him such a fright
to see such a terrible blade
that he knelt to beg
the pardon of the other *ranchero.*

---

[19] That is, tell him to go to!

244

SONGS OF THE MEXICAN MIGRATION

[*Norteño:*]

No vayas á dar por Dios
por San Antonio bendito,
no vayas á dar con fierro
no me pegues hermanito.

[*El que no había ido al norte:*]

No que eres la colmillona
que en el norte te has rifado
para que te incas de rodillas
levántate desgraciado.

No que no crees en los santos
ni tampoco en el demonio,
para que invocas cobarde
al glorioso San Antonio.

Se me hace que eres maldito
nada más de puro pico,
por eso de compasión
no te doy en el osico.

[*Man who had been north:*]

"Don't hit me, for God's sake;
in the name of blessed San Antonio,
don't strike me with the blade,
don't hit me, little brother."

[*Stay-at-home:*]

"Aren't you the bold fellow who
has done so much in the north?
What are you on your knees for?
Get up, miserable wretch.

"Since you don't believe in saints
nor even in the devil,
then, coward, why invoke
glorious San Antonio?

"It seems to me your bravery
is just a loud mouth;
that's why I am sorry for you
and don't push your face in."

The Enchanted
CITY OF MONTE ALBÁN

By E. R. SIMS

AT the time of the conquest of Mexico the territory of
Oaxaca was occupied by the flourishing Zapotec people.
Monte Albán, their strongest fortification, was kept well
garrisoned to resist Aztec invasion from the north and as a
precaution against the Mixtecs, who were not always friendly.
The remains of this fortress are on a huge truncated cone
rising abruptly more than a thousand feet above sea level.
Those who are entitled to an opinion say that the apex of the
cone was removed by human hands to form a level plaza 1,000
feet long by about 600 feet wide. Around the four sides of
this plaza, at the very edge, are enormous mounds, the ruins
of temples, altars inscribed with mysterious symbols, and forts.
The Fortified Hill, as the Zapotec name for it is to be translated,
was almost impregnable. Here the gods walked.

The ruins of Monte Albán have been studied at various times
for more than a hundred years, but the recent excavation of
tomb Number Seven, resulting in the finding of a wonderful
store of jewels and curiously wrought ornaments of silver and
gold, has centered the attention of the archæological world upon
the place. Our concern is not with archæology but with legend.

At the foot of Monte Albán are numberless mounds covered
with vegetation which conceals the ruins of houses, temples,
tombs. The Indians have always known that beneath these
mounds there lay an enchanted city. Four hundred years ago
the ancient gods, angry at the white man, who defiled both
temples and altars, cast a spell of enchantment over the people

and hid the city beneath the hills. So the Indians, direct descendants of the builders of the enchanted city, tell.

"And if the gods hid the city from the white man, how is it that a white man has found it?" you ask.

Unshaken in their faith, they will answer, *"Pues, había de ser así."* It had to be that way.

If you are still unconvinced, they will tell you the story:

High up on the mountain in the central plaza is a deep well from which there flows intermittently, but never except at dawn, a stream of pure water. Exactly in the center of the stream is a golden jar containing the sacred emblem of the gods, a silver fish, which comes to the surface to renew its colors in the morning sun. The fish knows the secret of the enchantment and if taken from the jar will reveal it as the price of liberty. As no one knows when the well will flow, great patience is required to wait night after night in all weather. The Indians say that Dr. Caso[1] has won the secret. They call him the *Desencantador*, the Disenchanter.

If no one had forced the fish to give up the secret, would the city have remained hidden always? Not necessarily. South of the main plaza on the summit of Monte Albán is a low hill almost hidden in a growth of shrubs and trees. It is an ancient temple. Natives may wander over it at will, unmolested, but let a white man approach and he is immediately attacked by dogs—a mother and four puppies. If the intruder defends himself, the animals vanish to reappear a short distance away. This play is repeated until the intruder tires of pursuit. If, however, he should be fortunate enough to capture one of the puppies, the others would give themselves up and the white man be told the secret of the enchanted city and given power to break the spell.

There is a third way to learn the secret of disenchantment—this by the direct intervention of the gods. This same hill, the Hill of the Four Gates, is penetrated by four passages that are

---

[1] Dr. Caso, archæologist of the National Museum of Mexico, was in charge of the party that opened tomb Number Seven. He has made many important discoveries at Monte Albán and other parts of Mexico.

so narrow and so low that they can be entered only by a man crawling on hands and knees. There are interesting objects on all sides, but nothing that can be carried away unless the curious one be fortunate enough to find a gold disc. Tradition says that should the gods desire to reveal the secret they will place in the path of the chosen a gold disc on which is written the secret of the enchanted city and the charm for breaking the spell.

There is a further tradition to the effect that during all the centuries since the conquest the city has lived for a brief time each year. On the 26th of June, at an hour of the night known only to the wise men of the village, the city is restored to its former glory. The altars and temples are thronged with priests and worshippers, warriors crowd the streets, and the markets are the scene of their former activity.

But the Indians like best to tell how Princess Donají, the Princess Great Heart, gave her life to restore the sacred city to her own people.

At the time of the conquest, Cosijoeza, the last and the greatest of the Zapotec kings, was engaged in a disastrous war with the Mixtecs, to whom he had lost Monte Albán. When Cosijoeza appealed to Cortés for aid, and Orozco was sent to make peace, the Mixtecs refused to put down their arms unless the Zapotecs gave a hostage as pledge that they would not attempt to retake Monte Albán. Princess Donají was surrendered to the Mixtecs. Imprisonment was intolerable to this spirited princess. She watched the invaders closely, and when the garrison seemed to have become careless and had been reduced to a handful, she sent a messenger to her father urging him to attack at once. It was only after repeated urgings that he would consent to risk his daughter's life, and only upon her promise to make her escape before the attack. Accordingly it was agreed that before the attack an arrow would be shot through the window of Princess Donají's room as a signal for her to flee. The attack was successful, but one of the guards saw the arrow and reported to his companions. The Princess was hurried away and secretly put to death. The Zapotecs searched in vain for the place of burial. After many months a strange story, originating no one knew where, was whispered among the people to the effect that the grave of the Princess would be found beneath a crimson lily. Search was made and the lily found on the banks of the Atoyac (Green) River. An excavation was made on the spot and the princess was found as natural as in life, lying on her side as if asleep. The roots of the lily were entwined in her hair. In recognition of the bravery of Princess Donají her head appears on the shield of the state of Oaxaca today.

Exploration goes on at Monte Albán. One of the most satisfactory results is the confirmation of Indian legends, or rather of stories that have been regarded heretofore as legends. Among the Zapotecs there is the story of entire armies that disappeared, sometimes reappearing in another place, sometimes never seen again. On one occasion Moctezuma laid siege to Mitla, another stronghold of the Zapotecs. After a stubborn defense of several weeks the Zapotec garrison disappeared during the night in spite of the fact that every avenue of escape had been closely guarded. The next morning they were found entrenched on a neighboring hill. This manoeuvre was repeated three times, and finally after a fourth disappearance they were never seen again. A network of tunnels has been uncovered at Monte Albán, which connect various fortifications with neighboring hills. Perhaps with further exploration a similar network may be found at Mitla and the story turn out to be based on fact.

PROCEEDINGS OF THE TEXAS FOLK-LORE SOCIETY

I. For 1934

Celebrating the twenty-fifth anniversary of its existence, the Texas Folk-Lore Society met in its twentieth annual session at Austin, April 19 and 20, 1934. There were three meetings: Thursday night, April 19, at the Y. M. C. A. Auditorium; Friday afternoon, April 20, at the same place; and Friday night for a dinner in the Union Building on the University of Texas campus. This dinner was in honor of the chief founders of the Society, John A. Lomax and L. W. Payne, Jr., both of whom responded, Frost Woodhull of San Antonio, President of the Society, acting as toastmaster. Each guest at the table announced his or her name with an old-time saying or proverb. A committee awarded the first prize, a copy of *American Ballads and Folk Songs* by John A. and Alan Lomax, to Chester F. Lay for what they considered the "best" saying; second prize, a copy of *Southwestern Lore*, issued by the Texas Folk-Lore Society, went to Dan Storm. Titles of papers read, with names of contributors, follow:

Traditional Proverbs and Ejaculations of the Río Grande Border, Jovita González, Saint Mary's Hall, San Antonio.

Walk Around My Bedside, Martha Emmons, State Home, Waco.

The Wonderful Chirrionera, Dan Storm, Austin.

Cowboy Songs from the Cedar Brakes, by four boys from the brakes.

Br'er Coyote, Sarah S. McKellar, Hda. La Mariposa, Múzquiz, Coahuila, Mexico.

Gallopin' Rheumatiz, H. B. Parks, State Apicultural Laboratory, San Antonio.

TEXAS FOLK-LORE SOCIETY

The Enchanted City of Monte Albán, E. R. Sims, University of Texas, Austin.

Voodoo Charms in Dallas, Virginia Waters, Southern Methodist University, Dallas.

Folk Nomenclature in Texas, E. G. LeStourgeon, San Antonio.

Kildare Lore, Tressa Turner, Kildare, Texas.

The Word on the Brazos, J. Mason Brewer, Dallas.

Negro Folk-Lore, A. W. Eddins, San Antonio.

The Mustang of the Mescalero Apaches, Joe Storm, Austin.

I Was Here When the Woods Were Burnt, L. W. Payne, Jr. University of Texas, Austin.

Folk-Lore Trails, John A. Lomax, Austin.

A Sixpence of British Song, Mabel Major, Texas Christian University, Fort Worth.

The Facts of the Case, J. Frank Dobie, Austin.

At the business session it was decided to hold the next meeting in Dallas and officers were elected as follows: President, John Lee Brooks, Southern Methodist University, Dallas; Vice-Presidents, Martha Emmons, Waco, Leon Denny Moses, School of Mines, El Paso, A. W. Eddins, San Antonio; Councillors, H. B. Parks, San Antonio, Rebecca Smith, Texas Christian University, Fort Worth, E. R. Sims, University of Texas, Austin; Treasurer, Marcelle L. Hamer, Austin; Secretary and Editor, J. Frank Dobie, Austin.

II. For 1935

The Society convened for its twenty-first annual meeting in the Palm Garden Room of the Adolphus Hotel, Dallas, Friday night, April 19, 1935, President John Lee Brooks presiding. A second meeting was held in the same room Saturday afternoon, April 20. The evening session of that day was accompanied by a subscription dinner in Virginia Hall on the campus of Southern Methodist University. At this Thomas A. Knight acted as toastmaster, each guest gave a folk anecdote, a saying, a rhyme or some other folk bit, and it was the most delightful occasion ever experienced by any folk-lore gathering.

A list of contributions to the general program follows:

Mister Coyote in Folk-Lore and Literature, J. Frank Dobie, Austin.

Collecting Folk-Lore on the Río Grande, Jovita González, Saint Mary's Hall, San Antonio.

Animal Tales from Mexico, Dan Storm, Austin.

I'se Sho Nuff Lucky, Aylett Royall, Southern Methodist University, Dallas.

Monte Diablo, H. B. Parks, San Antonio.

The Casey Jones Problem, Mrs. John Henry, Dallas.

Sandstorm Yarns, Henry Barton, Wichita Falls.

Cowboy Figures of Speech, Ramon F. Adams, Dallas.

Tall Tales of West Texas, Sue Gates, O'Donnell, Texas.

Dog Spirits, J. Mason Brewer, Dallas.

The Exposure of Pecos Bill, David Henry, Dallas.

A Negro Sermon, Mrs. Zelma Polly, Waco.

Remedies for the Home, Frost Woodhull, San Antonio.

The Adventures of Little Audrey (or *Little Emma*), Cornelia Chambers, Dallas.

Singing With Lead Belly, Alan Lomax, Austin.

At the business session the Secretary reported that during the year Publications No. VI of the Society, *Texas and Southwestern Lore,* had been reprinted; he announced that this year of three other volumes out of print (Volumes I, II, and III) Number II would probably be reprinted. Officers for the ensuing year were elected as follows: President, Martha Emmons, State Home, Waco; Vice-presidents, John Lee Brooks, Southern Methodist University, Dallas, Mabel Major, Texas Christian University, Fort Worth, A. W. Eddins, San Antonio; Councillors, John Green, Houston, Thomas A. Knight, Dallas, David Donoghue, Fort Worth; Treasurer, Marcelle L. Hamer, Austin; Secretary and Editor, J. Frank Dobie, Austin.

TEXAS FOLK-LORE SOCIETY

CONTRIBUTORS

Riley Aiken, now teaching modern languages in Kansas State Teachers College at Emporia, was reared on the Texas border and has made prolonged trips into Mexico for the purpose of collecting Mexican folk-tales. He understands the Kickapoo language, reads and writes Latin and Italian, and speaks French, German and Spanish, in addition to his own language.

Maude McFie Bloom, wife of Lansing Bloom, eminent historian of New Mexico, is a native daughter of the Spanish Southwest and a student of the history of Spanish-America as well as of Mexicans in the Southwest. She lives at Albuquerque, New Mexico.

Alice M. Crook, of Santa Fé, says, "Most of my childhood was spent in New Mexico, and sometimes I have gone to schools at which I was the only Anglo-American."

Elizabeth Willis DeHuff, of Santa Fé, New Mexico, has for years done work with the Pueblo Indians. She is a contributor to the *Southwest Review* and other magazines; her books of folk tales, *Five Little Katchinas, Taytay's Tales, Taytay's Memories* and *Swift Eagle of the Río Grande,* are well known.

Bertha McKee Dobie wrote "Tales and Rhymes of a Texas Household" for *Texas and Southwestern Lore,* 1927, and has written much on Texas gardens.

Josefina Escajeda belongs to one of the oldest Spanish families in El Paso County, Texas. She lived for a number of years at San Elizario, of the lore of which she writes.

Everardo Gámiz, who is connected with the Department of Education at Durango, Mexico, has made a very extensive collection of the songs, legends, *cuentos,* folk drama and other forms of folk-lore of his state; he has generously given the present editor free access to his collection.

Jovita González made her début as an exponent of border Mexican lore with a long and delightful article entitled "Folk-

PURO MEXICANO

Lore of the Texas-Mexican Vaquero" in *Texas and Southwestern Lore,* issued by the Texas Folk-Lore Society in 1927. At present she holds a grant from the Rockefeller Foundation of New York for the purpose of completing a book on the life and lore of the border Mexicans, "my people" as she calls them in an article. She has contributed generously to the *Publications* of the Texas Folk-Lore Society, and has written for the *Southwest Review.* She teaches in Saint Mary's Hall, San Antonio.

Sarah S. McKellar, native Texan, is the wife of a Scotch rancher in Mexico. Their hacienda, La Mariposa, in northern Coahuila, is famous for its hospitality and good talk.

E. R. Sims is Professor of Spanish in the University of Texas.

Catherine J. Stoker, a resident of Saltillo and Mazapil, Zacatecas, is another sympathetic listener to the *gente* of Mexico, whom she knows thoroughly.

Dan Storm used to live in Mexico and two years ago returned to the state of San Luis Potosí to hear what he might hear. A recent graduate of the University of Texas, he lives in Austin, where he is doing independent journalistic work.

Joe Storm, brother to Dan Storm, has spent a deal of his youth in New Mexico; he is editor-in-chief elect for the *Daily Texan,* student newspaper of the University of Texas, in which institution he is enrolled.

Hugh McGehee Taylor contributed "Spur-of-the-Cock," the best hero folk tale of America that this editor has ever read, to the volume issued by the Texas Folk-Lore Society in 1933. He is a civil engineer of many years' experience in Spanish-America and is now farming near Falfurrias, Texas.

Paul S. Taylor, of the Department of Economics in the University of California, has enjoyed several grants that enabled him to make studies of Mexican life both over the Southwest and in Mexico. He is the author of various books and pamphlets dealing with Mexican labor and social life, his latest work, published by the University of North Carolina Press, being *An American-Mexican Frontier,* a study of Mexicans in Nueces County, Texas.

Howard D. Wesley teaches school at Hebbronville, Texas, near the border.

Frost Woodbull, judge of Bexar County, Texas, in which San Antonio is located, expert on guns and fly-fishing, and an ornament to civilization, wrote "Ranch Remedios" and "Folk-Lore Shooting," highly interesting articles, for *Man, Bird and Beast* and *Southwestern Lore* respectively (two of the yearbooks issued by the Texas Folk-Lore Society).

INDEX

257

INDEX

Marriage customs, Mexican, 185-186

Maverick, county in Texas, 1

Mayas, 136, 137, 140

McKellar, Sarah S., vi, 254; "Br'er Coyote," 101-106

Mescaleros. *See* Apaches.

Mesquite. *See* under Plants.

Mexican, character of, 10-12; 215ff.

Mexican clothing. *See* under Clothing.

Mexican drinks. *See* under Drinks.

Mexican proverbs. *See* under Proverbs.

Mexican tales. *See* Aiken, Riley; DeHuff, Elizabeth W.; Dobie, B. M.; Dobie, J. F.; Escajeda, J.; González, J.; McKellar, S. S.; Sims, E. R.; Stoker, C. J.; Storm, D.; Storm, J.; Taylor, H. M.; Woodhull, Frost.

Mexicanisms current in southwestern United States: *adiós,* 10, 104; *administrador,* 29, 198; *amigo,* 14, 40, 42, 50, 54, 55; *aparejo,* 92; *arroyo,* 99; *baile,* 185; *bueno,* 59; *cabestro,* 74; *cabrito,* 215; *calabaza,* 219; *caporal,* 13, 15; *carreta,* 195; *chaparral,* 15; *chile,* 174; *compadre,* 29-36; *corral,* 29, 44; *corrido,* 52, 211, 222ff.; *dicho(s)* 211, 212, 214, 216; *fiesta,* 116, 166, 168; *frijoles,* 50, 73, 74, 143, 194; *gringo(s),* 227, 237; *hacendado,* 195; *hombre,* 37, 41, 217; *laguna,* 15, 26; *machete,* 88, 90, 107; *manada,* 104; *mancornada,* 9, 40, 73; *mescal,* 58, 59, 69, 88, 215; *mesquite,* 51, 52, 60, 88, 94, 99, 165, 166, 167, 201; *metate,* 184, 188; *monte,* 118, 214; *morral,* 91, 97; *nopal,* 94, 103, 203; *patrón,* 27-29, 195, 215; *pelado,* 137; *peon,* 180, 182; *pueblo,* 165ff.; *quintal,* 198; *ranchero,* 190, 195, 202, 212; *rancho,* 212; *remuda,* 65; *resaca,* 49; *sabe,* 220; *sarape,* 89, 100, 157, 158; *sendero,* 27, 198; *sombrero,* 11, 89; *sotol,* 6-7; *tequila,* 12, 215; *tortillas,* vii, 63, 120, 143, 194; *tunas,* 103, 214; *vaquero(s),* 75, 88, 104, 207, 210, 216, 217, 219

Mexicanos, 142

Mexico, 101, 152ff., 201, 222, 223, 246

Mexico City, 159

Michis, 162ff.

Mictlanteceutli, 143ff.

Mitla, 249

Mixtecs, 248ff.

Monster, 82

Monte Albán, 246ff.

Monterrey, 153ff., 208, 209

Moon, as cheese, 16, 214; dog that ran to the, 72-75

Munchausen, Baron, 1

Naranjal, El, lost gold mine, 173-174

New Mexico, 122, 184, 190

Nuevo León, 1

Nuevo Méjico, 177. *See* New Mexico.

Oaxaca, 135, 246

Oñate, Don Cristóbal, 165, 183

Oñate, Don Juan de, 176ff.

Oso Grande, 211

Plants: *Allegria,* 185; *alusema,* 187; *chile,* 73, 74, 188, 191; *coreopsi,* 201; *inmortal,* 184, 187; lily, 249; mesquite, 51-52, 60, 88, 94, 99, 165, 166, 167, 201; *nopal,* 94, 103; *ojía,* 187; *orégano,* 188; pine, 187; *pinque* weed, 187; poke-weed, 185; *punche,* 187; reed, 18; sunflower, 55; *yerba de víbora,* 187

Polecat. *See* under Animals.

Presidio, county in Texas, 1

Princess(es), 22ff., 123, 128, 138, 159ff.; Donají, 248; Harmonaca, 128

Proverbs and aphorisms, in English: It is the custom to repay good with evil, 4; Don't leave the highway for a trail, 8; Don't ask about things that don't pertain to you, 8; Don't lose your temper, 8; Sing to keep from crying, 41; The old sit best on the ground, 102; Birds of a feather flock together, 213; His head is as thick as a post, 213; He must have got up on the wrong side of the bed, 213; Belly full, heart easy, 216; He has bitten off more than he can chew, 216; Don't spill the soup, 216

Proverbs in Spanish: *Cante por no ponerse a llorar,* 41; *En su mismo pecado lleva Ud. la penetencia,* 41; *Ten cuidado que no te den gato por liebre,* 212; *Trae el rancho encima,* 212; *No*

259

INDEX

261